Dedication

To Jake DeRosier, Skinny Jim Davis, Shrimp Burns, Fred Ludlow,
Erwin Baker, Gene Walker, Ironman Ed Kretz and all the riders who ever
rolled their Indians up to the line.

The Indian

THE HISTORY OF
A CLASSIC AMERICAN MOTORCYCLE

Tod Rafferty

S

PUBLISHED BY
SALAMANDER BOOKS LIMITED
LONDON

Credits

A Salamander Book

This edition published in 2001 by
Salamander Books Ltd
8 Blenheim Court,
Brewery Road,
London N7 9NY
England

A member of the Chrysalis Group plc

ISBN 1 84065 300 0

Credits

Jacket Design
Phil Clucas
Design
Roger Hyde
Photography
Neil Sutherland
Project Editor
Philip de Ste. Croix
Indexer
Richard O'Neill
Production
Phillip Chamberlain

Art Director
John Heritage
Editorial Director
Will Steeds

Colour reproduction
Studio Tec, Leeds ,England

9 8 7 6 5 4 3 2 1

Printed in China.

The motorcycles pictured here come to you courtesy of their owners. Our thanks to all of them for the kindness and cooperation, without which there would be no book. We are grateful to Bob Stark, Max Bubeck, Chuck Vernon, Tom Hensley, Glenn Bator, Otis Chandler, Mike Tomas, Mark Dooley, Daniel Statnekov, Trev Deeley, John Eagles, Wilson Plank, Jim Lattin, David Hansen, George Gray, Rusty Kay, Eric Vaughan, Mort Wood, Bob and Robin Markey, Jeff Gilbert, Caryll Chriss, Gene Calidonna, Larry Struck, Vince Martinico, Bob Mercer, Thomas Kallos, Ron Sabay, Dave Bettencourt, Bob McClean, Leon Blackman, Jim Dennie, Milby Jones, Paul Pearce, Jim Quaintance, Elmer Lower, Tony Penachio, Louis Fisher, Gene and Tony Dodge, Marv Baker, Jeff Sierck, Vince Spadaro, Rocky Burkhart, Mike Parti, Ed Kretz, Jr., Stephen Wright, Peter Dunkel, Jim Smith, Tom Baker, Bob Romig, Ken Smith, Edwin Aucott, John Dufilie, Gary Myers, Dean Rigsby, Luke Walker, Barry Brown, Fran Guldenbrein, Larry Kahn, Dan Rouit, Doug Strange, Bob Shirey and Douglas Allen. Thanks also to Walt Behenke, Rich Holland and Karla Wilkinson at the Indian Motorcycle Company, Gilroy, California, the Petersen Automotive Museum, the Otis Chandler Vintage Museum, the Trev Deeley Museum and the National Motorcycle Museum in Birmingham, England.

The Author

Tod Rafferty is a veteran motorcycle junkie and former editor of *Cycle News*, *Big Bike* magazine and contributing editor for *Cycle Guide* magazine. He was also automotive editor of the Telegram-Tribune newspaper in San Luis Obispo, California. The author's other works include *Harley-Davidson: The Ultimate Machine* (Running Press, 1994); the companion volume to this book, *The Complete Harley-Davidson* (Motorbooks International, 1997); *Harley Memorabilia* (Chartwell Books, 1997); and *The Complete Illustrated Encyclopedia of American Motorocycles* (Courage Books, 1999). Rafferty and his family live on the central coast of California.

We recognize that some words, model names and designations, for example, mentioned herein are the property of the trademark holder. We use them for identification purposes only. This is not an official publication.

The information in this book is true and complete to the best of our knowledge. All recommendations are made without any guarantee on the part of the author or publisher, who also disclaim any liability incurred in connection with the use of these data or specific details.

CONTENTS

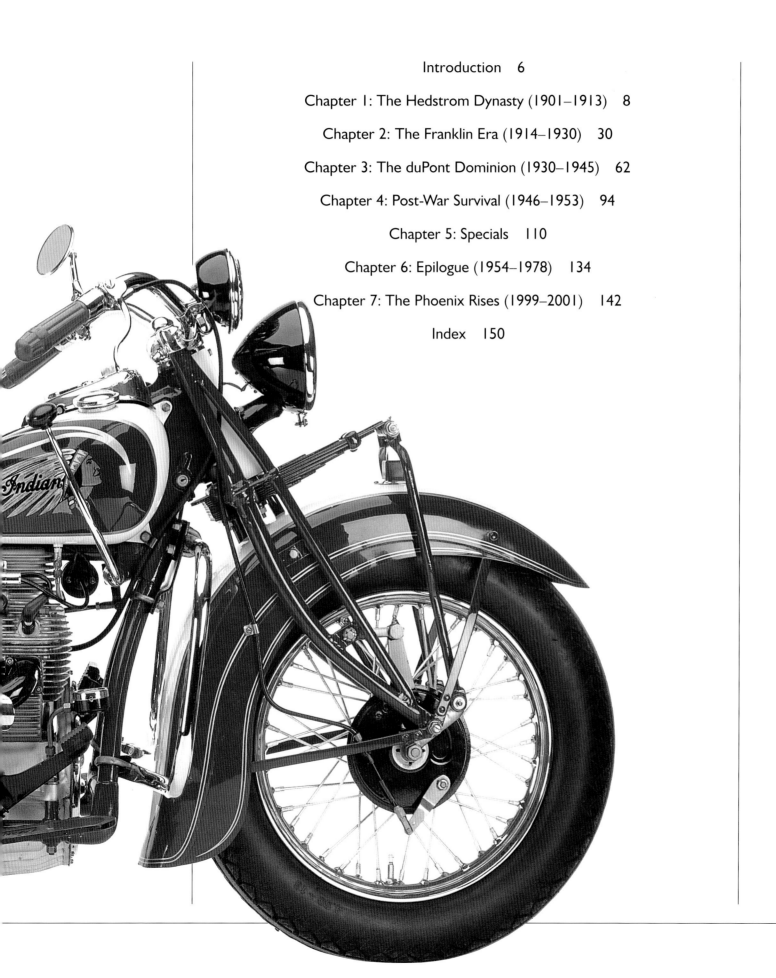

INTRODUCTION

The Indian Motocycle Company wrote a long chapter in the history of American motorcycling. As the dominant manufacturer for the first two decades of this century, Springfield, Massachusetts was at the hub of the international motorcycle scene. Then the effects of war, economic depression and galloping political disorientation shifted the American motorcycle industry from a global influence to a more provincial enterprise.

Between 1900 and 1917, when the United States entered World War I, about 150 domestic motorcycle companies came and went. Little more than a dozen remained in business following the war, and after the Great Depression of the early 1930s only two American manufacturers had survived: Indian and Harley-Davidson. Following the Korean war one remained. Indian was not the one.

Over the years, all manner of reasons have been offered for the ultimate failure of "America's Pioneer Motorcycle." Mismanagement, poor engineering, labor unions, greed, stupidity, arrogance, market myopia, flathead fixation, bad design, over-diversification, British duplicity and shameless profiteering have all appeared on the list. But two fundamental reasons led to the demise of Indian in 1953. One, the Indian Motocycle Company was never a family business. Two, Harley-Davidson was.

George Hendee was a bicycle racer, builder, entrepreneur and energetic promoter. Oscar Hedstrom was a bicycle racer, self-taught engineer and an inquiring, inventive mind. Together they were perfectly matched to create the first large-scale American motorcycle company, and did just that. But after little more than a decade, their individual visions diverged, and the motorcycle market had changed drastically. Both men were racing enthusiasts, but strong stockholders objected to the expense of a factory racing program. Plus, Hendee and Hedstrom began to disagree with one another on key manufacturing decisions.

Oscar Hedstrom resigned as chief engineer in 1913, and George Hendee retired as company president less than two years later. They had built in ten years the largest motorcycle company in the world, and both were wealthy men. In their absence the Indian Motocycle Company would fall under the control of one management group after another for the next 40 years But despite the changing names in the corporate boardroom, the distractions of wars and the economic rollercoaster of boom and bust, the people who designed, built and sold Indian motorcycles took genuine pride in their products. And they gave Harley-Davidson a good run.

The Milwaukee outfit, by comparison, was controlled by the same family for 65 years. The talents of William Harley and the three Davidson brothers were formidable, and they met Indian's challenge at each turn. Strongly conservative, in both engineering and economics, Harley-Davidson came only reluctantly to the racetrack. But once there they built the best machines, hired the finest riders, spent the most money and came away victorious.

It should be noted on Springfield's behalf that the brilliant Oscar Hedstrom was gone by the time Milwaukee fielded a factory team; and that after World War I, American motorcycle racing gradually shifted from professional to amateur competition, requiring far less financial support from the factories. Harley-Davidson, to its credit, maintained and eventually expanded its racing department when pro events made a comeback. But the fact remains that Milwaukee never would have built racing motorcycles if Springfield hadn't forced them to the line. In many respects, Harley-Davidson made better motorcycles because of the competition from Indian.

This book presents an illustrated hardware history of Indian motorcycles. We've covered the 52 years of Springfield machines, the handful of British and Italian cousins that followed, and a few of the Indian specials built by individual enthusiasts. Some are fully

*"If I had a Harley
I'd leave it for a thief,
And with the insurance
I'd buy an Indian Chief."*

Ancient tribal proverb

restored showpieces, others are original and a number are somewhere in between.

This revised edition has been expanded to include the new Indian motorcycles, manufactured in Gilroy, California since 1999. The former California Motorcycle Company offers the Chief, Scout and Spirit models, powered by the S&S V-twin. Indian plans to introduce its own proprietary engine in 2003.

Tod Rafferty
San Luis Obispo,
California, 2001

INTRODUCTION

Explanation of Terms

As motorcycle engines evolved they needed new names. The labels were invariably based on the disposition of the valves, and the first engines had an upper intake and lower exhaust valve. Thus the clever appellation, intake-over-exhaust, or IOE. These engines, which employed an atmospheric intake valve, were also known as pocket-valve motors.

With the advent of mechanical intake valves, the term F-head engine entered the lexicon. The valves remained in an over/under pocket. The next design put the valves parallel to each other beside the cylinder, which became the side-valve designation. (Or flathead; each generation of engines seemed to require two monikers, just to confuse the novices.) The next phase moved the valves to the top of the engine; overhead valves or ohv. When camshafts began migrating to the top, the name became overhead cam, or ohc engine. Neither of the latter two figured strongly in Indian production engines.

Specifications involving measurement can also be confusing. In the early days, tire sizes were specified by outside diameter, then switched in the Thirties to an inside measure. The system for rating horsepower was also subject to revision with the passage of time, and varied with the point of measurement as well as the prevailing socio-political winds of the day. Most of the early motors easily made double the advertised horsepower.

The weights cited in the specification tables are curb weights, the motorcycle with gas and oil aboard. Top speeds are a mix of factory claims, road tests, personal experience and pure guesswork.

Because Indian went through so many ownership changes, some documentation has been lost to history. Annual production figures are fairly accurate, but the numbers for specific models were often unavailable. Errors creep into the most meticulous research; if you come across mistakes in the specifications, let me know and we will correct them in the next printing.

Tod Rafferty
e-mail: traff@thegrid.net

1901 SINGLE

SPECIFICATIONS
ENGINE/DRIVETRAIN
Engine: IOE single
Displacement: 13ci (213cc)
Bore & stroke: 2.50 x 3.00in
(63.5 x 76mm)
Horsepower: 1.75
Carburetor: Hedstrom
Automatic
Transmission: Direct drive
Brake: Coaster
Batteries: Three 1.5-volt dry-
cell
Ignition: Coil/timer

CHASSIS/SUSPENSION
Frame: Steel, single downtube
Suspension: None
Wheelbase: 47in (119.4cm)
Weight: 110lb (50kg)
Fuel capacity: 0.85gal (3.2lit)
Oil capacity: 1qt (0.95lit)
Tires: 28 x 2in
Color: Blue
Number built: 3 to 6
Price: $200

Above: The original
Duckworth Number 3 chain
shows very little evidence
of wear.

Right: The earliest Indians
rolled on wooden rims, with
natural rubber tires glued on.
The first tires were not cast in
a mold, but extruded in
straight sections. The butt joint
was glued together and fixed
with a wooden dowel.

SINGLE (1901)

Both George Hendee and Oscar Hedstrom, the founders of the Indian Motocycle Company, were wheelmen. Bicycle racers. The velocipedes created a popular sport in the late 1800s, and the pedalers regularly drew crowds of 30,000 spectators at the major velodromes. By the turn of the century, the League of American Wheelmen had more than 100,000 members.

Hendee, a Boston native, was one of the top amateur riders in the country. In 1886, at age 20, he won the National Amateur High Wheel Championship. Hedstrom, a professional rider and five years Hendee's junior, was also an engineer. Intrigued by the possibilities of the new air-cooled, internal combustion engine, young Oscar built his own version of the bicycle pacer pioneered in France. The machine caught Hendee's attention.

George had been selling his own brand of bicycles for four years. Several other manufacturers had released motorized versions of their two-wheelers, and Hendee decided it was time to follow suit. In January of 1901 the two young men drafted a contract on the back of an envelope, and four months later the first Indian motorcycle was made public.

Why the name Indian? The two fledgling industrialists agreed that the name had to be recognizably American. Despite the misnomer, Native Americans were by then known collectively around the world as symbols of new world freedom, independence and pride. The burlesque version of cowboys, Indians and the US Cavalry attracted eager audiences at home and abroad. The term Indian implied courageous strength and bravery.

Why motocycle, with no r? Trademark concerns, primarily. Motorcycles were new, as was the word motorcycle. Other builders had already applied to register the word, so to avoid possible legal

Above: But for the engine and fuel
tank, the first Indian could easily be
mistaken for a bicycle from a
distance.

hassles, Hendee applied for a trademark on the word motocycle. Apparently the government granted neither term trademark protection.

Within a few years, the Hendee Manufacturing Company of Springfield, Massachusetts was the nation's leading motorcycle manu-

Right: Original fuel tanks held less
than one gallon, and created the
"camel-back" nickname. When
serious production got under way a
year later, Hendee Mfg. Co. was
added to the tank lettering.

Above: The rear frame geometry on
the first run of Indian motorcycles
was slightly steeper than it was when
the factory reached full production.
The early bikes had a shorter
wheelbase.

facturer. Some decades later, after the name was changed to the Indian Motocycle Company, collectors began wondering about the whereabouts of the first machine Oscar Hedstrom had built. The motorcycle would be a prized piece in any serious collection.

According to Indian biographer Harry Sucher, in 1954 Oscar Hedstrom said that the original had been disassembled and the parts used on another prototype, which he used as a demonstrator at velodromes. Six more motorcycles were built in the next few months. Two were sold and one was sent to England for exhibiting at the annual Stanley Bicycle Show. Following the exhibition, the machine was purchased by a Mr. McDermott, who later migrated to California and brought it with him.

Here the historical trail gets lost, but apparently the machine was sold shortly thereafter to Billy Jones of Los Gatos, California. In 1959, Jones sold it to Gordon Bennett, a collector from Oakland, California, who had the motorcycle restored in 1960. The machine's authenticity was confirmed by J. Worth Alexander, a veteran Indian enthusiast and expert on the early models. Gordon Bennett suffered a heart ailment, and was accompanied

everywhere by his right-hand man, Billy Ray Wilburn. Bennett pledged that upon his death, the Indian would be left to Billy Ray.

Gordon Bennett died in 1965. When his wife, Viola, passed on in 1988, the 1901 Indian went to Billy Ray. When Wilburn recently suffered a stroke, he directed his son, Port, to look into selling the motorcycle. The collector grapevine was soon buzzing with word of the bike, and the news reached Glenn Bator, manager of Otis Chandler's Vintage Museum in Oxnard, California. Accompanied by vintage Indian expert Gordy Clark, Bator examined the motorcycle closely.

Both were convinced of its authenticity. The parts were right: wooden rims, original sprockets, the hardware on the seat, and the lack of a serial number on the engine. No numbers were used until the production models of 1902. So the deal was closed.

Here then, by historical evidence and expert consensus, is one of the first few Indian motorcycles made. And 97 years later, the only complete 1901 model known to exist. Neat.

Below: Oscar Hedstrom had his first motorcycle designed before he and George Hendee agreed to undertake manufacturing. So once the young engineer set up his shop in the local bicycle factory, it only took him four months to have the first prototype ready for a public demonstration.

1901 Indian Single
Owner – Otis Chandler
Ojai, California

Above: Exactly when the first twist-grip spark control first appeared is still a matter of some dispute. Recent evidence indicates that Indian used the system before Glenn Curtiss adopted it in 1904.

SINGLE (1903)

George Hendee (1866–1943) was born near Boston, Massachusetts and started riding bicycles in his teens. A powerfully built lad with stout legs, he soon joined hundreds of other "wheelmen" in contests of speed throughout the northeast and midwest. Bicycle racing grew quickly as a popular spectator sport just before the turn of the century.

Hendee's career spanned the transition from the early "penny farthing" bicycle, with huge front and tiny rear wheel, to the "safety bicycle" with matched wheels. George won more than 300 races in a period of four years, losing only seven times. With the advent of the modern bicycle and professional board-track racing, Hendee retired from active competition in 1896 to concentrate on bicycle manufacturing. His first bikes, built in Middletown, Massachusetts were called the Silver King models.

Several other newfangled vehicles, variously termed horseless carriages, automobiles and motor-driven cycles, motocycles or motorcycles, were on more than a few drawing boards at this time. One sketcher was Carl Oscar Hedstrom (1871–1960), who was also a bicycle racer. He had developed a gasoline engine-powered bicycle for use as a pacer (and windbreaker) for bicycle racing. Setting new records for speed and distance became a common goal for racers, promoters and bicycle manufacturers.

New York and New England were then the seeding grounds for the rapidly growing sport of professional board-track bicycle racing. Hendee and Hedstrom met at the Madison Square Garden races in 1900. The two young enthusiasts struck an immediate friendship, and Hendee urged the young engineer to bring his pacer to Springfield for the velodrome races at the track Hendee owned in partnership.

Oscar Hedstrom was born in Sweden in 1871, the second of three children. When he was nine years old, the family emigrated to the United States and settled in Brooklyn, New York. Oscar attended public schools until the age of sixteen, when he left to take an apprenticeship in a watchmaking company. Later he took employment in a machine shop, and set to work on some of his ideas for a motorized bicycle.

1903 SINGLE

Below: The center tube connected to the cylinder head, making the engine a frame member.

Right: The first Indian motorcycles were called the diamond-frame models, for their basic bicycle-type frames. The fender-mounted fuel tank was the origin of the "camel-back" nickname, and was the standard tank on all Indian models for the first seven years of production.

Hedstrom's improvements to a French motorized bicycle pacer brought him immediate attention as both a designer and tuner. In Hendee he discovered someone equally enthused with the future of gasoline-powered two-wheelers, and likewise eager to develop new designs and materials.

So in 1901 Hendee and Hedstrom signed a contract to manufacture a "motor-driven bicycle that could be produced in volume, not for pacemaking, but for the every day use of the general public." They rented shop space in a Middletown, Connecticut bicycle plant and set to work. Hedstrom stipulated that his would be the only key to the shop, and that he could work day or night as he pleased. The first machine was completed in less than five months, and shipped to Springfield for Hendee's inspection. The 13-cubic inch (213cc) single, rated at 1.75 horsepower, propelled the 95-pound (43kg) cycle to a top speed of nearly 25mph (40km/h).

The grand opening demonstration, open to the public, the press and prospective investors, was conducted at Cross Street Hill in Springfield. The Indian easily climbed the 19-degree grade and impressed the onlookers with its power and speed. Hedstrom displayed the machine's tractability by stopping several times on the grade and pulling away from a stop. The chain-drive power train was obviously superior to belt drive, and the steady low-rpm pulling power was well received. Hendee instituted a national advertising program in 1902, and the Indian Motocycle Company was on the road to success.

Though his time in the motorcycle business would span little more than a decade, Oscar Hedstrom became the foremost motorcyle designer and engineer in the country, and arguably in the world. His refinements to the De Dion engine and improvements to the motorcycle chassis gained attention throughout the industrial nations. And for more than a decade his machines set the speed and distance records for others to chase.

Hendee had raised $20,000 in company shares and expanded the production space in the bicycle factory, but the demand for motorcycles required the services of a foundry to build engines. Indian chose the Aurora Automatic Machine Company of Illinois. The manufacturing agreement allowed Aurora to market the engines built in excess of Springfield's production capabilities. So variations of "the Hedstrom motor" soon appeared in other other motorcycles such as the Thor, America, Warwick, Royal and Rambler. But only the engines built for Indian, to Hedstrom's specifications, had the cases stamped Hedstrom Motor, and below that, Hendee Mfg. Co., Springfield, Mass.

Both Hendee and Hedstrom continued to participate in competitive motorcycle events as time allowed, and were joined by a young trainee named Jacob DeRosier, who proved a quick study in the new art of motorcycle racing.

DeRosier's family had moved from Quebec, Canada, to Massachusetts when he was four years old. A successful bicycle racer in his teens, at age 21 Jake began working and riding with Oscar Hedstrom. The young man's riding talent was apparent, but Hedstrom soon recognized that factory employment wouldn't hold his interest. DeRosier went to work as foreman in a Springfield garage, and rode as a privateer with support from the factory. He went on to win many major events throughout the country, and in 1908 became a full-time factory rider.

By 1903, Aurora had picked up enough pointers on motorcycle-building to pose a racing threat to Indian itself. Several other manufacturers were building worthy machines, Imperial, Pope, Monarch and Crescent among them, and the racing scene was starting to percolate. Record-setting performance, according to the prevailing axiom, meant record-setting sales. With more players showing the motive and the means, Oscar Hedstrom set to work improving both the single's power and durability. Meanwhile he was sketching the design for a new engine, in the increasingly popular V-twin configuration.

Total Indian production for 1903 reached 376 motorcycles, more than doubling the output of the previous year's mark of 143. Springfield, Massachusetts was securely on the motorcycle map.

Below: Early model handlebars were not required to support many of the machine's controls. But as motorcycles grew longer, and heavier, so did handlebars.

Left: The lever on the top frame tube was connected by rod to the carburetor throttle valve. The other lever controlled the ignition advance and compression release. Gas lights were accessories.

Above: The cylinder below the downtube housed the ignition coil. The upper cannister contained the dry-cell batteries. The muffler was tucked in below the frame.

1903 Single
Owner – Jim Lattin
Encinitas, California
Restored by Mike Parti

1905 SINGLE

SPECIFICATIONS
ENGINE/DRIVETRAIN
Engine: IOE single
Displacement: 13ci (213cc)
Bore & stroke: 2.50 x 3.00in
(63.5 x 76mm)
Horsepower: 2.25
Carburetor: Hedstrom
Automatic
Transmission: Direct drive
Brake: Coaster
Batteries: Three 1.5-volt dry-
cell
Ignition: Coil/timer

CHASSIS/SUSPENSION
Frame: Steel, single downtube
Suspension: Cartridge-spring
fork
Wheelbase: 48in (121.9cm)
Weight: 120lb (54.4kg)
Fuel capacity: 1.25gal (4.73lit)
Oil capacity: 1qt (0.95lit)
Tires: 28 x 2in
Top speed: 25mph (40km/h)
Colors: Blue, red
Number built: 1,181
Price: $200

SINGLE (1905)

Indian production for 1904 rose to 596 machines. A newly formed Milwaukee company named Harley-Davidson built a total of eight motorcycles that year. The Federation of American Motorcyclists (FAM) was in its second year, and the sport of motorcycle racing was in its formative phase in terms of organizing athletic events.

The FAM was a consortium of New York motorcycle clubs and dealers from Boston, Philadelphia, Baltimore and other major cities. Their efforts focused mostly on organized endurance runs, forerunners of the modern enduro. Professional racing was in the planning stages at this time, as more bicycle racers grew interested in the new sport.

During this period, George Hendee spent most of his time traveling the country, promoting the Indian brand and organizing new dealerships. At the same time he called on existing dealers and asked questions, and always solicited suggestions on how the motorcycles might be improved.

George had taken the title of President and General Manager of the Indian Motocycle Company, and Oscar served as Chief Engineer and Designer. Their product, and the marketplace, proved them a fortuitous team. Hendee changed the bicycle name from Silver King to Indian, capitalizing on the company's growing name recognition.

In 1904, Hedstrom was still a fit fellow of 33 and remained an active bicycle racer. He also rode the motorcycle of his own design in endurance runs, gaining first-hand knowledge of the machine's strengths and weaknesses and inspecting the competition's mounts. Between he and Hendee, the Indian founders won many of the local and regional events on their own machine, and the advertising value was significant.

Right: Twist-grip controls first appeared in 1905. Throttle and spark were now modulated without removing hands from the handlebar.

Right: The fuel tank was slightly larger by 1905, and a more substantial seat and springs were fitted.

Right: Few modifications were made to the diamond frame in the first few years of production. Oil was still carried in the forward section of the fuel tank, and the New Departure coaster brake remained standard. Most of Hedstrom's work was now devoted to the engine, controls and suspension components.

But more and more competitors were crowding the market, and new challengers appeared almost monthly. More than 70 motorcycle manufacturers had posted their claims to a place in the new industry. Most would fold within a few years, as the Henry Ford effect swept the country with affordable cars. Many motorcycle builders were gone by the 1920s, but a handful of determined engineers and entrepreneurs carried a number of marques on into the 1930s. Three forms of motorcycle competition formed the framework for the matches between competing manufacturers and riders. Endurance runs, hillclimbs and top speed events on the beaches.

In 1905, Indian adopted the twist-grip throttle pioneered by Glenn Curtiss. Before turning his efforts to aviation, Curtiss built a number of motorcycles, including one powered by a V-8 engine. The Springfield team of Hedstrom, DeRosier and a few others continued their winning ways in endurance and hillclimb contests. The single-cylinder machine now had a stronger cylinder, and the cam and valve timing had been revised for a broader power band. Engine failures were uncommon. And the new cartridge-type front fork, with

adjustable spring tension, brought a corresponding improvement in handling and comfort.

Hedstrom was now putting the finishing touches to the new V-twin, with the prototype cylinders set at 42 degrees and displacement at 26 cubic inches (425cc). He and DeRosier tested the engine in local events, continuing the Indian program of race-bred development. The first production twins, rated at 4 horsepower, were built for racing only. The first road version would appear in 1907, with the traditional camel-back fuel tank.

The racing motorcycles employed the "torpedo tank" on the backbone frame tube. In 1905, on the single, DeRosier set a new half-mile average with a speed of 46mph (74km/h). The young French Canadian-American continued posting impressive results, and grew to achieve national fame as a racer. Word of his prowess was also gaining notice in Great Britain and Europe, where motorcycle racing was also growing in popularity.

Indian production climbed to 1,181 in 1905, nearly double the figures for the preceding year. In Springfield, little note was taken that Harley-Davidson's output had also doubled that year, totaling 16 machines.

Left: The cartridge-spring front fork was the first Indian advance in suspension. The spring tension could be adjusted by a single bolt.

Above: Wooden rims had been replaced by steel rims a few years earlier. The sprung fork performed satisfactorily, but as engine power and speed increased, its shortcomings were apparent.

1905 Single
Owner – Mort Wood
Sparks, Maryland

1907 TWIN

SPECIFICATIONS
ENGINE/DRIVETRAIN
Engine: IOE 42° V-twin
Displacement: 38.61ci (633cc)
Bore & stroke: 2.75 x 3.25in
(70 x 82.5mm)
Horsepower: 4
Carburetor: Hedstrom
Automatic
Transmission: Direct drive
Brake: Coaster
Batteries: Three 1.5-volt dry-cell
Ignition: Coil/timer

CHASSIS/SUSPENSION
Frame: Steel, single downtube
Suspension: Cartridge-spring
fork
Wheelbase: 51in (129.5cm)
Weight: 135lb (61.2kg)
Fuel capacity: 1.25gal (4.73lit)
Oil capacity: 1qt (0.95lit)
Tires: 28 x 2.25in
Top speed: 35mph (56km/h)
Colors: Blue, red
Number built: 2,176 (including
singles)
Price: $240

Right: The first Indian V-twin
was introduced in 1907. The
oil supply was now in its own
tank behind the center
downtube, and featured a
hand-pump. The motorcycles
were gaining complexity and
weight, but also providing
additional speed and durability.

TWIN (1907)

The first spring fork, while an improvement on the rigid support, was not a complete success. The arrangement permitted more fore-and-aft wheel movement as speed increased, which had an undesirable effect on handling. So the first production racer, then on Oscar Hedstrom's drawing board, employed the rigid fork.

The V-twin, which would be introduced to the general public in 1907, had grown to 39 cubic inches (640cc) and was rated at 4 horsepower. The single for 1906 also grew to 19 cubic inches (311cc) and a rating of 2.25 horsepower. With the growing power output and subsequent increase in speeds, Hedstrom resolved to devote more attention to the motorcycle chassis and their systems of suspension.

But racing, as usual, took priority. The prototype V-twins were fitted to the existing diamond-frame chassis, with the seat repositioned lower and to the rear. Jake DeRosier was the primary development rider, and entered the machine in several races in the northeast. The engine performed well, and confirmed the design for production models. Hedstrom nonetheless disassembled the engines after each race and inspected the parts for wear and signs of premature failure.

The fifth annual FAM endurance run was held on the Fourth of July, 1906. Indian riders Stanley Kellog and Oscar Hedstrom finished 1-2. In August of the same year, two of the first Indian dealers rode the pre-production V-twins in a record-setting sprint across the country. George Holden of Springfield and Louis Mueller of Cleveland, Ohio made the 3,476-mile (5,594km) ride from San Francisco to New York in 31.5 days. No major mechanical difficulties were encountered.

The next site George Hendee chose to demonstrate the superiority of Indian motorcycles was Ormond Beach, Florida. The hard-packed sand of the coastal shoreline had attracted automobile speed contestants for several years, and Hendee saw no reason to omit motorcycles from the mix. By then Hedstrom had developed the first loop-frame chassis to replace the bicycle-type

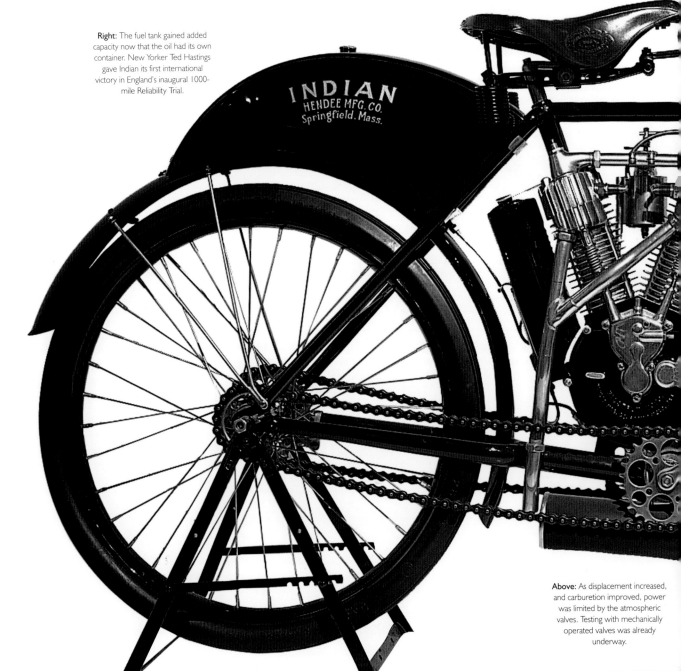

Below: The only non-Yankee parts
on the early Indian were the saddles,
made by Brooks of Great Britain.

Right: The fuel tank gained added
capacity now that the oil had its own
container. New Yorker Ted Hastings
gave Indian its first international
victory in England's inaugural 1000-
mile Reliability Trial.

Above: As displacement increased,
and carburetion improved, power
was limited by the atmospheric
valves. Testing with mechanically
operated valves was already
underway.

diamond-frame unit. The loop frame was stronger and allowed engines to sit lower, improving handling and aerodynamics.

The new frame wouldn't reach production until 1909, but at this phase in the heady sport of motorized competition, the magic figure was 60mph (96km/h). The first to reach the Mile-A-Minute mark was guaranteed a spot in history. Hedstrom fitted the prototype frame with a beefed-up version of the single for beach racing. Several impromptu match races with the car fellows ensued, and the motorcycle managed to keep pace. Hedstrom rode the machine to an unofficial record of 57mph (92km/h).

Indian production for 1906 totaled 1,698 motorcycles. But the relationship with Aurora was showing signs of strain as both companies worked to meet the growing demand for machines. Hendee and Hedstrom agreed that it was time for Indian to

duce their own engines, an undertaking that would require a new factory. They selected a building on State Street in the newly developed industrial section of Springfield, though frames and other components would still be produced at the Worthington Street facility.

1907

When the engine contract with Aurora expired in March, production of the new V-twin shifted to the State Street plant, which would come to be known as the Wigwam. With this expansion came new employees, and an abiding interest in the developing forms of motorcycle competition at home and abroad.

Charles Gustafson of Minnesota joined the company in 1907. He had designed the V-twin engine for the Reading-Standard motorcycle built in Reading, Pennsylvania. Charlie was an astute mechanic/machinist/engineer with a scrupulous eye for detail and a measure of Scandanavian humor. He was put second in command to Oscar Hedstrom in the engineering department. Indian's annual production totaled 2,176 machines

1907 also saw the inception of two seminal racing events in Great Britain. The first was the Tourist Trophy race at the Isle of Man, the other the 1000-Mile Reliability Trial. The Island meet grew steadily to become the foremost international event for road machines, and the reliabilty trial evolved into the International Six Days' Trial. Teddy Hastings, the first American rider/machine entrant in a British event, won the inaugural trial on an Indian V-twin. Hastings, a member of the Crescent Motorcycle Club of New York, was not a factory rider. But his victory established Springfield as a world-class player in the exciting new sport of motorcycle racing.

The advantages of chain drive were well demonstrated by the American rider, who scored a remarkable 994 out of 1000 points in the event. Most of his competitors rode belt-drive machines. Hastings, who financed his own trip abroad, rode the civilian model with spring fork and camel-back tank. The pioneer international racer later became an Indian dealer in Melbourne, Australia.

Below: Indian's "patented, leverless, double grip, twist-of-wrist system." Left grip controlled the throttle, right grip for electrical spark and exhaust valves.

Above: The 39-cubic inch (640cc) V-twin was rated at 4 horsepower; the 60-inch (983cc) racing model at 7hp.

Left: Attempting better to control the increase in fore-and-aft wheel movement at high speeds, Hedstrom lengthened the fork spring for a wider range of adjustment. Racing bikes retained the rigid fork.

1907 Twin
Owner/restorer – Mike Parti
North Hollywood, California

1908 TWIN RACER

SPECIFICATIONS
ENGINE/DRIVETRAIN
Engine: IOE 42° V-twin
Displacement: 61ci (1000cc)
Bore & stroke: 3.25 x 3.44in (82.5 x 87.4mm)
Horsepower: 7
Carburetor: Hedstrom Automatic
Transmission: Direct drive
Brake: Coaster
Ignition: Battery/coil (magneto opt.)

CHASSIS/SUSPENSION
Frame: Steel, single downtube
Suspension: None
Wheelbase: 51in (129.5cm)
Weight: 130lb (59kg)
Fuel capacity: 1.5gal (5.68lit)
Oil capacity: 1.5qts (1.42lit)
Tires: 28 x 2.25in
Top speed: 70mph (97km/h)
Colors: Royal blue, black, red
Number built: Unknown
Price: $350

Right: The factory racing model, available with 633 or 1000cc engine, was nicknamed the "monkey-on-a-stick" model, after a popular children's toy. B.A. Swenson ("The Terrible Swede") rode one to a new record between New York and Chicago, covering 978 miles (1,574km) in 33 hours, 26 minutes.

TWIN RACER (1908) AND TWIN (1908)

Motorcycle racing in America was now a growth sport, and by 1908 had developed most of the framework that would stay in place for the rest of the century. The fork in the road had arrived, and amateur competition took one path as professional racing created venues of its own. Endurance racing, hillclimb and cross-country became fundamentally amateur events. Professional motorcycle racing, dictated by the engineering contest for market share and the public thirst for daredevil action, moved to enlarged versions of the bicycle velodromes. The steeply banked board-track motordromes brought drama and excitement to the scene, and a new level of danger.

Motorcycle design had shifted as well, as the standard bicycle frame was forsaken for stronger, heavier chassis to meet the demands imposed by more powerful engines. Soon all the components were reconfigured to higher standards for strength and durability, as the disciplines of metallurgy and precision machining were joined in the refinement of internal combustion engines. Annual production in 1908 reached 3,257 machines.

Hedstrom recognized that professional racing required machines built specifically for competition. The factory racers were fitted with a smaller fuel tank on the main frame tube, and the seat attached to a strut between the rear downtube and a yoke bolted to the axle. The 61-cubic inch (1000cc) V-twin was rated at 7 horsepower, and the motorcycle weighed 130 pounds (59kg). These first Indian factory racers were the also the final versions of the diamond-frame chassis.

The most significant change to the Sixty-one and the Thirty-fifty single was the incorporation of mechanical intake valves. The engines were also fitted to the new loop-frame chassis, with new factory rider Jake DeRosier race-testing the machines. On the short track velodrome in New Jersey he set a quarter-mile record at 68mph (109km/h) and won the 3-mile race.

Below: The "torpedo"-style gas tanks were made in several sizes to suit various racing requirements and distances. The standard tank held 1 gallon (3.79lit).

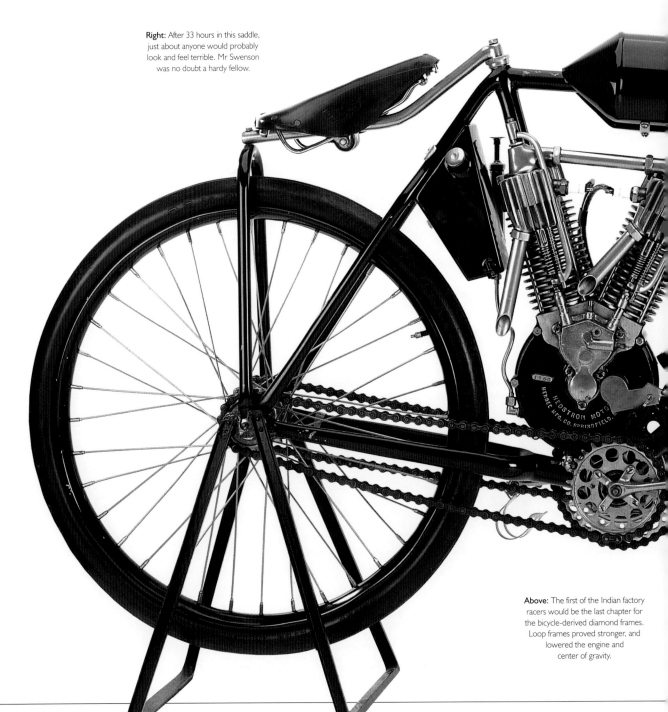

Right: After 33 hours in this saddle, just about anyone would probably look and feel terrible. Mr Swenson was no doubt a hardy fellow.

Above: The first of the Indian factory racers would be the last chapter for the bicycle-derived diamond frames. Loop frames proved stronger, and lowered the engine and center of gravity.

1908 Twin
Owner – Otis Chandler
Ojai, California

Above: The standard twin was offered with atmospheric or mechanical intake valves. Mufflers got larger, as did the mudflaps. The magneto was $40 extra, bringing the price to a hefty $300.

Professional motorcycle racing now had a number of accomplished tuners and riders ready to go the line for the glory of championship competition. The third essential component for market success, the promoter, appeared in the form of New Jersey engineer/entrepreneur Jack Prince. As a former builder of velodromes, Prince turned his skills to larger facilities for motorcycle racing, and became the premier developer of board tracks in the country.

By now Aurora was supplying engines to a half-dozen firms, and building their own Thor motorcycles with a 1000cc V-twin engine. The loop-frame racer was long and low, with the engine canted forward. The bike was developed by William Ottaway, who later headed the Harley-Davidson racing effort. One development rider was California star Paul "Dare Devil" Derkum, who also raced Indian and Reading-Standard machines. Derkum became the manager of the Los Angeles Coliseum board track built by Jack Prince in 1909.

Teddy Hastings returned to Great Britain in 1908, this time with support from the Indian factory, and won the 1000-mile Reliabilty Trial once again. On the domestic front, B.A. Swenson, "The Terrible Swede," won the New York-to-Chicago endurance race aboard an Indian. Springfield basked contentedly in the glow of international acclaim.

Harley-Davidson was not a serious player in the professional ranks at this point. The Milwaukee firm chose not to field a factory team, lending its support to amateur endurance riders. But Harley production rose to 450 machines in 1908, and would triple the following year. The showdown lay ahead.

Above: Early racers normally had the carburetor positioned between the cylinders, while road models located the carb in front.

Above: The most famous name in American motorcycling, chosen for its Americanness.

1908 Twin Racer
Owner – Tony Penachio
Millwood, New York
Restored by Stephen Wright

1909 LIGHT TWIN

SPECIFICATIONS
ENGINE/DRIVETRAIN
Engine: IOE 42° V-twin
Displacement: 38.61ci (633cc)
Bore & stroke: 2.75 x 3.25in (70 x 82.5mm)
Horsepower: 5
Carburetor: Hedstrom Automatic
Transmission: Direct drive
Brake: Coaster
Ignition: Magneto

CHASSIS/SUSPENSION
Frame: Steel, single downtube
Suspension: Cartridge-spring fork
Wheelbase: 56in (142.2cm)
Weight: 195lb (88.5kg)
Fuel capacity: 2gal (7.57lit)
Oil capacity: 2qts (1.9lit)
Tires: 28 x 2.50in
Top speed: 50mph (80km/h)
Colors: Royal blue, black, red
Number built: 4,771 (including singles)
Price: $265

Right: The bicycle era ended in 1909 with the introduction of the full loop frame. Diamond frames remained optional until supply was exhausted. The luggage rack is an Excelsior item.

TWIN (1909) AND SINGLE (1908)

The 60mph (96km/h) goal was already ancient history by 1909. Motorcycles had got faster quickly and the new ambition, the 100mph (161km/h) mark, reflected the accelerating lust for speed. In 1909, George Hendee expanded the factory racing team with the addition of Robert Stubbs, Red Armstrong, Walter Goerke and A.G. Chapple.

The State Street plant was growing as well, with a new wing on the building and the purchase of adjacent property for additional expansion. More factory and administrative employees were hired on, and all the motorcycle operations were transfered to the new site. The Worthington Street plant was given over to bicycle production only.

Prince's Los Angeles Coliseum board track opened in March. With the turns banked at 25 degrees, the track measured just over 1,500 feet (457m); 3.5 laps to the mile. "Daredevil" Derkum was then the top racer in southern California, and Jack Prince recognized the promotional possibilities in an East vs. West shootout at the new motordrome. So he queried the Indian factory, soliciting their interest in sending their best rider out west for a match race. Without hesitation, Hedstrom chose Jake DeRosier and endorsed his choice of amateur support rider, who was young Freddie Huyck from Chicago.

The team arrived in Los Angeles with two loop-frame, 1000cc V-twins with atmospheric intake valves, and six spare engines set up by Hedstrom. The competition roster included Derkum on the Reading-Standard, Al Lingenfelder on a Thor and Ron Mitchell on a Neckarsulm (NSU), made in Germany.

Jake DeRosier smoked everybody at the Coliseum. He had the benefit of superior equipment, but he was also light, shrewd in terms of racing tactics, and an immensely talented rider. Probably the most adept practitioner in the new art of high-speed drafting, DeRosier rarely abused his engine and was cat-quick to take advantage of a competitor's error. After Los Angeles he was a racing star, effectively becoming the USA's first national champion.

The flavor of the 5-mile final race was described by a local newspaper reporter:

"DeRosier and Derkum shot away from Lingenfelder as if he were anchored. Together they flew side by side, gaining or losing not an inch for half way around the lap, when DeRosier began to pull ahead.

"Derkum has been accused by his detractors of having a streak of yellow because of one or two flukes in other races. But those who saw him open up his throttle and proceed to wear down De Rosier's lead yesterday will never accuse him of being anything else than one of the gamest, the nerviest and the headiest drivers ever to turn a handlebar. No more magnificent burst of speed

Below: The later model fuel tank is from a 1915 twin; original tanks still featured the Indian logo in block lettering. The loop frame offered the additional advantage of lower seat height.

Above: The oil tank was now a rectangular 2-quart (1.9lit) container fitted to the center frame tube. Mechanical intake valves were standard. The 633cc model was called the Light Twin.

1908 Single
Owner – Mort Wood
Sparks, Maryland

Above: The bicycle origins of the 1908 single show starkly when juxtaposed with the loop-frame model of the following year.

Above: Many owners now prefer to leave the early models unrestored, since some machines are over-restored and actually diminish in value.

Left: Many of the classic Indians have been restored for regular use, rather than as showpieces. The late Dewey Bonkrud built this '09 as a rider, thus the horn, rearview mirror and luggage rack. Authenticity isn't everything.

1909 Light Twin
Owner – Chuck Vernon
La Mirada, California
Restored by Dewey Bonkrud

could be imagined. Inch by inch Derkum pushed the nose of his machine nearer to De Rosier's until they were first even on terms and then Derkum's nose as steadily went ahead and a mighty cheer from 10,000 throats hailed Derkum as the leader. And again the desperate battle was renewed, this time with DeRosier striving for the lead and calling on his machine as it never was called on before. Slowly but as surely he repeated the thrilling hair-raising trick turned by Derkum, and when the race was perhaps half through 'Jake' again resumed his place at the front...

"Again Derkum called on his mount, which had apparently tired under the grueling pace for the moment, and again it responded, and still once again did Derkum creep steadily toward De Rosier, inch by inch, but still creeping turning corners with a swish and a rush that seemed so terrific as to be demonical, and tearing into the straightaways with not a trace of perceptible change in the mad work. And as grimly and as desperately as Derkum laid down to his work, as equally grim and desperate was the fight made by DeRosier in maintaining his lead.

"It was a battle royal, which is doubtful any other two men in the world today could duplicate, much less excel, and there was not a man, woman or child present but who felt a thrill of admiration for two men with such steady heads, such nerveless bodies as these two riders, who held their machines true to the lines of the track as they followed its changing contour from high banks into more level straightaway and back into high banks again.

"Try as he would, Derkum could not again gain in equal footing with Jake, though it was apparent that he was cutting down the lead, and at the finish pistol he was two wheel lengths behind."

Derkum's California cheering section was disappointed, but all agreed it had been a thrilling race indeed. The Indian contingent gathered more bragging rights when Freddie Huyck decimated the amateur 5-mile final with a time only two seconds slower than DeRosier's. When the celebration ended in Springfield, the founders agreed on the need for a local motordrome in their own backyard, and helped fund construction of the Springfield Stadium.

The ⅓-mile track, completed in August, was of circular rather than oval configuration. The bowl was blisteringly fast, and DeRosier's time for the flying mile translated to 84mph (135km/h). Professional motorcycle racing on board tracks was dashing headlong for disaster; top speed was the all-consuming goal, and issues of handling, suspension and braking were low on the engineering agenda. The fastest machine was the best machine, with the bravest rider, and racing victories were directly correlated to higher sales figures. But the horsepower race was creating a corresponding roster of liabilities for the manufacturers, the riders and ultimately the spectators as well. Indeed, for the entire sport of motorcycling. All of which became perfectly clear in hindsight.

The original diamond-frame Indians remained available in 1909 as less expensive models, but were supplanted within the year by the new loop-frame models. With a number of racing glories to its credit, and increased production capacity in the growing factory, the output for 1909 reached 4,771 machines. Near the end of the year George Hendee established a publicity department in Springfield, and hired John J. O'Connor as its head. Also a former professional bicycle racer, O'Connor's fanciful pen would promote the Indian cause for many years. Support in this effort came from W.F. Hapgood, Editor of the company magazine, *The Motocycle News*.

SPECIFICATIONS
ENGINE/DRIVETRAIN
Engine: IOE single
Displacement: 19.30ci (316cc)
Bore & stroke: 2.63 x 3.58in (67 x 91mm)
Horsepower: 5
Carburetor: Hedstrom Automatic
Transmission: Direct drive
Brake: Coaster
Batteries: Two 1.5-volt dry-cell
Ignition: Coil/timer

CHASSIS/SUSPENSION
Frame: Steel, single downtube
Suspension: Leaf-spring leading link fork
Wheelbase: 56in (142.2cm)
Weight: 175lb (79.4kg)
Fuel capacity: 2gal (7.57lit)
Oil capacity: 2qts (1.9lit)
Tires: 28 x 2.50in
Top speed: 45mph (72km/h)
Colors: Blue, red, green
Number built: 6,137 (all models)
Price: $215

SINGLE (1910) AND SINGLE (1911)

The V-twin engine, now the standard powerplant for most of the top-ranking motorcycles, was being steadily refined. In its new loop frame, the Hedstrom motor moved forward and down, the rear cylinder no longer integrated with the frame tube.

The first two-speed transmission was offered in 1910 as an option on the 500cc single and the 1000cc twin. The clutch was also standard on the direct drive model. The leaf-spring front fork, which became an Indian trademark, was also introduced.

Meanwhile the racing department was busy preparing machines for shipment to England, where they would be run at the famous Brooklands circuit in Surrey. The paved 2.8-mile (4.5km) banked concrete raceway, completed in 1907, was the site of numerous record-setting runs for both cars and motorcycles, and the testing facility for all the British manufacturers.

The premier Jack Prince creation for 1910 was the one-mile Playa del Rey motordrome near Los Angeles. DeRosier had lost his 100-mile title to Morty Graves at the Coliseum track the previous year, and was keen to regain it at the new facility. The national star was running well ahead of his competitor's time, but ran out of fuel on the penultimate lap and had to push his machine for nearly five minutes to cross the finish line. But he still recaptured the record. That fall DeRosier returned to the Coliseum and turned the mile at just over 85mph (137km/h).

Above: The Indian script logo was phased in during 1910, though some models were still produced with the traditional block lettering. Footboards were optional equipment.

Below: The accessory dual spring-post seat suspension was designed for the loop frame. A luggage rack or passenger seat were options.

Right: The first use of chrome-vanadium steel came in 1910, creating an even stronger frame. The cartridge spring fork was replaced by the leaf spring, trailing link assembly that provided better suspension compliance and ride control. The leaf spring acted as part of the front fender.

Above: In 1910 the single-speed model was augmented by an optional two-speed with a clutch. The battery/coil model was $25 less than the magneto version.

Above: Acetylene lights were offered in various sizes and candlepowers. Basic units such as this had small integral tanks; larger systems employed remote tanks connected by hose to the light.

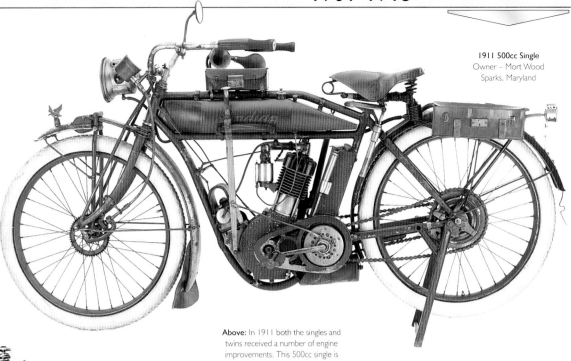

1911 500cc Single
Owner – Mort Wood
Sparks, Maryland

Above: In 1911 both the singles and twins received a number of engine improvements. This 500cc single is accessorized with fender tip, speedometer and tool box.

The long-distance touring honors for 1910 went to rider Volney Davis, who traveled from San Francisco to New York by indirect routes. He then rode the same Indian twin back to the west coast, covering a total of 10,400 miles (16,737km) without any major mechanical problems.

By now Indian had secured most of the major motorcycle contracts with police departments throughout the country. One of the reasons given for Indian's left-hand throttle was that it allowed the patrolman use of his right hand for his sidearm. Indian motorcycles were also finding wider use for mail and commercial delivery. Springfield's total production for 1910 was up again, to a total of 6,137 machines.

1910 316cc Single
Owner/restorer – Marv Baker
Vallejo, California

Above: Electric horns were years away. The bicycle oo-gah horn was usually enough to notify horsemen, bicyclists and pedestrians of your approach.

Above: The Jones Speedometer indicated 5-mph increments until running out of room on the right. Roads of 1911 were exciting at 60mph (97km/h).

1911 BIG-BASE 8-VALVE

SPECIFICATIONS
ENGINE/DRIVETRAIN
Engine: OHV 8-valve V-twin
Displacement: 61ci (1000cc)
Bore & stroke: 3.25 x 3.67in (82.5 x 93.2mm)
Horsepower: Approx. 16
Carburetor: Hedstrom
Transmission: Direct drive
Brakes: None
Ignition: Magneto

CHASSIS/SUSPENSION
Frame: Steel, single downtube
Suspension: Leaf-spring leading link fork
Wheelbase: 53in (134.6cm)
Weight: 245lb (111.1kg)
Fuel capacity: 2gal (7.57lit)
Oil capacity: 1.5qts (1.42lit)
Tires: 28 x 2.25in
Top speed: 100mph (161km/h)
Color: Red
Number built: Approx 6-10
Price: Unknown

8-VALVE RACER (1911)

At its tenth anniversary, the Hendee Manufacturing Company staked legitimate claim to being the world's premier manufacturer of motorcycles. And the events of 1911 would serve to reinforce that position.

Oscar Hedstrom instituted a number of significant changes in the new machines. The cartridge-spring fork was now completely replaced by the leaf-spring unit with trailing link suspension. The new "free engine" was fitted with a stronger clutch and a new forward-kick starting mechanism. The 300cc single was dropped from the roster, and the belt-drive model developed in 1910 lost its planetary clutch, which was too expensive to produce. Indian now offered a selection of eight models, and in the wings were two new racing models; a four-valve single and an eight-valve V-twin.

Racing remained Hedstrom's primary concern, and he realized that progress in both engine and chassis design would be necessary to keep Indian in its dominant position. The most prominent threat to Springfield was the Excelsior motorcycle from Chicago, ridden by Joe Wolters. Another strong contender would be the Flying Merkel, built in Middletown, Ohio.

DeRosier started the 1911 season with a strong showing at the Los Angeles Coliseum motordrome, establishing new records for all distances from two to 90 miles (3.2 to 145km). The 100-mile (161km) mark was within reach when Jake ran out of fuel.

New motordromes had been built in Oakland, California; Denver, Colorado; Cleveland, Ohio; Buffalo, New York; Detroit, Michigan and Chicago, Illinois. More amateurs were making the leap to professional competition, many of them with plenty of dirt-track racing under their belts. Speeds were still climbing, over 80mph (129km/h), matching the ascension of racers' heroic reputations and their salaries. Motordrome banking grew steeper each year, increasing from 25 to 40 degrees and ultimately to 60-degree inclines.

Motorcycle frames, suspension and tires were subjected to correspondingly higher loads. The concurrent escalation in danger produced more accidents, more serious injuries to the riders and more expressions of distaste in the general press. Motorcycle racing, and by association motorcycling itself, was rapidly developing a Bad Reputation.

European motorcycle racing was more civilized by comparison, conducted as it was mostly on public roads. Except in Great Britain, which held to a strict 20mph (32km/h) speed limit and no closure of public roads. So the Isle of Man, or simply The Island, had become the premier international event on the calendar. The fifth annual event held in 1911 was the first use of the 37.5-mile (60.3km) Mountain Course, which the contestants would navigate five times for a total race distance of 187.5 miles (302km).

Both Hendee and Hedstrom were certain that Indian motorcycles, with the best riders aboard, could win at the Isle of Man. Most of the competing machines would be belt-drive, or single-speed chain-driven motorcycles. Indian's two-speed, chain-drive

Below: The exact number of big-base 8-valve racing bikes built is unknown. From racing results, old photos and the consensus of the few remaining old-timers, the number was from six to ten.

Above: Auxiliary ports at the top and bottom of the cylinders vented excess exhaust. Second generation 8-valves of 1914 used standard crankcases. This is the only known big-base to survive.

Right: One of the first serious challenges to Indian's racing dominance came from Excelsior of Chicago. In 1911 the firm brought to the line a big-valve IOE racing engine. Oscar Hedstrom responded with the Indian 8-valve racer.

Above: Direct drive at its most direct. The bikes were towed to start the engines. Rigidly mounted pedals served only as footrests.

Below: Board-track speeds had reached 90mph (145km/h). The Indian racer had one throttle position: wide open. Only a kill button slowed the machine.

Above: The Indian racer took its name from the over-sized crankcases, which contained jumbo flywheels. The oil pump was mounted low for easy reach.

Above: The oil tank was channeled for direct exit of the rear exhaust pipe. The 8-valves raced from 1911-1915.

1911 Big-Base 8-Valve
Owner – Jim Dennie
Palmyra, New York
Restored by Milby Jones

V-twins with front suspension would have the advantage. Early in the year they contacted British Indian agent Billy Wells and outlined the plan. A former TT competitor, Wells agreed to form a team of the best British riders for the event. They would be joined by Hedstrom and Jake DeRosier for an assault on The Island.

The Isle of Man TT was conducted by Britain's Auto-Cycle Union (ACU), established in 1903. The 1911 meet was the first to feature a Senior class, for 500cc singles and 585cc twins, in a curious bit of British logic. Hedstrom sleeved the Indian twin's cylinders to meet the displacement rule, and set about building six machines to take abroad.

Billy Wells selected three riders for the big event: Oliver Godfrey, A.J. Moorhouse and Charles Franklin. Hedstrom, DeRosier and three mechanics from the factory arrived at the island several weeks before the event, so the riders could familiarize themselves with both the course and the machines. The British enthusiast press enthused at length over the forthcoming showdown between the foremost racers from both countries, the highly reputed Jake DeRosier from America and Britain's own Charlie Collier of Matchless. The other major marques represented were NSU, Triumph, Rudge and Scott.

Despite his deserved reputation as a speed merchant, it was soon apparent in practice that DeRosier was out of his element on the Isle of Man. His experience on board tracks and the groomed dirt ovals of American fairgrounds found him ill prepared for the island's rough roads. DeRosier crashed six times while practicing, and commented to reporters that, "this race ain't going to be no tea party." He came to the line on race day bruised and battered, but game nonetheless.

DeRosier actually led on time for the first lap, but was overtaken by Collier when the Indian developed valve problems. With the problem sorted out, the American was underway once again, only to suffer a serious crash on the third lap which left him dazed. His tool kit had come adrift on the previous lap, and DeRosier had to ride three miles (4.8km) on one cylinder before repairs could be made. Still disoriented from his crash, DeRosier finished twelfth.

British champ Charlie Collier ran into problems when he ran out of fuel, and Oliver Godfrey took over the lead. Collier brought his Matchless in second, but was disqualified for receiving outside assistance and taking on fuel at an unauthorized stop.

This moved Indian riders Franklin and Moorhouse into second and third positions, meaning a top-three sweep for Indian motorcycles. Fewer than half of the 59 entrants in the Senior TT finished the event.

BELT-DRIVE SINGLE (1912) AND 4-VALVE RACER(1912)

1912 BELT-DRIVE SINGLE

SPECIFICATIONS
ENGINE/DRIVETRAIN
Engine: IOE single
Displacement: 30.50in (500cc)
Bore & stroke: 2.63 x 3.58in (67 x 91mm)
Horsepower: 4
Carburetor: Hedstrom Automatic
Transmission: Pulley/belt
Brake: Coaster
Batteries: Three 1.5-volt dry-cell
Ignition: Coil/timer

CHASSIS/SUSPENSION
Frame: Steel, single downtube
Suspension: Leaf-spring leading link fork
Wheelbase: 56in (142.2cm)
Weight: 230lb (104.3kg)
Fuel capacity: 2gal (7.57lit)
Oil capacity: 2qts (1.89lit)
Tires: 28 x 2.50in
Top speed: 45mph (72km/h)
Colors: Blue, red, green
Number built: Unknown
Price: $215

Americans were still celebrating the Isle of Man victory a week later, when DeRosier arrived at Brooklands to learn the track for his upcoming match race with Charlie Collier. The paved surface was much more to his liking, and the Yank quickly set new speed records for the kilometer, mile and 5-mile marks. The first Anglo-American match race was set for the following weekend.

Hedstrom had prepared Jake's machine specifically for Brooklands. Despite the concrete surface, the raceway was much more bumpy than American board tracks. The leaf spring was shortened to control front wheel movement, the pedal cranks were removed and the footrests rigidly mounted. Knee pads were fitted to each side of the tank for extra grip, and the tallest possible gearing installed. Wider handlebars were employed to improve leverage on the rough surface.

Cheers erupted from the large crowd as the two riders took to the track behind the starter car for the first two-lap race. It was a clean start and Collier took a slight lead, which grew to three bike lengths on the first lap. But DeRosier closed the gap and passed the Englishman into the final turn. Collier regained some ground on the straightaway but was unable to pass, as round one went to the American.

In the five-lap second event Collier again took the early lead and DeRosier tucked in behind him. They rode inches apart for two and a half laps, until Jake's front tire burst on the back straight at over 80mph (129km/h). Somehow he managed to stay upright and limped in. USA – 1, Great Britain – 1.

The front wheel and tire from Oliver Godfrey's bike was fitted to DeRosier's machine, and the two riders lined up for the 10-lap final. Once again Collier set the pace and the American sat on his tail, but by lap three the Matchless had pulled a 10-bike lead, running at 85mph (137km/h) on the front straight. Collier's machine seemed to have a handling advantage coming off the banking, but a few laps later one of his plug wires came adrift and DeRosier overtook him. By the time the Englishman regained full spark he had lost nearly a half lap. Though Collier made up some of the distance, the Indian rider was home first with an average speed of 78.64mph (126.56km/h).

A few weeks later, just before his return to the States, DeRosier returned to Brooklands for a few more record runs. He upped the kilometer speed to 88.77mph (142.86km/h) and the mile to 88.23mph (141.99km/h). DeRosier sailed for the USA the next

Below: The tank-mounted toolbox was standard Indian practice in the early years, but later moved to the lower frame.

Right: The leaf spring was accompanied by a notched fender in 1912, which helped control the spray of mud and water from the tire.

1912 Belt-Drive Single
Owner – Mort Wood
Sparks, Maryland

Right: Though Indian made its reputation largely on the superiority of chain drive, a number of dealers asked for a belt-drive model. The first version, in 1910, had an elaborate internal gear system to control belt slippage. This proved too costly and was eliminated for the following year.

day, hailed by the enthusiast press as a world champion. But as it turned out, his homecoming would be nothing to celebrate.

Concurrent with this period of dramatic successes in racing, the management and production situation in the Hendee Manufacturing Company was in a state of revision. With a roster of some 1,200 dealers nationwide, and growing numbers overseas, the company was struggling to keep up with its own growth. Ambitious plans for factory expansion and additional tooling were undertaken early in 1911, including plans for an additional plant east of town. A number of new officials and managers were hired, and the executive offices remodeled.

The scale of this expansion required the sale of more shares in the company, most of which were purchased by local investors. The future of Indian Motocycles looked uncommonly bright, and the growing demand for sidecars made the appeal even stronger. Hendee had little trouble raising capital investment in the flourishing enterprise. But within a year the issues of policy, profit, racing expense and engineering standards would collide, and drastically alter the course of Indian's development.

Springfield listed record numbers for both production and profits in 1911. The factory produced 19,585 machines, and showed profits of $502,000.

No historical record indicates what exactly transpired between DeRosier, Hedstrom and Hendee upon the racer's return from Great Britain. But the issue hinged on the new 8-valve racing machine built to challenge the Excelsior, and who would ride the new bikes. As the factory's star rider, DeRosier naturally expected to receive one of the machines, which in his absence had been ridden by amateurs Eddie Hasha and Ray Seymour. But following a heated argument, DeRosier left Springfield for Chicago and was quickly signed to a factory Excelsior ride by owner Ignaz Schwinn. A new 1000cc Big Valve twin was prepared for Jake to ride at Jack Prince's new Los Angeles Stadium motordrome.

1912 4-Valve Racer
Owner – Dan Rouit
Clovis, California

Above: A limited number of 4-valve racing singles were built in 1911 and 1912, most raced on dirt tracks. The rider braced his right leg against the taped bar attached to the top frame tube.

Right: The 4-valve singles were purpose-built race engines, rather than modified twins. The crankcase breather tube doubled as a drip oiler for the primary chain. The Bosch magneto was standard.

Above: The final belt drive configuration included a conventional lever and roller belt tensioning system. The last models were sold in 1912.

Left: Indian red became the standard color in 1912. The rear stand was improved for both ease of operation and better stability when starting the engine.

BOARD-TRACK RACER (1912) AND TT TWIN (1912)

**1912 BOARD-TRACK
V-TWIN**

SPECIFICATIONS
ENGINE/DRIVETRAIN
Engine: IOE V-twin
Displacement: 61ci (1000cc)
Bore & stroke: 3.25 x 3.67in
(82.5 x 93.2mm)
Horsepower: 12
Carburetor: Hedstrom
Transmission: Direct drive
Brakes: None
Ignition: Magneto

CHASSIS/SUSPENSION
Frame: Steel, single downtube
Suspension: Leaf-spring leading
link fork
Wheelbase: 53in (134.6cm)
Weight: 240lb (109kg)
Fuel capacity: 2gal (7.57lit)
Oil capacity: 1.5qts (1.42lit)
Tires: 28 x 2.75in
Top speed: 90mph (145km/h)
Color: Red
Number built: Approx. 30
Price: $235

Speculation, of course, is even cheaper than talk. Perhaps Hendee foresaw the impeding demise of motordrome racing; maybe he was under pressure from new investors to cut the racing budget, or it could have been that DeRosier demanded more money to match his international fame. Whatever the case, the new factory racing team consisted of Ray Seymour and Eddie Hasha, with additional support from a freelance rider named Erwin G. Baker, who would figure strongly in the Indian legend.

Preoccupied with other issues, Springfield didn't send a factory effort to the Isle of Man in 1912. Hedstrom did provide Charles Franklin with a new big-base 8-valve for another record attempt at Brooklands. The young Irishman turned in a remarkable ride on the rough surface, completing 300 miles (487km) in 4.6 hours for a new record.

The factory offered a number of the new 4-valve single racing machines for sale to the public, possibly to mollify investors' concerns over the competition expenditures.

To capitalize on the Isle of Man victory, Indian released TT models in both single and twin versions. The clutch lever was now fitted to the right side of the fuel tank, and footboards and kickstarter added. The larger rear hub incorporated both internal expanding and external contracting brakes, and knockout axles were employed on both wheels.

Royal blue was dropped as an optional color in 1912 and Indian red became the standard color. The belt-drive model, less than successful the previous year, was refitted with a conventional pulley and belt-tensioner and sold as the 1912 model. Production numbers on this model have been lost to history, but relatively few were built and even fewer remain today.

Two horrendous racing accidents occured in 1912, which combined to alter the course of both racing history and the future of the Hendee Manufacturing Company. The Los Angeles Stadium motordrome opened in February, and the three fastest men on the track were Jake DeRosier, Joe Wolters and "Fearless" Charlie Balke, all mounted on Excelsiors. For whatever reason, DeRosier and Balke disliked one another immediately, a fact played up by the race promoters and the press. So a match race was set for the next event.

In the final event, when the racers were side by side, Balke neared the baseline where the track angle changes pitch. His pedal touched down and Balke lost control of his machine, which hit DeRosier and sent him tumbling. Balke's injuries were minor, but DeRosier was unconscious with a leg broken in three places. He was rushed to the hospital for surgery. He barely survived but then seemed to be on the mend. But a few months later his condition deteriorated, requiring another operation. De Rosier's savings

Below: The aerodynamics of speed dictated a riding position as low as possible. Riders crouched down with their chins on the tank.

Below: Racing machines were built to minimums in terms of comfort and lightness. Fenders were unnecessary but for a strip in front of the rear wheel.

Above: Board-track racers had cylinders ported to scavenge excess exhaust and crankcase pressure. Some factory racing machines were sold to the public in 1912, both to defray expenses and encourage privateer entries.

Right: The 1912 racing season was dominated by Indian motorcycles. This is the standard factory board-tracker.

Right: The TT model, built to capitalize on Indian's victory sweep at the 1911 Isle of Man, was introduced in 1912. This was effectively the first café racer.

Left: The leaf-spring fork proved itself in competition at the Isle of Man. The machines were originally fitted with front fenders.

1912 TT Twin
Owner – Gene Calidonna
Seal Beach, California

Right: The entire valve train on Indian racers and production models was strengthened and improved for the 1912 season. Hedstrom favored straight exhaust pipes.

were soon depleted, his racing trophies were sold to raise money, and the racers held a benefit meet at the motordrome to help with his expenses. Accompanied by his wife and mother, DeRosier returned home to Springfield.

In September, at the new motordrome in Newark, New Jersey, the final event of the day was a five-lap handicap main. On the third lap, Eddie Hasha on the Indian overtook Johnnie Albright for the lead. At this point Hasha's engine mis-fired, and he reached down with his left hand, presumably to the spark plug lead. The engine caught immediately and bike and rider surged to the right and up to the railing.

Reports say Hasha rode the rail for 100 feet, until hitting a post which sent the rider into the grandstand and the bike cartwheeling down the banking. Four boys who had their heads out over the railing were killed instantly. The rear wheel of Hasha's Indian was clipped off by the post and landed on an infield spectator, who died several days later. The tumbling bike hit Albright in the shoulder, crashing the rider and both machines to the bottom of the track. Albright, Hasha and another grandstand spectator all died, which brought the total to eight deaths in single accident.

Headlines of outrage appeared in the press, calling for an end to "murderdromes" and senseless carnage in the name of entertainment. The New Jersey track closed forever shortly thereafter. The motordrome era had effectively ended.

1912 Board-Track V-Twin
Owner – Tony Penachio
Millwood, New York

1913 1000cc TWIN

SPECIFICATIONS
ENGINE/DRIVETRAIN
Engine: IOE V-twin
Displacement: 61ci (1000cc)
Bore & stroke: 3.25 x 3.67in
(82.5 x 93.2mm)
Horsepower: 7
Carburetor: Hedstrom
Transmission: Direct or 2-speed
Brake: External contracting
Ignition: Magneto

CHASSIS/SUSPENSION
Frame: Steel, single downtube
Suspension: Leaf-spring leading
link fork
Wheelbase: 59in (149.9cm)
Weight: 355lb (161kg)
Fuel capacity: 2.2gal (8.33lit)
Oil capacity: 2qts (1.89lit)
Tires: 28 x 3.00
Top speed: 55mph (88km/h)
Color: Red
Number built: 31,950 (all
models)
Price: $250

Right: In 1913 Indian became
the first major American
motorcycle manufacturer to
offer rear suspension. The
cradle-spring frame, designed
and developed by Oscar
Hedstrom, was a dandy piece
of engineering.

TWIN (1913) AND SINGLE (1913)

This would be the all-time record year for Indian motorcyles, in terms of both production volume (31,950 machines) and profit ($1.3 million). It would also be the worst year ever in terms of personal loss for Oscar Hedstrom and Jake DeRosier.

Hedstrom had invested more than a year of development and testing on the new cradle-spring frame. Rear-wheel suspension had been largely ignored by other manufacturers since it created numerous problems in chassis design and construction, frame flexing and maintaining chain tension foremost among them. Not to mention the costs of new tooling, materials and production. So most builders settled for suspending the rider at the seat and leaving the rear wheel solidly attached to the frame.

But Springfield's phenomenal growth, and the driving motivation to set the industry standards, made rear suspension the next logical engineering and marketing steps for Indian. The object: make motorcycling more comfortable, which will attract more customers. This, and Oscar Hedstrom's creative impulse as an engineer and rider, were manifest in the cradle-spring frame.

As a tribute to his considerable skills, the design proved out in its original form. The system utilized two 8-leaf inline springs of chrome vanadium steel, attached at the rear frame junction to a U-shaped boss. At the rear the springs fitted to a hinged loop carried

by bar struts bolted to the swingarm above the axle. Rubber bumpers damped the recoil stroke. (Or rubber dampers bumped it.) The new frame also provided a 1.5-inch (3.8cm) reduction in seat height, covering another important consideration in riding comfort and safety.

Despite dire warnings from traditionalists on the probable consequences of a hinged rear wheel (rubbery handling, wheel misalignment, broken chains), Hedstrom's suspension worked well. With four inches (10.2cm) of wheel travel (two in each direction), the system made easier work of the more punishing roads in the American countryside. Motorcyclists could simply travel farther, in more comfort, by virtue of the fatigue reduction for both bike and rider. And, of course, ride faster in the process.

The following year Erwin G. Baker, a rider of uncommon physical strength and stamina, would ride the cradle-spring Indian across the country and into history. His accomplishment, and those to follow, would reinforce the image of the Springfield marque for the company's lifetime and beyond. The big fellow from Indianapolis, "Bake" to his friends and soon "Cannonball" Baker to the world at large, would become the most famous motorcyclist of all time.

But despite the remarkable advances in engineering, production and the positive publicity to follow, the Hendee Manufacturing Company and the Indian Motocycle now approached the end of

Below: Dual leaf springs and a swing
arm combined to diminish the jolts
of early motorcyling, when most
roads were rough and unpaved.

Above: Public apprehension abou
rear-wheel suspension was mitigat
by the results of the first San Dieg
to Phoenix race. Paul Derkum wo
the 441-mile (710km) event, mos
over scraggly desert terrain, on a
cradle-spring Indian.

1913 Single
Owner – Jim Lattin
Encinitas, California

Above: The 500cc overhead-valve singles were winning dirt-track races for more than a decade. Later versions were "made over" engines, V-twins with one cylinder removed and a plate bolted to the crankcases.

Below: Indian suspension was based on established automobile engineering of the period; simple leaf springs at both ends.

1913 1000cc Twin
Owner – Otis Chandler
Ojai, California

their Golden Age. The firm had grown by the proverbial leaps and bounds in a decade, established an international reputation for quality and advanced design, and set virtually all the speed and distance records in the books. Now the forces of time, economics and individual principle combined to close the first chapter of an extraordinary story.

In retrospect the dissolution of Springfield's pioneering team seems to almost caricature Murphy's Law, revising it to read "If almost everything can go wrong, it will." The friction between the founders and the new stockholders began generating heat a year earlier, when the board of directors pressured Hendee to improve the profit picture. Building good motorcycles, still a manual process, with the best materials was not inexpensive. Expenditures for the new models, the 8-valve racers and the factory expansion looked alarming. Hedstrom, now in charge of two plants plus design and engineering, began to chafe under the imposition of more restrictive policies.

He was also less than enthused about Hendee's proposal for an electric starting system for the big twins. The president reasoned that starting ease was the next most important leap in technology, since more people would be attracted to a thumb-start machine. Sidecarists in particular, and Springfield had become the leading manufacturer of sidecars. Charles Kettering had just established the workability of the electric starter for the automobile.

Hedstrom's misgivings were based on simple matters of practical physics and chemistry. Batteries were large, heavy and easily drained of their charge. And there was more than a little doubt that they could withstand the jarring shocks administered by rugged roads to a motorcycle. The chief engineer undertook work on the project nonetheless, but would not see it to completion.

Jacob DeRosier entered the Springfield hospital for another operation in February. The two-and-a-half hour surgery appeared successful, and Jake seemed to be recovering. But a few days later he failed, and died at the age of 33. The transplanted French-Canadian had arguably been the greatest motorcycle racer in the world, and easily the most widely known. Hedstrom, his friend and mentor, was stunned. A few days later the racer's funeral procession passed the Indian factory, with the flag at half mast and production suspended in his honor. Oscar Hedstrom resigned four days later.

EIGHT-VALVE RACER (1915) AND TWIN (1914)

Control of the Hendee Manufacturing Company was no longer in the hands of pioneer enthusiasts of the motorcycle sport. The majority stockholders and new board of directors were investors and businessmen, most of whom would never ride a motorcycle. Budgets, production figures, sales, profits and dividends composed the framework in which they worked.

Historical scuttlebutt also suggests that some business practices of these men were less than scrupulous. This era of unprecedented technological development and unbridled industrial growth also multiplied the accompanying elements of greed and corruption. By manipulating stock values and creating the public impression that company fortunes were growing at amazing rates, corporate owners were able to generate windfall profits for themselves. Absent government restrictions, this version of capitalism grew fat and happy until 1929 when the charade collapsed.

Neither Hendee nor Hedstrom had the stomach for this sort of business. The death of Jake DeRosier had quickened Hedstrom's departure, but his decision came months earlier. The reign of George Hendee would end two years later, but the direction of Indian Motocycles effectively changed forever in 1914.

The electric-start Hendee Special was introduced with considerable fanfare. The 7-horsepower twin also featured electric lights and two batteries. Unfortunately the batteries were not built to withstand the rough roads of the day. At $325 the Special was competitively priced, but even the convenience of thumb-starting failed to attract legions of customers and the model lasted only one year. "Ahead of its time," as the saying goes.

Both the 1000cc V-twin and 500cc single were offered in 2-speed and direct drive models, and the Light Twin was dropped from the lineup. Development work was underway on the 3-speed transmission for the next model year, and the 8-valve big base racing engine was reconfigured with standard twin crankcases.

Some irony attaches to the decline of Indian's racing program and the concurrent ascension of factory racers from Harley-Davidson. Springfield had long regarded the Milwaukee bunch as novice upstarts, and the Silent Gray Fellows were perceived as mostly uncompetitive utility machines. But Harley-Davidson production had gone from fewer than 4,000 motorcycles in 1912 to over 16,000 in 1914. The heavy-duty iron obviously had some

Below: Lean and purposeful, the Indian 8-valve racing machines set the early standards for speed.

Right: The second generation of 8-valve racing engines employed the standard crankcases and bottom ends. Cost cuts imposed by the new management led Franklin to modify the engine.

Above: The small-base engine allowed a lower frame, and center of gravity, compared to the big-base models. The two Charlies, Franklin and Gustafson, cooperated on development.

Above: In 1914, the racing singles were equipped with what would later come to be called Ricardo heads. The squish-band combustion chamber boosted horsepower.

1914 IOE V-Twin
Owner – Chuck Vernon
La Mirada, California

Above: This 1914 2-speed has been stroked to 65ci (1025cc), and equipped with a Schebler bellmouth carburetor and a quick-change magneto.

Below: At the first 300-mile race in Dodge City, Kansas, July 4, 1914, Charles Gustafson set a fast lap time on the new small-base eight valve. His average speed was 91mph (146km/h). Glen "Slivers" Boyd won the event on a pocket-valve Indian.

Left: On board tracks, high-pressure tires often slung splinters at following riders. Slivers Boyd got the nickname for the lumber removed from his body after a nasty tumble on the boards.

appeal, and privateer racers who cherished the underdog role took some delight in challenging Indian's supremacy.

While Harley-Davidson development engineer Bill Ottaway, formerly of Thor Motorcycles, was at work on Milwaukee's 8-valve racer, Indian was shifting its emphasis to the new side-valve engines. Although the racing singles were granted the latest squish band-type cylinder heads, which would later be called Ricardo heads after their British designer, Harry Ricardo.

Erwin G. Baker began his legendary cross-country run from San Diego, California on May 14, 1914. Departing in a rainstorm, big Bake reached clear sailing when he made the high desert and enjoyed good weather all the way to the midwest. At about 6

foot-four, with a face variously described as strong with character or just flat-shovel ugly, Erwin was an imposing presence in the saddle. He possessed the requisite physical strength, self-discipline and true grit to ride staggering distances without sleep, roads or not. Women and small children loved him. He was a hero.

Baker carried a reasonably large-caliber revolver to discourage wild dogs and other critters that might slow his pace, and had occasion to use it. His transcontinental time was 11.5 days, establishing a new national record that would be the first of many. Erwin was effectively the first professional free-agent racer, setting his own financial terms and riding for whomever he chose. Baker became the motorcycle sport's first prominent ambassador, and he didn't mind the nickname Cannonball.

Oscar Hedstrom was succeeded as chief engineer by Charles Gustafson, who served in that capacity until the arrival of Charlie Franklin from Ireland. Born in Dublin in 1880, Franklin was a young bicycle and motorcycle enthusiast who went on to study electrical engineering. His amateur performances were noted by Indian's British agent, Billy Wells, who signed Franklin to ride for the factory at the 1911 Isle of Man TT, where he finished third.

Charles was a studious, soft-spoken young man who could go like hell on a motorcycle. And he was smart. Franklin didn't affect fancy racing outfits, chase women or "drink like an Irishman." Nor did he crash often. But he rode well and developed an abiding fascination with motorcycle design and performance. So when the call came from America, Charlie immediately gave up his secure civil engineering job and packed his bags.

To his dismay, Franklin's first project in Springfield would be the design of a lightweight two-stroke motorcycle to be produced without undue expense. His other more important challenge would be refining the new F-head engine to meet the growing threat from Harley-Davidson. The Milwaukee crew served notice with its first factory team at the Savannah, Georgia 300-mile national championship, where Irving Janke finished third on the Harley-Davidson.

1915 8-Valve Racer
Owner/restorer – Stephen Wright
Huntington Beach, California

1915 BIG TWIN

SPECIFICATIONS
ENGINE/DRIVETRAIN
Engine: IOE V-twin
Displacement: 61ci (1000cc)
Bore & stroke: 3.25 x 3.67in
(82.5 x 93.2mm)
Horsepower: 15
Carburetor: Indian Automatic or
Schebler
Transmission: 3-speed
Primary drive: Duplex chain
Final drive: Chain
Brake: External contracting
Battery: 6-volt
Ignition: Splitdorf magneto

CHASSIS/SUSPENSION
Frame: Steel, single downtube
Suspension: Leaf-spring leading
link fork
Wheelbase: 59in (149.9cm)
Weight: 370lb (167.8kg)
Fuel capacity: 2.2gal (8.33lit)
Oil capacity: 2qts (1.89lit)
Tires: 28 x 3.00
Top speed: 55mph (89km/h)
Color: Red
Number built: 21,000 (all
models)
Price: $275

TWIN (1915) AND RACING SINGLE (1914)

The last of the "Hedstrom Motors" powered the Indian Motocycles for 1915, with the 1000cc twin supplemented by a 700cc Little Twin rendition. The original F-head machines would come to establish a cachet among purists as the "real" Indians, the first editions in the 50-year span. One contemporary vintage organization is called simply the Pre-16 Club, limiting its group rides to the original Springfield mounts and other early models of original marques of the period.

In addition to the optional 3-speed transmission, generators were fitted to the new models with electric lights, and the new kickstart mechanism featured a rear-swing lever. Economies of production were reflected by painted spokes, rims and hubs, and Schebler carburetors replaced the more expensive Hedstrom units. The D-1 racing model, listed in the catalog with a rating of 20 dynamometer-tested horsepower, was priced at $250. The short-wheelbase bike had the leaf-spring fork, rigid-mount rear wheel and a guaranteed speed of 70mph (113km/h).

Charles Gustafson and his son Charles, Jr., convinced management that side-valve engines could be produced more cheaply, last longer and go faster than the F-head models. Their first attempt at proof was the Powerplus model that would appear in 1916, following another convincing cross-country dash by the redoubtable Erwin G. Baker.

The endurance ace rode from Vancouver, British Columbia to Tijuana, Mexico in just under 3.5 days. The cradle-spring frame was credited with a large measure of his success, and ads quoted Baker saying that "without this device he could never have stood the hardships or his Indian the rough usage in his record-breaking trip across the continent." According to the factory, "It is the greatest achievement in motorcycle construction for comfort since the introduction of pneumatic tires."

But the Springfield bunch had their hands full for the 1915 racing season, which would witness a full-scale factory assault by Harley-Davidson, who was obviously no longer just messing around.

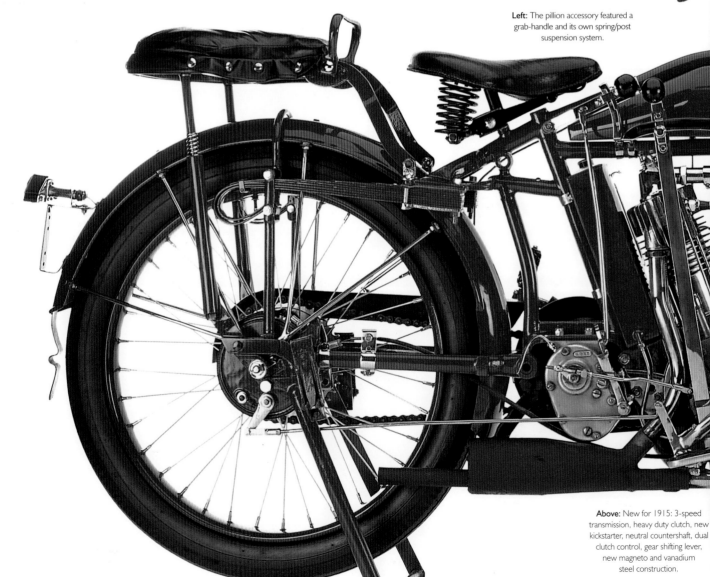

Left: The pillion accessory featured a grab-handle and its own spring/post suspension system.

Right: In 1915 the Big Twin was offered in three models: single speed ($225), two-speed ($260) or three-speed ($275). Corresponding Little Twin (700cc) models were $210, $245 and $260 respectively.

Above: New for 1915: 3-speed transmission, heavy duty clutch, new kickstarter, neutral countershaft, dual clutch control, gear shifting lever, new magneto and vanadium steel construction.

1914 IOE Racing Single
Owner – Tony Penachio
Millwood, New York

Above: These were the final renditions of the Hedstrom pocket-valve single racers. The next generation of side-valve engines were developed by Franklin and Gustafson.

1915 Big Twin
Owner – Fran Guldenbrein
Vallejo, California
Restored by Marv Baker

Indian had won the Dodge City 300-mile National in 1914 on a side-valve twin, ridden by Glen Boyd. The factory had entered both ohv 8-valves and flatheads for testing and evaluation. Harley-Davidson built a few 8-valves in response, which were as yet unproven. But in the spring Harley-Davidson factory riders Otto Walker and Red Parkhurst were 1-2 in the 300-mile roadrace through the streets of Venice, California. And the Excelsiors of Carl Goudy and Bob Perry were third and fourth. Indian riders Fred Ludlow and Morty Graves finished in fifth and sixth places. That summer Walker and the "Harley Wrecking Crew" dominated the Dodge City 300 and effectively toppled the mighty Indian factory racing team.

And the automobile industry, Henry Ford in particular, was posting record production and sales figures. Ford had not only perfected the assembly line manufacture of cars, but doubled the wages of his workers. The results were more cars on the market at lower prices and, since other industries were pressured to raise wages, more customers who could afford them. The motorcycle industry was effectively demoted as a contender in the production of practical transportation vehicles.

History suggests that George Hendee foresaw much of this a few years earlier, when he bought a large farm in Connecticut. In 1914 he appeared less often in his factory office, and delegated much of the daily management responsibility to treasurer Frank Weschler. His friends and associates would later report that Hendee was never the same after Hedstrom's departure, and that he grew increasingly disenchanted with the business practices and directives of the board of directors.

George Hendee resigned as general manager in April at the age of 49. He had been a bachelor for 20 years, but a few months later he married Edith Hale, his personal secretary. A year later he retired to his estate in East Suffolk, Connecticut. Hendee's title of president and his stock in the company went to board member John F. Alford, for a reported figure of $950,000.

Both production figures and profits dropped for 1915, the second year running.

POWERPLUS (1916) AND POWERPLUS EXPORT (1915)

1916 POWERPLUS
MODEL F

SPECIFICATIONS
ENGINE/DRIVETRAIN
Engine: Side-valve 42° V-twin
Displacement: 61ci (1000cc)
Bore & stroke: 3.13 x 3.97in
(79.5 x 100.8mm)
Horsepower: 18
Carburetor: Schebler
Transmission: 3-speed
Primary drive: Duplex chain
Final drive: Chain
Brake: External contracting
Battery: 6-volt
Ignition: Splitdorf magneto

CHASSIS/SUSPENSION
Frame: Steel, single downtube
Suspension: Leaf-spring leading
link fork
Wheelbase: 59in (149.9cm)
Weight: 405lb (183.7kg)
Fuel capacity: 2.2gal (8.33lit)
Oil capacity: 2qts (1.89lit)
Tires: 28 x 3.00
Top speed: 60mph (97km/h)
Color: Red
Number built: 22,000 (all
models)
Price: $350 (with sidecar)

For 1916 Springfield's board of directors discovered another corollary of Murphy's Law: "If something looks too good to be true, it probably is." In this case, the promise of greater profits took the form of World War I.

But the investors could hardly be charged with war profiteering, since they somehow managed only a slim margin of profit during the hostilities. In the absence of an experienced team that knew how to run the company, the new owners depended on novice managers to establish the costs, production schedules and pricing for military contracts. And despite Indian's position as the top supplier of motorcycles for the armed forces, the return for investors was less than it would have been in the civilian market. Indeed the lust for war profits turned out to be a double whammy for Springfield, which neglected its traditional dealers and customers in the process. And by alienating many dealers, the Indian management would make a costly mistake.

As if to add insult to perjury, Harley-Davidson and Excelsior combined to demolish Indian's racing effort, winning between them all the major championship meets of 1916. By mid-season it was apparent that Springfield's vaunted racing reputation was in deep stew, so the call went out for help. Naturally the call went to Oscar Hedstrom, who had spent a comfortable three years sailing on the Connecticut River and tinkering with speedboats. Then a wealthy man, he had built an expansive workshop behind his house, and enjoyed life with his wife, Julia and their 17-year-old daughter, Helen. Oscar wasn't keen on returning to the factory.

But the combined efforts of the Charlies, Gustafson and Franklin, and Hedstrom's own racing enthusiasm drew him back to Springfield to lend a hand. No doubt he was paid handsomely as well. For some three months Hedstrom was nominally in charge of both production and racing, though in correspondence he listed himself simply as Mechanical Engineer.

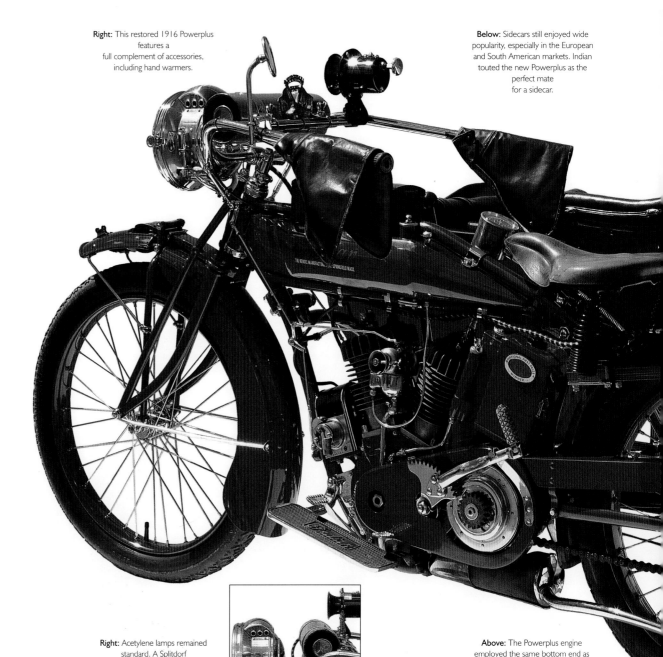

Right: This restored 1916 Powerplus features a full complement of accessories, including hand warmers.

Below: Sidecars still enjoyed wide popularity, especially in the European and South American markets. Indian touted the new Powerplus as the perfect mate for a sidecar.

Right: The new side-valve engine, designated the Powerplus, was met with more than a little skepticism by veteran devotees of the Hedstrom pocket-valve motor. But the performance was sufficient to satisfy all but the most die-hard doubters, and the Powerplus would establish its own merits.

Right: Acetylene lamps remained standard. A Splitdorf magneto/dynamo for ignition and lighting was an extra-cost option.

Above: The Powerplus engine employed the same bottom end as the Hedstrom design. Displacement remained 1000cc, but the new engine had slightly smaller bore and longer stroke.

Above: A few Powerplus engines were fitted to export models in 1915. These machines were equipped with front-wheel stands and the last of the remaining aluminum footboards.

1915 Powerplus Model F
Owner – Chuck Vernon
La Mirada, California

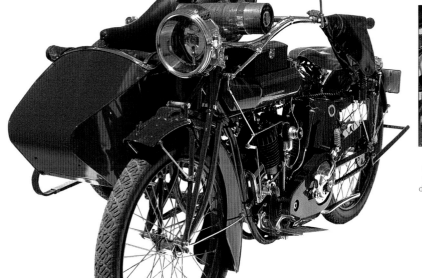

Above: A thoughtful accessory for midnight riders in the early years; a detachable gas-powered flashlight for roadside emergencies.

Above: Sidecar-equipped big twins sold well in Canada and Africa as well, since the supply of British machines had been curtailed by the war.

Indian managed to save some racing face late in the year with a victory in the major desert race, held for the first time in Arizona. The team, headed by Cannonball Baker, included cross-country record-holder Roy Artley, Alan Bedell and Jack Dodds. Harley-Davidson fielded a full team, and Joe Wolters represented Excelsior. Indian riders took three of the top four places, with Artley first into Phoenix in the middle of the night. He had crossed 441 miles (710km) of Arizona desert at better than a 33mph (53km/h) average speed.

A few weeks later Speck Warner, former Indian factory employee, won the inaugural San Juan Capistrano hillclimb in southern California. The spirits of Indian dealers in the west were buoyed by these two late-season victories. But racing was then shelved by mutual consent of the factories, as the prospect of American involvement in the European war loomed large.

The initial version of the Powerplus also put to rest many concerns expressed by Indian dealers, who had considerable faith in the redoubtable Hedstrom motor. The side-valve, with slightly smaller bore and longer stroke than the F-head, was standard with the Schebler carburetor. The Hedstrom carb remained available as an option. The bottom end was fundamentally the same, but featured stronger wristpins and crankpin. The 3-speed transmission was improved and accompanied by a stronger clutch.

Most importantly, the new engine produced a boost of about two horsepower over its predecessor, and promised more ease and economy of maintenance. The war department ordered 20,000 standard 1000cc V-twins for the conflict overseas.

1916 Powerplus Model F
Owner – Bob Romig
Pottstown, Pennsylvania

Above: The Corbin Screw Corporation of Chicago supplied components for both Indian and Harley-Davidson. The firm also made brakes, hubs and sprockets.

MODEL O (1917) AND MODEL K (1916)

1917 MODEL O

SPECIFICATIONS
ENGINE/DRIVETRAIN
Engine: Opposed side-valve twin
Displacement: 15.7ci (257cc)
Bore & stroke: 2 x 2.5in (51 x 63.5mm)
Horsepower: 2.75
Carburetor: Indian Automatic
Transmission: 3-speed
Primary drive: Chain
Final drive: Chain
Brake: External contracting
Ignition: Dixie magneto/distributor

CHASSIS/SUSPENSION
Frame: Steel, double loop
Suspension: Cartridge-spring fork
Wheelbase: 49.5in (125.7cm)
Weight: 235lb (106.6kg)
Fuel capacity: 2gal (7.57lit)
Oil capacity: 1qt (0.95lit)
Tires: 26 x 2.25in
Top speed: 45mph (72km/h)
Color: Red
Number built: Unknown
Price: $180

Above: Acetylene lamps were offered as accessories. The O didn't last long enough to get electrics.

Right: The Model O opposed twin was too little, too late. Or perhaps too early. Despite technical achievement and a smooth-running engine, the Light Twin only lasted three years. The $180 price was considered too expensive.

Although Hedstrom's return to active duty was brief, it had a positive effect on morale among the workforce, and his production experience brought more efficiency to the manufacturing processes and assembly lines. The net result brought production expenses back into line.

Several changes were made to the Powerplus for 1917. The new rounded two-piece fuel tank fit over the frame rails, and could be produced more cheaply than the earlier tank. The toolbox moved from the top of the tank to the rear frame tube below the seat. The bicycle-style T-stem fork crown was replaced by a stronger triple stem assembly, and push-pull controls replaced the earlier jointed rods.

Although the Model K two-stroke had failed and been withdrawn from production, Springfield was convinced of the need for a lightweight model for economical utility, younger riders, women and short folks in general. Plus, market research indicated that many bicycle riders were intimidated by the big V-twin, and less than enthusiastic with the vibration of a single. The success of the Douglas brothers' opposed twin in Great Britain led Indian to develop the Model O, which detractors would quickly label the Model Nothing.

Although the double-downtube frame was different from the K model, the rest of the opposed twin derived heavily from the earlier lightweight. The Model O employed the same cartridge spring fork, fenders, wheels, tires and luggage rack. The 16-cubic inch (257cc) engine also had an external flywheel and sliding-gear 3-speed transmission. The O was 20 pounds (9kg) heavier and 3 inches (7.62cm) longer than the K, and made slightly more than half again the horsepower. The top speed was 45mph (72km/h).

With bore and stroke of 2 x 2.5 inches (51 x 63.5mm), and a large flywheel, the little twin was a smooth-running motor. But its shortage of power and opposed configuration put it well out of the American mainstream. A leaf-spring fork was fitted to the 1918 model, but not even the appeals of low cost, light weight and 80 miles to the gallon (34km/lit) were sufficient inducements to attract many paying customers.

The Light Twin faced a sea of opposing forces, and lasted only three years in production. Dealers were generally less than aggressive in marketing the lightweight, preferring to concentrate on the traditional popularity of the V-twin. The last Model O appeared in 1919, ironically the same year Harley-Davidson introduced its own Douglas-based twin with a 36-cubic inch (584cc) engine. The Milwaukee version was a larger and heavier machine than the Indian, but produced only six horsepower. It lasted five years, but was no match for the next Indian middleweight that would appear in 1920. The Scout, designed by Charles Franklin, would put Indian back on the right road.

Below: Easy riding: "Truly, this is a machine for every man, every woman, every boy, and every girl who yearns for ideal lightweight motoring!"

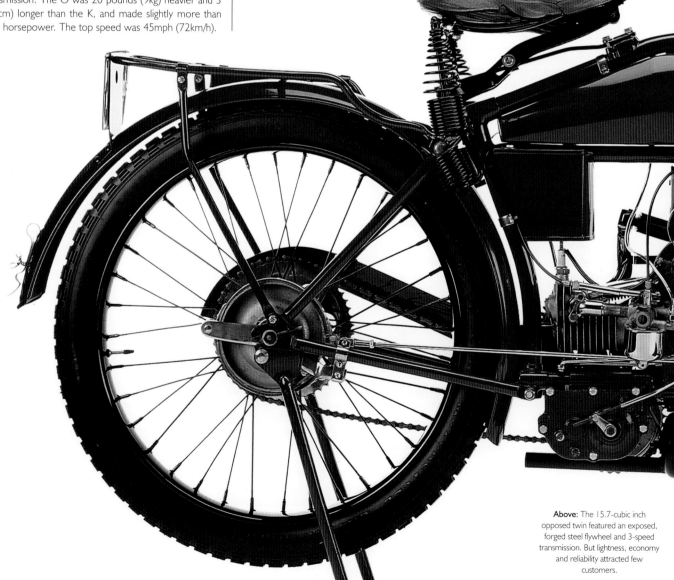

Above: The 15.7-cubic inch opposed twin featured an exposed, forged steel flywheel and 3-speed transmission. But lightness, economy and reliability attracted few customers.

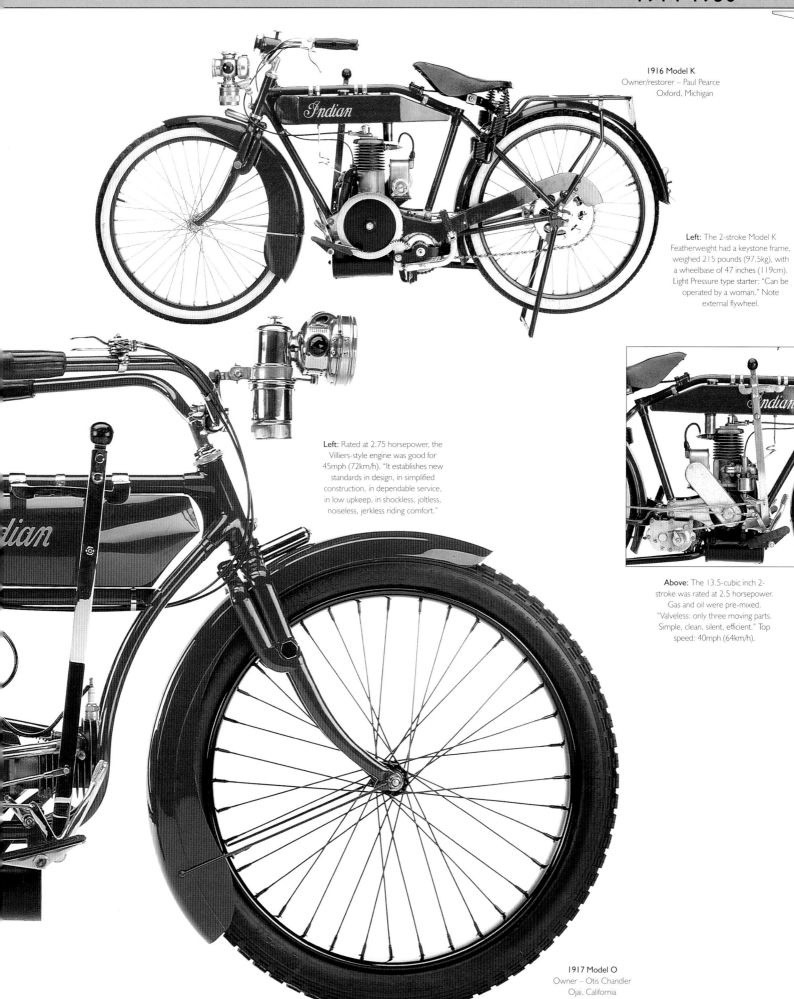

1916 Model K
Owner/restorer – Paul Pearce
Oxford, Michigan

Left: The 2-stroke Model K Featherweight had a keystone frame, weighed 215 pounds (97.5kg), with a wheelbase of 47 inches (119cm). Light Pressure type starter: "Can be operated by a woman." Note external flywheel.

Left: Rated at 2.75 horsepower, the Villiers-style engine was good for 45mph (72km/h). "It establishes new standards in design, in simplified construction, in dependable service, in low upkeep, in shockless, joltless, noiseless, jerkless riding comfort."

Above: The 13.5-cubic inch 2-stroke was rated at 2.5 horsepower. Gas and oil were pre-mixed. "Valveless: only three moving parts. Simple, clean, silent, efficient." Top speed: 40mph (64km/h).

1917 Model O
Owner – Otis Chandler
Ojai, California

8-VALVE RACER (1918) AND POWERPLUS RACER (1920)

1918 8-VALVE RACER

SPECIFICATIONS
ENGINE/DRIVETRAIN
Engine: OHV 8-valve twin
Displacement: 61ci (1000cc)
Bore & stroke: 3.13 x 3.97in (79.5 x 100.8mm)
Horsepower: Approx 20
Carburetor: Indian Automatic
Transmission: Single-speed
Primary drive: Chain
Final drive: Chain
Brakes: None
Ignition: Dixie magneto

CHASSIS/SUSPENSION
Frame: Steel keystone
Suspension: None
Wheelbase: 53in (134.6cm)
Weight: 260lb (118kg)
Fuel capacity: 1.5–2.5gal (5.68–9.46lit)
Oil capacity: 2qts (1.89lit)
Tires: 28 x 3.00in
Top speed: 115mph (185km/h)
Color: Red
Number built: Unknown
Price: $350

Springfield's production and profit figures for 1917 had been the lowest marks in six years. The boondoggles with military contracts had taken a toll; engine castings and other components were now purchased from outside sources rather than produced in-house, and the second factory had been sold to a local foundry.

In the spring of 1918, with the USA now commited to the raging battle in Europe, Indian negotiated another contract to supply motorcycles to the military. This agreement was more beneficial to the company, but did nothing to address the problem of dis-affected dealers and customers, many of whom had switched to Harley-Davidson. Milwaukee had drawn even with Springfield the previous year, and by the end of 1918 had surpassed Indian's pro-duction for the first time.

Harley was also building military models, but in far fewer num-bers than Indian. And Milwaukee had taken care to maintain and support their dealers and civilian customers at the same time. But Indian was recovering from the effects of mismanagement, and by the end of the war would be on equal footing with Harley in terms of production. The peacetime economy created a new playing field, and the resumption of racing would surely be conducted on one part of it.

Few modifications were made to the Powerplus in 1918. The combined magneto-generator was replaced by separate com-ponents. The Splitdorf generator was mounted low in front of the front downtube, a position that left it prone to damage from road debris, ruts and water. Dealers and customers both expressed their dislike for the new system, which was discontinued the following year.

The hand clutch was fitted to the right side of the tank in order to synchronize its operation with the left-hand throttle. With its dual-control clutch system, 3-speed transmission and added horsepower, the Powerplus was easier to ride than the F-head series it replaced. The engine also operated more quietly and ran slightly cooler. Riders could still choose between the cradle-spring and rigid frame models, the latter being less expensive.

As World War I, the first war powered by the internal combus-tion engine, wound down, Springfield prepared for the return to peacetime production and marketing. Rumors of peace had been circulating all year, but not until August was it clear that the German military machine was crumbling. Peace negotiations among the involved nations took several months, and the armistice was final on November 11. In addition to a large inven-tory of motorcycles originally destined for the military, Indian faced the prospect of regaining the confidence of dealers and customers.

In September the factory embarked on a public relations cam-paign to polish its image and reassure dealers of its intent to meet their needs. Bulletins in the trade magazines were headlined, "Indian Deliveries Contingent on Needs of Government." The text explained that "the Indian motorcycle has been drafted for the duration of the war."

The news release promised that Powerplus twins, opposed twins, sidecars and parcel vans would all be available for civilian buyers in 1919, but the number and time of availability depended on the needs of the military. Given the uncertainty, dealers were urged to get their orders in early, since delivery would be first come, first served.

Right: The Model H racing frames were subjected to numerous modifications just before World War I. In response to Harley's Model 17 and its low center of gravity, Springfield began to experiment with keystone frames.

Above: Curved rear frame tubes were apparently an early attempt to lower the racer's overall height. An extra rear sprocket was fitted to facilitate quick changes of gearing.

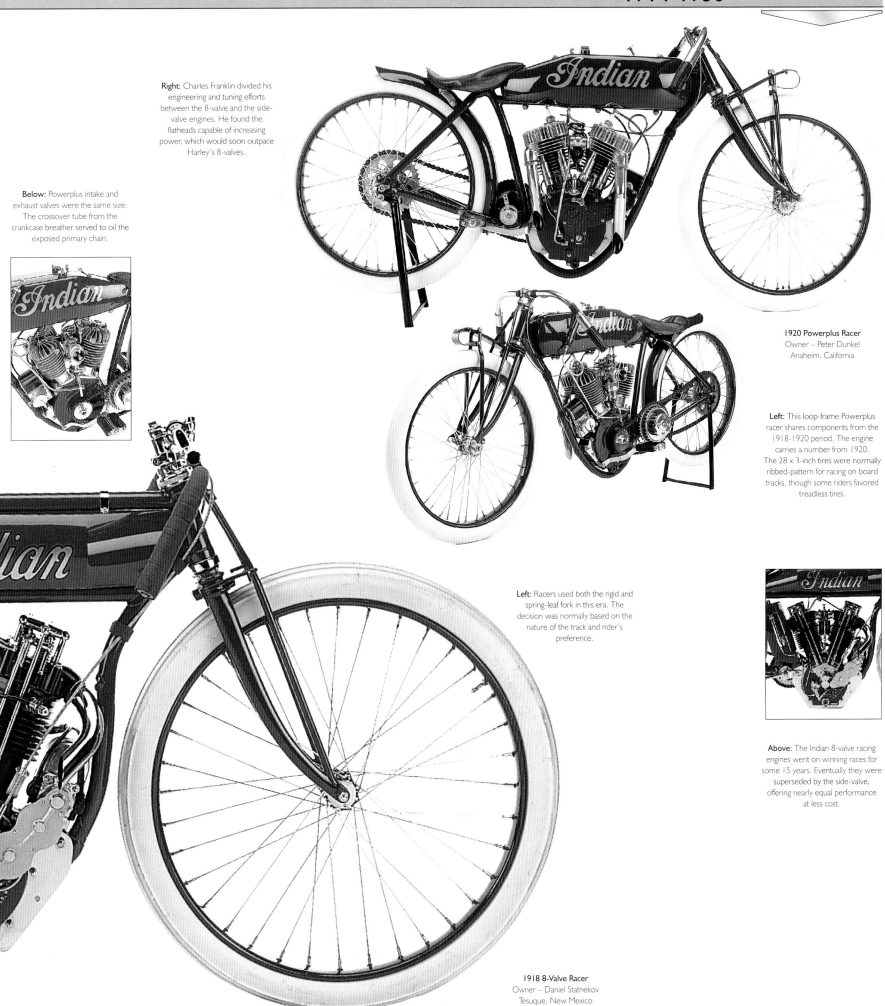

Right: Charles Franklin divided his engineering and tuning efforts between the 8-valve and the side-valve engines. He found the flatheads capable of increasing power, which would soon outpace Harley's 8-valves.

Below: Powerplus intake and exhaust valves were the same size. The crossover tube from the crankcase breather served to oil the exposed primary chain.

1920 Powerplus Racer
Owner – Peter Dunkel
Anaheim, California

Left: This loop-frame Powerplus racer shares components from the 1918–1920 period. The engine carries a number from 1920. The 28 x 3-inch tires were normally ribbed-pattern for racing on board tracks, though some riders favored treadless tires.

Left: Racers used both the rigid and spring-leaf fork in this era. The decision was normally based on the nature of the track and rider's preference.

Above: The Indian 8-valve racing engines went on winning races for some 15 years. Eventually they were superseded by the side-valve, offering nearly equal performance at less cost.

1918 8-Valve Racer
Owner – Daniel Statnekov
Tesuque, New Mexico
Restored by Brad Wilmarth

POWERPLUS (1919) AND DAYTONA TWIN (1920)

**1919 POWERPLUS
MODEL F**

**SPECIFICATIONS
ENGINE/DRIVETRAIN**
Engine: Side-valve 42° V-twin
Displacement: 61ci (1000cc)
Bore & stroke: 3.13 x 3.97in
(79.5 x 100.8mm)
Horsepower: 18
Carburetor: Indian Automatic
Transmission: 3-speed
Primary drive: Duplex chain
Final drive: Chain
Brakes: External contracting,
internal expanding
Battery: 6-volt
Ignition: Dixie magneto

CHASSIS/SUSPENSION
Frame: Steel, single downtube
Suspension: Leaf-spring leading
link fork
Wheelbase: 59in (149.9cm)
Weight: 430lb (195kg)
Fuel capacity: 2.2gal (8.33lit)
Oil capacity: 2qts (1.89lit)
Tires: 28 x 3.00
Top speed: 60mph (97km/h)
Colors: Red, gray
Number built: Unknown
Price: $290

Following the post-war celebration, the Springfield fellowship returned to civilian production with enthusiasm and high hopes. Two new models, the Scout and the Chief, had been delayed by the war, and Charles Franklin now gave his full attention to the machines' development. His experience as an enthusiast, racer and engineer would find its full application in these designs.

Frank Weschler had joined the company in 1905 as an office manager and bookeeper. His devotion to the firm was notewothy, and through successive shifts in management he ascended to treasurer and then general manager. Now, with the company's financial base and its dealer network weakened, he faced the prospect of a far more competitive market than Indian had yet confronted. Fewer manufacturers would participate in the post-war marketplace, but the new strengths of Harley-Davidson and Excelsior were challenge enough.

Hedstrom and Weschler confronted the additional obstacle of a board of directors still moody over the nominal military profits, and aggravated by the costs of developing new models. Not to mention another round of frivolous racing expenses. Weschler did everything in his power to convince the board of the importance of both new technology and racing, and that to neglect Indian's traditional strengths in the developing market could spell disaster. The directors considered Weschler's brief, conferred with the stockholders and subsequently decided to divest themselves of the Hendee Manufacturing Company.

A reduced catalog of three models appeared in 1919. The Powerplus was offered in a standard (N) model and electrically equipped (NE), available in either the cradle-spring or rigid frame configuration. The 560cc single with 3-speed transmission was available as a commercial model, many of which were exported.

The organizing framework for motorcycle racing had fallen into disarray during the war. Everyone agreed that it was time to get the competition program underway, but the FAM no longer had the management, finances or membership to get things rolling. While the racing reorganization process was underway, Weschler decided the best way to start restoring the Indian name was another cross-country record run. Naturally he would turn to Cannonball Baker.

With a sidecar attached to a 1000cc standard twin, Baker and passenger Erle Armstrong set off from Springfield in May. The run went well until the twosome reached the Mississippi River, where heavy rains slowed their progress. They carried on into Kansas, until the mud became impassable and the sidecar rig was disintegrating. The record run was abandoned.

The pre-war motordromes were replaced by longer board tracks with less precipitous banking, and the FAM was replaced by the Motorcycles and Allied Trades Association (MATA). The trade organization appointed a committee to serve as an interim governing body until a new racing association could be formed. Several years later the group would evolve into the American Motorcycle Association.

Below: Cannonball Baker continued his record-setting ways in Australia, on a machine nearly identical to this one. The same engine powered numerous Indian racing bikes.

Right: In 1918 the Powerplus got separate magneto and generator, replacing the earlier unit.

Above: The 1000cc Powerplus was a smooth and strong engine. The dry clutch and 3-speed transmission were well mated. Top speed was close to 60mph (97km/h), but optimum cruising was 45mph (72km/h).

Above: The Daytona racer housed a special Powerplus engine in a custom-built keystone frame. Gene Walker set a new record of 106mph (170.6km/h) on the beach at Daytona, Florida.

To no-one's surprise, Harley-Davidson held a commanding position in the post-war racing program. Headed by Los Angeles ace Ralph Hepburn, the Milwaukee team captured the top five places in the 200-mile championship dirt-track race at California's Ascot Park. The top Indian and sixth place went to Percy Coleman of New Zealand. The race attracted more than 10,000 spectators.

Young Gene Walker emerged as the rising star on the Indian team for 1919, winning four of the nine dirt-track nationals. But the Harley team dominated the standings, finishing 1-2-3 at the 200-mile Marion, Indiana, race and 1-2 at the Sheepshead Bay,

New York, board track. Albert "Shrimp" Burns was the winner, followed by Maldwyn Jones and Fred Nixon on the first Indian.

The New York meet marked the debut of the new FLXI sidecars designed by Hugo Young. Manufactured by the Flxible Company in Loudonville, Ohio, these rigs featured a third wheel that leaned in unison with the motorcycle. The new hacks were to provide plenty of excitement for dirt-track fans in the 1920s.

In December, Indian was sold to a new group of investors, headed by Springfield banker Henry Skinner. Frank Weschler remained in charge of operations.

1919 Powerplus
Owner/restorer – Marv Baker
Vallejo, California

Right: Dual electric headlights were accessory items for serious nighttime travelers. Enthusiasts praise the handling of the spring-frame Powerplus.

Below: Control lever handles (left to right) operate compression release, clutch and transmission. With a bit of practice, it's second nature.

1923 SCOUT

SPECIFICATIONS
ENGINE/DRIVETRAIN
Engine: Side-valve 42° V-twin
Displacement: 36.4ci (596cc)
Bore & stroke: 2.75 x 3.06in (69.8 x 77.7mm)
Horsepower: 11
Carburetor: Schebler
Transmission: 3-speed
Primary drive: Helical gear
Final drive: Chain
Brake: External contracting
Battery: 6-volt
Ignition: Splitdorf magneto

CHASSIS/SUSPENSION
Frame: Steel, double downtube
Suspension: Leaf-spring fork
Wheelbase: 54.5in (138.4cm)
Weight: 340lb (154.2kg)
Fuel capacity: 2gal (7.57lit)
Oil capacity: 2qts (1.89lit)
Tires: 26 x 3.00in
Top speed: 55mph (88.5km/h)
Color: Red
Number built: 7,036 (all models)
Price: $325

SCOUT (1923) AND FLXI RACER (1920)

Fortunately by 1919 the prototype work on the new Scout was too far along to be abandoned by the distressed board of directors. Even though lightweight motorcycles had not proven out in the marketplace, the conviction remained that an agile middleweight with sufficient power would find broad acceptance. Weschler and Franklin were both convinced of the truth of this, and proceeded accordingly.

After the war it was even more apparent that American motorcycling had been cast forever as a recreational, rather than practical, form of transportation. A decade earlier more than a hundred motorcycle manufacturers were firmly convinced that motorized two-wheelers would replace bicycles as an inexpensive means of transport. They shared the belief that people would ride to work, ride to the market and ride to church, because the automobile was well beyond the reach of common folks. Then they proceeded to build large, powerful motorcycles while Henry Ford built small, utilitarian cars that common folks could afford. And the rest is history.

This socio-economic turn of events reduced the number of American motorcycle manufacturers to a handful, and subsequently to just two, Indian and Harley-Davidson. For the next 30 years these two companies would conduct a vigorous, sometimes vicious and often comical battle for control of the motorcycle market. This wasn't just business, it was personal. Springfield and Milwaukee were at war, with skirmishes fought in the showrooms, in the press, in the boardrooms, on the roads and the racetracks. The object: to be Number One. Of two.

Neither company had been able to produce much in the way of positive market results with lightweight machines. But Charles Franklin, with his extensive experience in Britain and Europe, knew that a middleweight machine would succeed. He reasoned that not every rider needed or wanted a large-displacement touring machine, and that the new emphasis on sport motoring would favor his ideas.

Franklin and Tommy Butler had toured the eastern states, interviewing dealers and riders on their opinions about new motorcycles. Butler, former Excelsior dealer, salesman, amateur engineer with the Irish gift for gab, and Franklin became fast friends. The two men were polar opposites in terms of demeanor and personality, but their combined efforts were responsible for both the Scout and the later Chief models.

Franklin's design for the Scout engine was fundamentally a compressed Powerplus. But the 37-cubic inch (600cc) side-valve V-twin featured helical gear primary drive rather than the single chain primary of the Powerplus, and the system was hell-for-strong. The Scout immediately eclipsed Harley-Davidson's 600cc sport twin, and set Milwaukee to work on a middleweight V-twin.

The 1920 Scout went a long way to restore the reputation that Springfield had been steadily losing for five years. The chassis consisted of a cradle frame, with a dual downtube splitting at the mid-point and tubes running below the engine to the rear wheel, with a modified leaf-spring fork in front

Below: The Scout generated enthusiastic responses worldwide. When cheers subsided, riders asked for more power.

Right: Powerplus fans were more than a bit dubious about the Scout, considering its 600cc engine a weak sister. But the performance of the new machine belied the size of its engine.

Above: The Scout engine was a two-cammer, each with a single lobe for intake and exhaust valves. The total package was under 350 pounds (159kg).

1920 Daytona/Flxi
Owner – Tony Penachio
Millwood, New York

Above: The sidecar classes were among the popular events of the late Teens and early Twenties. The leaning Flxi hacks allowed thrilling corner speeds.

The wheelbase was 54.5 inches (138.4cm), curb weight 340 pounds (154kg) and seat height 28 inches (71.1cm). The 3-speed transmission bolted to the rear of the big-valve engine, which produced 10 to 12 horsepower. Cylinders and heads were still cast in common, but unlike the single-cam Powerplus the Scout had a camshaft for each pair of valves. Connecting rods and main shaft rode ball bearings. The package looked altogether unremarkable on paper, but on the road the Scout proved more than the sum of its parts. The machine handled with ease compared to the Powerplus, was easy to start and offered shorter riders an easier reach to the roadway. The power was easily manageable and sufficient to propel the rider close to 60mph (97km/h), which on most roads was plenty.

The sporty twin produced an immediate response in the marketplace, and orders began arriving from overseas. Springfield added a second factory shift in the spring to meet the growing demand. The Scout's performance was sufficient to draw fleet orders from police departments in several states.

The 1000cc Powerplus was joined by a 74-inch (1200cc) version in response to requests from sidecar owners for more power. Many solo touring riders also enjoyed the added grunt of the big twin. The single remained in production as a commercial machine, not listed in the general catalog.

Above: The Scout was distinguished by its double-loop cradle frame, which provided a stout foundation for the engine and running gear. It also proved a bonus in handling.

1923 Scout
Owner – Eric Vaughan
Monrovia, California

1920 DAYTONA/FLXI

SPECIFICATIONS
ENGINE/DRIVETRAIN
Engine: Side-valve 42° V-twin
Displacement: 61ci (1000cc)
Bore & stroke: 3.13 x 3.97in
(79.5 x 100.8mm)
Horsepower: 22
Carburetor: Schebler Special
Transmission: 3-speed
Primary drive: Duplex chain
Final drive: Chain
Brake: External contracting
Batteries: 6-volt
Ignition: Dixie magneto

CHASSIS/SUSPENSION
Frame: Steel, single downtube
Suspension: Leaf-spring leading link fork
Wheelbase: 53in (134.6cm)
Weight: 350lb (159kg) (with sidecar)
Fuel capacity: 2.2gal (8.33lit)
Oil capacity: 2qts (1.89lit)
Tires: 28 x 2.75in
Color: Red
Number built: Unknown
Price: Approx. $425

Right: Sidecar racing enjoyed immense popularity in the early Twenties. Fans were surprised by the speeds attained by the 3-wheelers, and the courage of the passengers or "monkeys."

RACING HACKS (1920)

Prospects were bright for the 1920 racing season, and the big three of Harley-Davidson, Indian and Excelsior were well prepared. Some few riders remained aboard Reading-Standard machines, but Merkel, Pope, Thor, Emblem and Cyclone were no longer in the game.

The season began on a terrible note when Excelsior's Bob Perry, practicing for the opening race at Ascot Park, crashed and died. A recent mechanical engineering graduate from the University of Illinois, Perry had worked on the design of the new overhead cam Excelsior X that he was riding. The Excelsior team withdrew from the 100-mile event to be held two days later. Bob Perry had been held in high favor by company owner Ignaz Schwinn; there was no further development on the ohc twin.

With nearly 25,000 racing fans in attendance, the Harley Wrecking Crew again swept the top positions. The finishing order was Otto Walker, Ralph Hepburn, Red Parkhurst and Fred Ludlow. Roy Artley and Gene Walker's Indians ran fifth and sixth.

Springfield's hopes were restored a week later at the Ascot 25-mile national championship race. Shrimp Burns, who had defected from Harley-Davidson after reportedly being refused an 8-valve racer, was entered on an Indian 8-valve. Attrition claimed a number of top riders in the heated sprint race, as Wells Bennett on the Excelsior X fell and unfortunately broke an arm. Otto Walker, Joe Wolters and Bill Church all crashed as well but they were not seriously hurt. Burns went on to win the event, with a record time that was nearly one and a half minutes faster than the previous mark.

The national championship series was back up to 17 events in 1920, and Indian riders won 14 of them. But the overall title went to the team winning the most miles, and Harley-Davidson had dominated the long-distance events at Dodge City, Kansas and Marion, Indiana.

The jovial Shrimp Burns was a prankster and a daredevil, but also an extraordinary rider. When lots were drawn for starting positions at Marion, he drew last place, and promptly announced that he would be in the lead after one lap. He made good on the promise, and set a new record for the first 100 miles (161km), but two successive broken chains would put him out of the running. In nearly every photo taken of Burns at the races during his career, he's wearing a grin.

Below: The sidecar wheel was fitted to an axle containing a spring-loaded rod. This enabled the wheel to lean with the motorocycle. With the passing of sidecars, the Flxible Company built commercial buses.

Above: The Flxicar was made by the Flxible Company of Loudonville, Ohio. The brand was not labeled Flexible because it was not legally possible to trademark a common word.

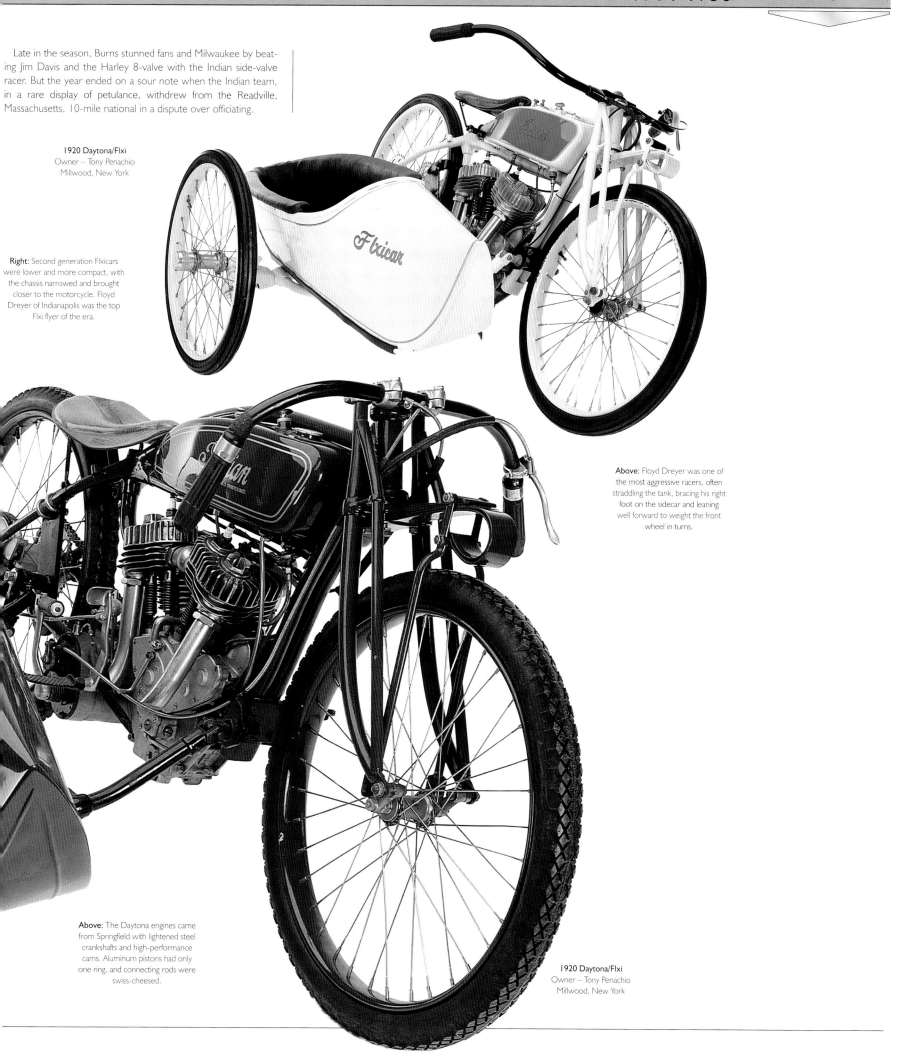

Late in the season, Burns stunned fans and Milwaukee by beating Jim Davis and the Harley 8-valve with the Indian side-valve racer. But the year ended on a sour note when the Indian team, in a rare display of petulance, withdrew from the Readville, Massachusetts, 10-mile national in a dispute over officiating.

1920 Daytona/Flxi
Owner – Tony Penachio
Millwood, New York

Right: Second generation Flxicars were lower and more compact, with the chassis narrowed and brought closer to the motorcycle. Floyd Dreyer of Indianapolis was the top Flxi flyer of the era.

Above: Floyd Dreyer was one of the most aggressive racers, often straddling the tank, bracing his right foot on the sidecar and leaning well forward to weight the front wheel in turns.

Above: The Daytona engines came from Springfield with lightened steel crankshafts and high-performance cams. Aluminum pistons had only one ring, and connecting rods were swiss-cheesed.

1920 Daytona/Flxi
Owner – Tony Penachio
Millwood, New York

1923 CHIEF

SPECIFICATIONS
ENGINE/DRIVETRAIN
Engine: Side-valve 42° V-twin
Displacement: 74ci (1200cc)
Bore & stroke: 3.25 x 4.44in (82.5 x 112.7mm)
Horsepower: 34
Carburetor: Schebler Automatic
Transmission: 3-speed
Clutch: Wet multi-disc
Primary drive: Helical gear
Final drive: Chain
Brake: External contracting
Battery: 6-volt
Ignition: Splitdorf magneto

CHASSIS/SUSPENSION
Frame: Steel, twin downtube
Suspension: Leaf-spring fork
Wheelbase: 60.5in (153.7cm)
Weight: 440lb (200kg)
Fuel capacity: 3.1gal (11.7lit)
Oil capacity: 3qts (2.84lit)
Tires: 26 x 3.00in
Top speed: 75mph (121km/h)
Color: Red
Number built: 7,036 (all models)
Price: $435

Above: Sold as an accessory, the pillion assembly included a deluxe saddle, handhold and footrest system. The Big Chief actually did produce sufficient grunt to carry both a sidecar and pillion passenger, though acceleration and hill-climbing were compromised.

CHIEF (1923) AND DAYTONA PP (1920)

Although most of the other American motorcycle companies had by now drifted to history, two outfits remained as challengers to both Springfield and Milwaukee. One was the Excelsior of Chicago, headed by bicycle entrepreneur Ignaz Schwinn. The company had acquired the Henderson four-cylinder in 1917, and hired founders Tom and William Henderson to oversee production. But within two years the Hendersons soured on Schwinn's dictatorial style and left the company.

William Henderson, with funding from Philadephia bicycle builder Max Sladkin, founded the Ace Motorcycle Company and built a new version of his inline four. The handsome, smooth-running Ace made its debut in 1920, and was instantly popular. With a 75-cubic inch (1229cc) engine, seat height of 29 inches (73.7cm) and weighing only 385 pounds (175kg), the machine was fast and comfortable. Both Indian and Harley-Davidson had cause for concern. The fours were finding favor with both police departments and hillclimbers looking for more horsepower.

But two other concerns dominated the Springfield agenda in 1921. One was the overwhelming might of Milwaukee's racing effort, and the other a motorcycle market that was eroding rapidly. Ford announced another reduction in automobile prices, and inflation had increased production costs.

Harley-Davidson, having survived the war in better financial condition, was now the world's largest motorcycle manufacturer. Indian, unaccustomed to being in the catch-up role, scrambled for ways to restore some of their past glory. For 1921 an optional electrical system was offered for the Scout, with a Splitdorf lighting system and generator.

The worldwide popularity gained by the Scout served to make the Powerplus, now called the Standard, seem archaic by comparison. The more compact machine signaled the next chapter in motorcycle development, representing an integrated overall design that scored well in terms of performance, comfort and ease of maintenance. So, reflecting the inevitable call for more horsepower, the next version would naturally have a larger engine.

Several of Springfield's executives were understandably reluctant to undertake the expense of a new model, given the weakened market. Others insisted that an enlarged Scout was an absolute necessity, that it would improve their position against Harley-Davidson and serve well in overseas markets where sidecars remained popular forms of transportation. The arguments rattled back and forth, but ultimately the larger model won approval and Charles Franklin was charged with the responsibility for its design and engineering.

On the racing front, Milwaukee opened strong with an exciting win at the 1-mile board track in Fresno, California. Otto Walker set new records in the 1-, 15- and 50-mile events, and became the first rider to average over 100mph (161km/h) in competition. His speed in the opener was 107.78mph (173.45km/h). Shrimp Burns put his Indian a close second in the 10-mile race at 104.65mph (168.41km/h).

A new 1.25-mile board track, built by Jack Prince, hosted motorcycle racing for the first time in Beverly Hills, California. Shrimp Burns blitzed Harley's Otto Walker in the last turn to win the 10-mile race, but in the 25-mile event a seized engine sent him sliding and he collected numerous splinters. Burns was forced to miss the 50-mile national while his wounds were treated. Returning in bandages for the consolation race, he received a roar of acclaim from the 15,000 spectators. Burns passed the two leading Harley 8-valve riders in the final turn to win at 102.55mph (165.03km/h), the fastest time yet for a side-valve engine.

But the talented and well-equipped Harley-Davidson factory racing team went on to win every national championship event in 1921. In August, at a dirt-track race in Toledo, Ohio, Shrimp Burns and Harley's Ray Weishaar were dicing for position. Burns clipped his competitor's rear wheel and was high-sided head-first into the outside fence. He died of his injuries shortly thereafter. The court jester of racing was gone.

Harley-Davidson had fielded a factory racing effort for seven years, longer than most railbirds, or Harley itself, had ever reckoned. But by 1922, having spent considerable sums on the competition enterprise, Milwaukee officially withdrew from factory-sponsored racing. They would continue to support selected riders on a privateer basis.

Indian's racing budget was already stretched mighty thin, but Frank Weschler was determined that Springfield maintain its presence in professional competition. Milwaukee may have demonstrated its strength in convincing fashion, but Indian had been a racing company from the beginning, and Weschler considered himself honor-bound to uphold the tradition.

Two of the top Harley factory riders, Jim Davis and Ralph Hepburn, both joined the Indian team and raced against their former teammates. Californian Hepburn emerged as the prominent race star of 1920s and later became a top racing-car driver.

The Indian Scout was compiling a winning record in amateur endurance events, and special overhead-valve Powerplus engines

Right: By the early Twenties, sidecars experienced diminishing popularity in the USA, but remained top sellers in Europe and South America.

1923 Chief
Owner – Vince Spadaro
Burlingame, California

Above: This sidecar rig is 1927 vintage. The four-point leaf-spring mounting system was lighter than earlier models. Ride was surprisingly comfortable.

Left: Speedometer was driven off the rear wheel. Corbin remained a primary supplier for many years.

successfully powered many hillclimb machines. But the financial picture in Springfield was not in a corresponding frame-work, and the company had shown a net loss in 1921. Frank Weschler was forced to go to the bankers hat in hand.

Meanwhile, back at the factory, Charles Franklin's work on the Scout's bigger brother was pro-ceeding apace. The first Chiefs appeared in the fall, accompanied by a new advertising program and considerable public relations work. The Standard remained in the lineup, and was fitted with a new generator, fenders and fork assembly. The price for the traditional model was $370, compared to $435 for the Chief.

1920 Daytona Powerplus
Owner – Tony Penachio
Millwood, New York

Above: The 1000cc Daytona Powerplus twins continued to win major board and dirt-track races in the mid-Twenties. Harley withdrew its factory team.

Above: Automotive-style instrument panels were still a few years away. Motorcycle components retained individual identities.

1923 BIG CHIEF

SPECIFICATIONS
ENGINE/DRIVETRAIN
Engine: Side-valve 42° V-twin
Displacement: 74ci (1200cc)
Bore & stroke: 3.25 x 4.44in
(82.5 x 112.7mm)
Horsepower: 34
Carburetor: Schebler
Automatic
Transmission: 3-speed
Clutch: Wet multi-disc
Primary drive: Helical gear
Final drive: Chain
Brake: External contracting
Battery: 6-volt
Ignition: Splitdorf magneto

CHASSIS/SUSPENSION
Frame: Steel, twin downtube
Suspension: Leaf-spring fork
Wheelbase: 60.5in (153.7cm)
Weight: 440lb (200kg)
Fuel capacity: 3.1gal (11.7lit)
Oil capacity: 3qts (2.84lit)
Tires: 26 x 3.00in
Top speed: 75mph (120.7km/h)
Color: Red
Number built: 7,036 (all
models)
Price: $435

Right: The Big Chief was a
bigger Chief, which had been
a bigger Scout, rather than a
modified Powerplus. The leaf-
spring fork carried over from
the Hedstrom model, but the
rear wheel was solidly
mounted.

BIG CHIEF (1923)

The Scout generated enthusiasm among riders as more reports on its performance circulated by word of mouth. In Colorado, former Harley racer and dealer Floyd Clymer had switched his allegiance to Indian and opened a dealership. Clymer rode a Scout to the top of Pike's Peak, the first ascent by motorcycle.

Although domestic motorcycle sales were still in decline, and more manufacturers dropping out, Springfield's export business remained strong. Great Britain, South Africa, Australia and South America were the major overseas markets. But at home the Indian financial picture was grim. The combined effects of post-war inflation, an expensive experiment with engine-wheels for bicycles and increased labor costs, resulted in a record loss of more than one and a quarter million dollars for 1922.

Dick Richards had been elevated to a position of market research and product planning. Several top executives retired or were given limited responsibilities. A number of factory workers were laid off and production and assembly lines reduced in scale.

Better news came from the racing front, where Jim Davis recorded the fastest mile of all time with a 110.67mph (178.1km/h) lap at the Beverly Hills board track. Ralph Hepburn won the big 300-mile Dodge City race, which had been moved to Witchita, Kansas on the traditional Fourth of July date. And a new hillclimb celebrity named Orrie Steele won the national championship for Indian at Egypt, New York. The popularity of hillclimbing was still growing, and both Springfield and Milwaukee built over-head-valve engines for the sport. But the year ended on a sad note for the industry when William Henderson was killed in a road accident while testing the new Ace Four.

The immediate success of the Scout and the 61-cubic inch (1000cc) Chief led directly to the development of the 74-inch (1200cc) version, called the Big Chief. The big-bore rendition came in response to dealer requests and the Harley Seventy-four which appeared in 1921. The Standard remained in the lineup, but

it was the last year for the venerable Powerplus engine. Indian powerplants were now in their third generation, and Charles Franklin remained the chief designer.

Even though Indian remained the sole manufacturer with direct factory support for racing, the budget was seriously trimmed from previous years. Without the factory money for expensive contracts, professional racers became free agents and rode for whomever they chose. Many purchased their former factory bikes and solicited support from dealers. For several years Ludlow and Davis switched back and forth between Indian and Harley-Davidson. Both factories vied for the service of these two stars, since both riders could win on either machine.

Cross-country record runs were now officially discouraged by the factories, at the behest of police departments and civic groups, but numerous independent attempts were made. In May, Paul Remaley took his Scout from Mexico to Canada in just under 47 hours, breaking the earlier mark set by Wells Bennett on a 1300cc Henderson. In June, Bennett regained the record with a time 49 minutes quicker. In July, Remaley made the run again and clipped nearly three hours of Bennett's time.

In August, Remaley set off to challenge the east-west trans-continental record, also held by Henderson. The Scout made the run in 5 days, 17 hours, nearly a day quicker than the old record. Overseas, Britain's Freddie Dixon won the Belgian Grand Prix on an Indian 500cc single, and, slowed by tire trouble, finished third in the Isle of Man Senior TT.

With the death of William Henderson, it appeared that only Excelsior and Cleveland would remain as manufacturers of four-cylinder machines. But Ace investors hired engineer Art Lemon away from Schwinn and told him to build the

1923 Big Chief
Owner/restorer – Rocky Burkhart
Birdsboro, Pennsylvania

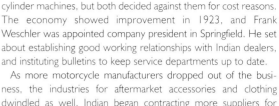

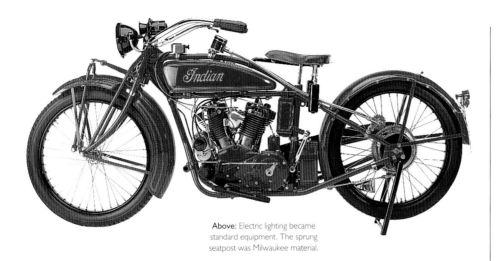

Above: Electric lighting became standard equipment. The sprung seatpost was Milwaukee material.

Both Indian and Harley-Davidson considered building four-cylinder machines, but both decided against them for cost reasons. The economy showed improvement in 1923, and Frank Weschler was appointed company president in Springfield. He set about establishing good working relationships with Indian dealers, and instituting bulletins to keep service departments up to date.

As more motorcycle manufacturers dropped out of the business, the industries for aftermarket accessories and clothing dwindled as well. Indian began contracting more suppliers for instruments, luggage racks, seats and other accessories. Springfield also added more types and styles of riding clothing, boots, helmets and foul-weather gear. And dealers were encouraged to work on maintaining regular contact with their customers, and implementing ways to improve service for the riders.

Spirits in Springfield ran high when the 1923 season showed profits of nearly $208,000, and Indians captured six of the eight national championship races. Orders for the Scout were running ahead of production, the export market was quite healthy and the time seemed ripe for renewed expansion. The company decide to go public with a stock offering on Wall Street.

And although track racing was now mostly limited to 500cc machines, the singles were capable of considerable speeds on some tracks. The 1924 season was dimmed by the deaths of two prominent riders, Gene Walker and Ray Weishaar.

world's fastest motorcycle, cost was no object. The result was a powerful 80-cubic inch (1320cc) four designated the Ace XP4, which clocked the record speed of 129.61mph (208.58km/h). A second version powered a sidecar rig to 106.82mph (171.9km/h), the first hack to exceed 100mph (161km/h).

Left: High top speeds were good for bragging rights, but most riders wanted power enough to provide comfortable cruising speeds. On the better roads of 1923 that was 45-50mph (72-80km/h).

Left: The leaf-spring fork remained in service for many years. The mechanical simplicity, and easy action of the trailing link system, were sufficient until higher speeds led to hydraulics.

Above: The rear wheel-driven speedometer remained one of the traditional touches on the Big Chief. And it continued in use for the next thirty years.

Above: The 1200cc Chief was well received by sidecarists, police and torque enthusiasts. The frame was reinforced with bracing at key points.

Above: Simple gauges were standard components on motorcycles of the era. Later styling trends led to decorative housing for instruments.

PRINCE (1926–1928) AND FOUR-VALVE SINGLE (1926)

1928 PRINCE

SPECIFICATIONS
ENGINE/DRIVETRAIN
Engine: Vertical side-valve single
Displacement: 21.25ci (350cc)
Bore & stroke: 2.75 x 3.58in (69.8 x 90.9mm)
Horsepower: 7
Carburetor: Schebler
Transmission: 3-speed
Clutch: Dry disc
Primary drive: Chain
Final drive: Chain
Brakes: F & R. Drum
Battery: 6-volt
Ignition: Magneto

CHASSIS/SUSPENSION
Frame: Steel keystone
Suspension: Girder/spring fork
Wheelbase: 54in (137.2cm)
Weight: 265lb (120kg)
Fuel capacity: 2.75gal (10.4lit)
Oil capacity: 3qts (2.84lit)
Tires: 26 x 3.30in
Top speed: 55mph (88.5km/h)
Color: Red
Number built: Unknown
Price: $195

Despite nearly all historical encouragement to the contrary, Springfield was determined to produce a lightweight motorcycle in the European fashion. So the big news for 1925 was the introduction of the single-cylinder Prince, designed by Charles Franklin. The 21.25-cubic inch (350cc) side-valve single was advertised as "The Personal Motor," with an illustration of a female rider, and sold for $185.

At 250 pounds (113kg) the Prince was a lightweight by the standards of the day, and hopes were high for its success. The single featured an adjustable-feed oil pump and an auxiliary hand pump for high-speed work or hot running. With modest compression of 5.5:1, the Scout started easily and turned in nearly 60 miles per gallon (25km/lit). The engine was rated at six horsepower.

Franklin developed an overhead-valve version for the following year, with an eye on both the European sporting market and the continuing diminution of engines for American motorcycle racing. He also produced a few prototypes of an overhead-cam rendition of the Prince engine, which achieved only limited production. Harley-Davidson also introduced a 350cc single, in side- and overhead-valve iterations in 1926. The bikes were almost identical to the Indians in terms of weight and power, but had about two inches longer wheelbase.

To the misfortune of both companies, the budget-priced singles arrived just before the British raised protective tariffs and effectively eliminated foreign competition in Great Britain and its empire nations. Since the export market was a prime target for both firms, their expectations were diminished considerably.

Domestically the Prince sold fairly well, and was popular with students and other riders of limited means, light delivery services and women riders. Many dealers were less than enthused by the single, but some in larger metropolitan areas found a reasonable market for the lightweights. Economy, and the 29-inch (73.7cm) seat height, were the major selling points.

The racing rules for 1925 reflected the fluctuating forces at work in the industry and the sanctioning organization, as the 1000cc class was back as a national category. The 500cc class was a shootout between the two new ohv singles from Harley and Indian, and a new 350cc class was instituted. The latter came to be called the Peashooter class, after the staccato sound emitted by the Harley ohv 350.

Indian's Johnny Seymour was outfitted with a new 4-valve 500cc single developed by Charles Franklin and tuned by Charles Gustafson, Jr. The machine was remarkably fast for a 500, handled well and Seymour rode exceptionally. At the Syracuse Mile national he set new records winning the 5-, 10- and 25-mile events against top Harley riders Jim Davis, Joe Petrali and Curly Fredericks. Seymour won four of the five national 500cc titles.

Charles Franklin had designed detachable heads for all the Indian engines for 1925. He had also been at work on several upgraded 8-valve engines for hillclimbs and high-speed runs, as well as a racing version of the 1000cc side-valve engine. Gustafson and Seymour took one of the 8-valves to Daytona Beach, Florida in January for some record attempts. Seymour was able to set a new 1000cc world record at 132mph (212km/h), and a 500cc record on a 4-valve at 112.63mph (181.25km/h).

Another noteworthy change in 1925 was the company name, which was changed from the Hendee Manufacturing Company to the Indian Motocycle Company.

The Prince was slightly modified for 1926, with a Scout-style gas tank and curved top frame tube. The new frame and Mesinger

Right: The Prince went through several detail changes following its introduction in 1925. An overhead-valve version, built primarily for racing, appeared in 1926. Low seat height and ease of handling were not enough to bring the Prince to the throne.

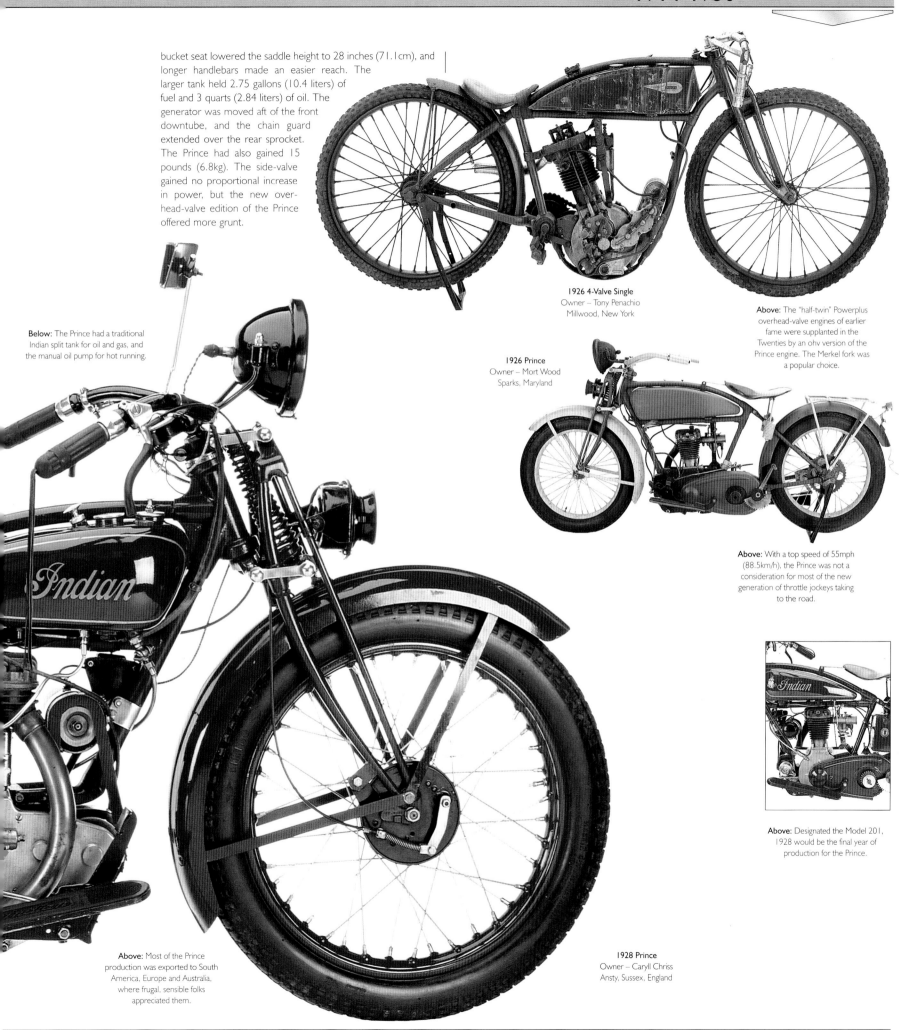

bucket seat lowered the saddle height to 28 inches (71.1cm), and longer handlebars made an easier reach. The larger tank held 2.75 gallons (10.4 liters) of fuel and 3 quarts (2.84 liters) of oil. The generator was moved aft of the front downtube, and the chain guard extended over the rear sprocket. The Prince had also gained 15 pounds (6.8kg). The side-valve gained no proportional increase in power, but the new overhead-valve edition of the Prince offered more grunt.

1926 4-Valve Single
Owner – Tony Penachio
Millwood, New York

Above: The "half-twin" Powerplus overhead-valve engines of earlier fame were supplanted in the Twenties by an ohv version of the Prince engine. The Merkel fork was a popular choice.

Below: The Prince had a traditional Indian split tank for oil and gas, and the manual oil pump for hot running.

1926 Prince
Owner – Mort Wood
Sparks, Maryland

Above: With a top speed of 55mph (88.5km/h), the Prince was not a consideration for most of the new generation of throttle jockeys taking to the road.

Above: Designated the Model 201, 1928 would be the final year of production for the Prince.

Above: Most of the Prince production was exported to South America, Europe and Australia, where frugal, sensible folks appreciated them.

1928 Prince
Owner – Caryll Chriss
Ansty, Sussex, England

CHIEF (1927) AND BIG-VALVE POWERPLUS/SCOUT (1920)

1927 CHIEF

SPECIFICATIONS
ENGINE/DRIVETRAIN
Engine: Side-valve 42° V-twin
Displacement: 74ci (1200cc)
Bore & stroke: 3.25 x 4.44in
(82.5 x 112.7mm)
Horsepower: 34
Carburetor: Schebler
Automatic
Transmission: 3-speed
Clutch: Wet multi-disc
Primary drive: Helical gear
Final drive: Chain
Brake: Rear external contracting
and internal expanding
Battery: 6-volt
Ignition: Splitdorf magneto

CHASSIS/SUSPENSION
Frame: Steel, twin downtube
Suspension: Leaf-spring fork
Wheelbase: 60.5in (153.7cm)
Weight: 650lb (295kg) (with
sidecar)
Fuel capacity: 3.1gal (11.7lit)
Oil capacity: 3qts (2.84lit)
Tires: 26 x 3.00in
Top speed: 75mph (120.7km/h)
Color: Red
Number built: Approx. 3,000
Price: $435 (with sidecar)

Just when both Indian and Harley figured they had the market covered with 500, 1000 and 1200cc machines, Excelsior threw a Spaniard in the works with a 750cc V-twin. The engine carried the traditional F-head valve arrangement, replacing the 1000cc, 50-degree Excelsior V-twin. The new Super X incorporated the transmission and engine case in a single unit, the term for which became, unit construction. Primary drive arrived by helical gears.

The Super X was roughly the size of an Indian Scout, but had considerably more urge. On some tracks the 750 would take the measure of bikes running 1000 or 1200cc engines. Excelsior had effectively created the 750 class, which would became the basis of American Class C competition from then on.

So Franklin fashioned a 750cc version of the Scout. About two dozen motorcycles were built with overhead valves, most set up in hillclimb chassis, some for dirt track and a few in road-racing trim. The 1926 national championship series was divided into displacement classes for 1000, 750, 500 and 350cc engines. The question of relative importance between the bike and rider was answered early on, when Jim Davis won the first 750 national on an Indian 500cc 4-valve single. Indian riders won five of the nine championship races for the year.

Franklin also put together several 1000cc side-valve engines in modified hillclimb frames. The engine was fitted with two Zenith carburetors and two oil pumps, and made some serious power. Curly Fredericks and Jim Davis raced the machines with great success for two seasons. At Rockingham, New Hampshire, Fredericks set the all-time board-track speed record with a lap at 120mph (193km/h).

The Prince was quickly drafted for competition in response to the Harley-Davidson ohv 350 single. Corollary to the racing version was a street model called the Prince Sport, available in red or white. The Sport, which featured a handlebar-mount hand clutch, was produced in limited numbers, most of which were exported.

The Scout and Chief were fitted with larger tires in 1926, and the fatter rubber was optional on the Prince. Indian experienced another good year, with production nearing 17,000 machines and a reasonable profit picture. President Weschler announced that the factory had reached total production of 275,000 motorcycles since its inception. The company president spent considerable time during the year negotiating with the proprietors of Michigan Motors, owners of the remains of the Ace Motorcycle Company. The Detroit firm had hoped to restore the Ace to the stature of the Henderson era, but were unable to secure sufficient financing. After more than a year of negotiations, Indian acquired the Ace assets in early 1927. Weschler had campaigned forcefully to get hold of the four-cylinder machine, reasoning that it would give Indian the most comprehensive model roster in the market.

Right: With the widespread availability of affordable cars in the United States, most of the sidecar business for both Indian and Harley-Davidson was overseas. Most domestic rigs went to racing or commercial use.

Right: This Chief is an export model for 1927, indicated by sidecar on the left. The domestic models had the kickstart lever fitted to the left side, and the hack on the other.

Right: The Chief engine remained available in 1000 and 1200cc sizes, the latter being the preference of sidecar owners. The detachable heads, which first appeared two years earlier, improved the engine's respiration.

Above: The long vertical rod just forward of the gearshift lever is the compression release. These large V-twins were assembled of large, stout pieces that would hold together for quite some time if properly maintained.

Right: This club racer was built by Noel McIntyre, who would later tune Floyd Emde's Daytona-winning big-base Scout. Built in 1922, the standard Scout frame holds a 1920 1000cc big-valve Powerplus engine and gearbox.

Below: Even though sidecars lost out to automobiles, few things were more pleasant, of a summer's day, than riding along in the open air, watching the world unfold before you.

1920 Big-Valve Powerplus/Scout
Owner – Tony Penachio
Millwood, New York

Above: The fittings atop the tank, right to left, are the oil tank cap, oil pump handle, fuel tank cap and fuel shut-off valve. The motorcycle name is prominently displayed tankside.

1927 Chief
Owner – Jim Smith

1929 SCOUT

SPECIFICATIONS
ENGINE/DRIVETRAIN
Engine: 42° side-valve V-twin
Displacement: 45ci (750cc)
Bore & stroke: 2.88 x 3.50in
(73.2 x 88.9mm)
Horsepower: 22
Carburetor: Schebler
Transmission: 3-speed
Clutch: Wet multi-disc
Primary drive: Helical gear
Final drive: Chain
Brake: F & R. Drum
Battery: 6-volt
Ignition: Magneto

CHASSIS/SUSPENSION
Frame: Steel, twin downtube
Suspension: Leaf-spring fork
Wheelbase: 57in (144.8cm)
Weight: 370lb (168kg)
Fuel capacity: 2.75gal (10.4lit)
Oil capacity: 3qts (2.84lit)
Tires: 25 x 3.85in
Top speed: 75mph (121km/h)
Color: Red
Number built: Approx. 3,000
Price: $300

Right: Fans of the original Scout were less than pleased to hear that the new 101 model was larger and heavier. But in action it proved to be an improvement on the earlier generation, and went on to establish itself as one of the most popular models ever built.

101 SCOUT (1929)

The first civilian Scout 45 appeared in 1927, in the guise of a police model. This was interpreted as either a clever marketing ploy or a means to assure the sale of the bulk of the production run. Or both. The term Police Special has a dramatic ring to it. And, as numerous peace officers discovered, the 750 was easier to handle in the city.

And the 750cc engine did add a new dimension to the Scout's performance profile. This was good news to sporting riders, who quickly determined that it could be made even faster with a stroker kit. With the advent of the larger engine, the Scout shifted its image from middleweight utility bike to hot rod. Or the original term, "alley racer." Of course, the Scout in its standard form continued its growth as a popular choice with riders more interested in reliability, handling ease and moderate cost.

Given the market success of the Scout 45, and the growing roster of wins on the racetrack, Franklin's efforts shifted from the 8-valve and 1000cc side-valve engines to the 750. Harley-Davidson, willing as ever to let Indian make the first move, followed up with a 750 side-valve for 1929. The Excelsior 750 that set the pattern had been designed by engineer Arthur Constantine, who had worked for Harley-Davidson.

The work of another competitor's engineering appeared in Indian showrooms for the first time in 1927. William Henderson's Ace was revived in its final form and sold in selected dealerships without modifications. The single downtube Ace frame would be retained through the following year, with the Indian leaf-spring front fork grafted on. The machine was called the Indian Ace, which developed a hybrid frame of combined Ace and Indian components. In 1929 it would emerge as the Indian Four, with an all-Springfield chassis.

Thus the new Indian Motocycle Company appeared well positioned in the sales arena, even though the market had diminished with the growing availability of low-priced cars. And the profit picture remained in reasonable shape as well. Unfortunately this period also produced another board of directors eager to expand into market categories other than motorcycles. Despite opposition from Frank Weschler and other Indian veterans, the board decided to invest in shares of outside companies rather than in motorcycle tooling and development.

Weschler now realized that Indian would not survive another dilution of its motorcycle emphasis, at least not with the standards he had long worked to uphold. Weschler resigned and the Springfield ownership deteriorated into another period of profit-taking and mismanagement.

Right: The 750cc engine quickly proved its worth.

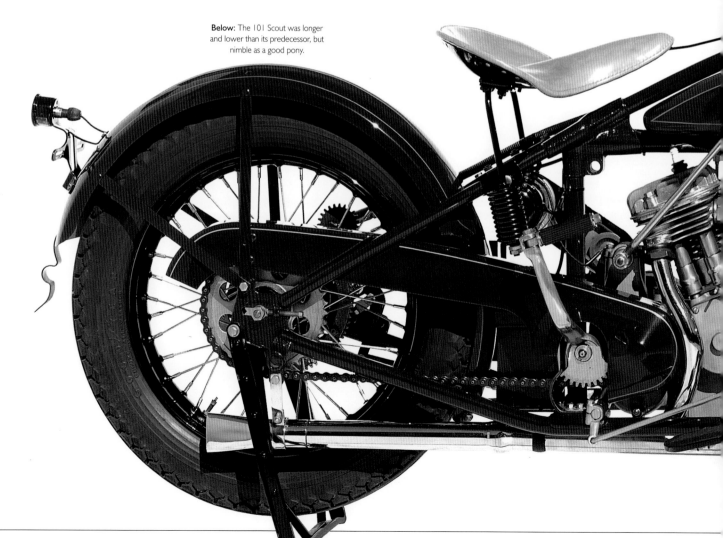

Below: The 101 Scout was longer and lower than its predecessor, but nimble as a good pony.

The motorcycle industries in Europe and Great Britain now developed quite independent of Yankee influence. Most countries imposed restrictive duties on the products of others, and the mix and match of international racing had dissolved not long after the war. Old world craftsman in Britain, Germany, Italy and other countries continued to tinker and refine. Research and development attended to valve systems, overhead cams, chassis, suspension and brake technologies. European racing was largely the realm of single-cylinder machines.

By contrast, the USA had adopted a V-twin orthodoxy that would be maintained to the present day. So for more than 30 years there was little interchange between the racing fraternities here and abroad. With board tracks receding to history, the prominent venue for American competition became the traditional fairgrounds dirt oval; horse-racing tracks of half- and one-mile lengths. And short quarter- to third-mile ovals built for sprint cars and assorted fairground festivities.

The 101 Scout was made to order for this formula, which evolved as amateur racing on modified road machines. With the addition of a semi-professional class in which top riders received assistance from factories and/or motorcycle dealers.

Indian's product roster for 1928 was impressive, including the Prince, 600 and 750cc Scouts, 1200cc Chief and 1220cc Four. The 1000cc Chief was discontinued. But it was the new Scout, designated Model 101, which achieved the most acclaim from riders. Charles Franklin's racing experience produced a Scout that had nearly three inches (7.62cm) more wheelbase and a fork with increased rake and trail. Seat height was nearly two inches (5cm) lower than the original Scout.

And for the first time, the motorcycle was fitted with a front brake. The 101 Scout was nearly 30 pounds (13.6kg) heavier than its predecessor, but handled better at low and high speeds. The Chief and Four were also fitted with front brakes in 1928, but few other modifications were made to either model.

Below: The 101 Scout became Charles Franklin's crowning achievement as a motorcycle designer and engineer. The looks, weight, power and handling were spot on for a market lacking a sporting middleweight twin. Stripped for racing, the new Scout weighed about 300 pounds (136kg).

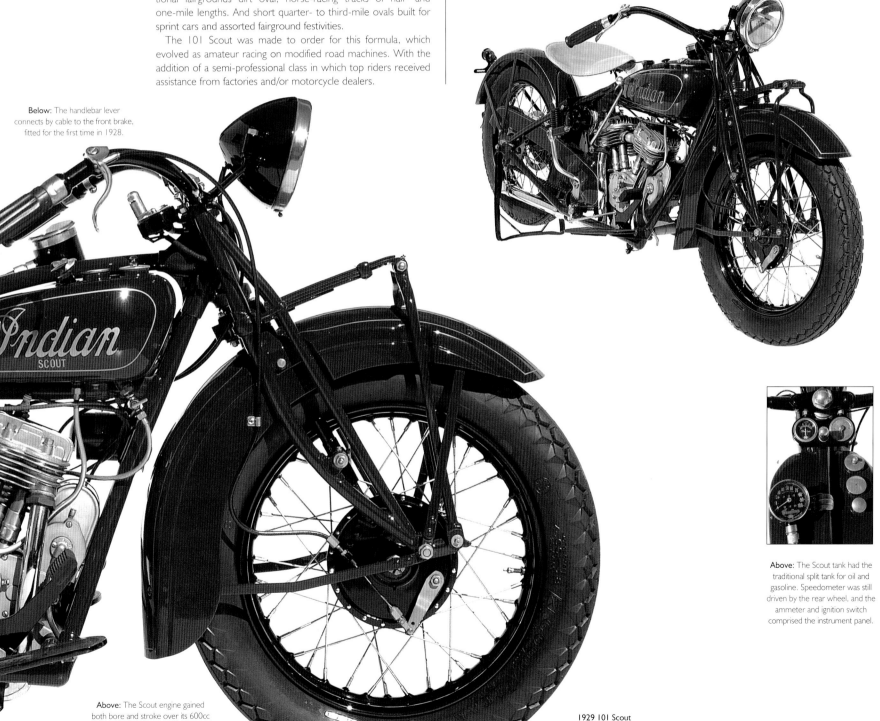

Below: The handlebar lever connects by cable to the front brake, fitted for the first time in 1928.

Above: The Scout engine gained both bore and stroke over its 600cc ancestor. And racers quickly learned that it could readily be stroked to make it even faster than the Chief.

Above: The Scout tank had the traditional split tank for oil and gasoline. Speedometer was still driven by the rear wheel, and the ammeter and ignition switch comprised the instrument panel.

1929 101 Scout
Owner – Vince Martinico
Auburn, California
Restored by Gene Grimes

ACE FOUR (1928) AND 1000cc HILLCLIMBER (1928)

1928 INDIAN ACE

SPECIFICATIONS
ENGINE/DRIVETRAIN
Engine: IOE inline four
Displacement: 77ci (1265cc)
Bore & stroke: 2.75 x 3.25in (69.8 x 82.5cc)
Horsepower: 35
Carburetor: Schebler
Transmission: 3-speed
Clutch: Wet multi-disc
Primary drive: Helical gear
Final drive: Chain
Brake: Double rear drum
Battery: 6-volt
Ignition: Splitdorf magneto

CHASSIS/SUSPENSION
Frame: Steel cradle, single downtube
Suspension: Trailing link girder/spring
Wheelbase: 59in (150cm)
Weight: 395lb (179kg)
Fuel capacity: 3.75gal (14.2lit)
Oil capacity: 3qts (2.84lit)
Tires: 25 x 3.85in
Top speed: 80mph (129km/h)
Color: Red
Number built: Approx. 400
Price: $425

Indian racers dominated the 1928 season, winning all the national championship events on the calendar. The overhead-valve Scouts, in the hands of Jim Davis, Bill Minnick and Curly Fredericks, won both the 750 and 1000cc classes at Rockingham, New Hampshire. The ohv Prince racers also logged good results in dirt-track races throughout the country.

Springfield's new board of directors had named Ohio industrialist Louis Bauer as the company president. His son Jack, recent automotive engineering graduate from the University of Wisconsin, took a job in the engineering department. Within a period of two years, the Bauers would undertake the manufacture of an automobile with a Chief engine, a car with a 4-cylinder Continental engine, auto shock absorbers and home refrigerators. Every project failed, at a cumulative cost to Indian of more than a million dollars.

The Ace, last of the mighty fours, had considerable history prior to its acquisition by Indian. In its original Henderson form, the 1910 four had matching competition from Pierce and a few others. Most were derived from the design originated by Belgian engineer Paul Kelecom and built as the FN marque in 1904.

William Henderson was born in Glasgow, Scotland in 1875 and emigrated with his family to the United States when he was three. In 1910 he and his younger brother Tom built a prototype inline four with mechanical inlet valves in the head and exhaust valves on the cylinders' sides. The configuration was known in the United States as the F-head design.

The motorcycle performed well, and by 1911 the Hendersons had raised enough money to set up a production facility in Detroit,

Michigan, with a schedule of 1,000 machines for 1912. Good publicity was assured when adventurer Carl Clancy made an 18,000-mile (29,000km) trip around the world on a new Henderson Four. The new machine sold for $325.

The Fours were popular for their smooth operation and good power. Production increased annually, and by 1916 the Henderson engine was 1000cc with wet sump lubrication and a 3-speed transmission. The wheelbase had shrunk from the protoype's 65 inches (165cm) to 58 inches (147cm). To establish the marque's reputation for speed and durability, Henderson hired racer Alan Bedell to make a run at Cannonball Baker's transcontinental record. In 1917 Bedell made the trek from Los Angeles to New York in 7 days, 16 hours, knocking nearly four days off Cannonball Baker's time.

Despite the machine's credentials, William Henderson's business and financial acumen didn't match his engineering prowess. The Hendersons sold the company to the Excelsior firm in 1917, and hired on in Chicago to direct production of the machine, which would be called the Henderson X. The relationship soured quickly when Excelsior owner Ignaz Schwinn insisted on a re-design of the four, and the Hendersons departed a year later. The new Henderson X would be designed by Arthur Lemon, former engineer with the Hendersons, who chose to stay on in Chicago.

To avoid legal disputes with Excelsior, William Henderson designed a new four-cylinder engine displacing 80 cubic inches (1300cc). With financing from Schwinn competitor Max Sladkin of Philadephia, Henderson undertook the manufacture of Ace motorcycles. The first machines appeared in 1920, and achieved

Right: The history of the Indian four traced a crooked trail from William Henderson's first design. The path traveled from Detroit to Chicago to Springfield, where it came to its final form as the Indian Four.

Below: The Indian Ace was subtitled The Collegiate Four, an appeal to the well-heeled young gentlemen sport riders of the Twenties.

1928 Indian Ace
Owner – Mort Wood
Sparks, Maryland

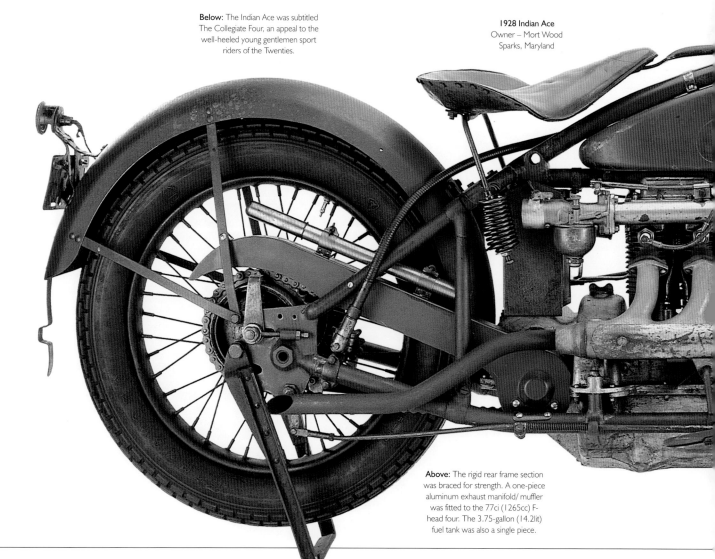

Above: The rigid rear frame section was braced for strength. A one-piece aluminum exhaust manifold/ muffler was fitted to the 77ci (1265cc) F-head four. The 3.75-gallon (14.2lit) fuel tank was also a single piece.

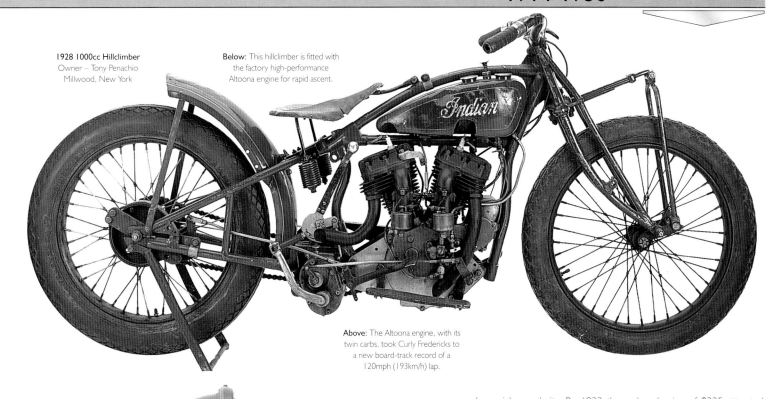

1928 1000cc Hillclimber
Owner – Tony Penachio
Millwood, New York

Below: This hillclimber is fitted with the factory high-performance Altoona engine for rapid ascent.

Above: The Altoona engine, with its twin carbs, took Curly Fredericks to a new board-track record of a 120mph (193km/h) lap.

quick popularity. By 1922 the reduced price of $325 attracted numerous police contracts, and Cannonball Baker knocked 17 hours off Bedell's cross-country record of 1917.

But in 1923, while road-testing a new model in Philadephia, William Henderson was struck and killed by an automobile. His former protégé Arthur Lemon resigned at Excelsior and moved to Philadelphia to continue Henderson's work. A number of improvements were made to the engine during the year, but the company's financial position remained fragile. Production of the Ace was terminated late in 1924, and the tooling and inventory passed through several hands before being acquired by Indian three years later.

The initial Indian Ace was little changed from the 1924 model. Springfield would undertake a number of design changes to the engine and chassis in subsequent years, producing a quite different machine. But many enthusiasts welcomed the survival of William Henderson's handiwork, and he came to be widely regarded as a seminal figure in American motorcycle engineering.

Left: The Indian Ace was little changed from Henderson's original design. Later versions would adopt more standard Indian features, including the fork, frame and fuel tank. Springfield now advertised its roster as the most complete line of motorcycles.

1929 101 SCOUT

SPECIFICATIONS
ENGINE/DRIVETRAIN
Engine: 42° side-valve V-twin
Displacement: 45ci (750cc)
Bore & stroke: 2.88 x 3.50in
(73.2 x 88.9mm)
Horsepower: 22
Carburetor: Schebler
Transmission: 3-speed
Clutch: Wet multi-disc
Primary drive: Helical gear
Final drive: Chain
Brake: F & R. Drum
Battery: 6-volt
Ignition: Magneto

CHASSIS/SUSPENSION
Frame: Steel, twin downtube
Suspension: Leaf-spring fork
Wheelbase: 57in (144.8cm)
Weight: 370lb (168kg)
Fuel capacity: 2.75gal (10.4 lit)
Oil capacity: 3qts (2.84lit)
Tires: 25 x 3.85in
Top speed: 75mph (121km/h)
Color: Red
Number built: Approx. 3,000
Price: $300

Among Indian enthusiasts, the Franklin model most widely cherished as a regular rider is the 101 Scout. The combined considerations of riding comfort and durability account for its popularity. The collectibility quotient, since the 101 had only a three-year production run, has taken many of the machines off the road. And a sizeable portion have been upgraded through the years as dirt-track racers, many of which are still raced regulary in vintage contests.

John Eagles' 101 Scout remains a touring mount, and as this is written may well be on the road in Washington or British Columbia. Eagles specializes in the care and feeding of 101s for other customers, though he has no problem working on Harleys if the need arises. The headlight is a period aftermarket item. The owner has logged some 75,000 miles (120,700km) on the Scout.

But speaking of racing (*for which you will note the author has a strong affinity – Editor*), the years 1928 and '29 were bright highlights for Indian racers, who won all the national championship meets both years. Phenomenal, and never done before or since. Among those riders, the sole remaining survivor is Jim Davis of Ohio, who likely rode one or more of the machines shown here. Jim, who still attends several races a year, recently celebrated his 101st birthday.

Below: The 350 and 500cc overhead-valve engines shared a common frame for racing. In 1929, Indian won all six of the 350cc national events. Jim Davis took four and Curly Fredericks two.

1928 350cc ohv Racer
Owner – Tony Penachio
Millwood, New York

Right: The 101 Scout achieved wide appeal among riders who wanted a more agile machine than the Chief, but one still capable of touring duty. Stroked to 935cc with Chief flywheels, the Scout offered a nice balance between speed, comfort and handling.

1929 500cc ohv Racer
Owner – Tony Penachio
Millwood, New York

Above: Springfield turned out both two-valve and four-valve ohv racing engines in the Twenties. Johnny Seymour was quite successful with the singles, and set several world records.

This was the closing segment of the second great racing era, as competition moved closer to production equipment and fewer specialized racing machines were built. Class C dirt-track and hill-climbs would maintain their grassroots support, but big-bore pro racing succumbed to the economic grip of the Great Depression.

The Indian Powerplus had established the performance standards for big-bore road machines of the Twenties, but Harley-Davidson's engineering department had not been idle. The twin-cam JD models, in 1000 and 1200cc versions, incorporated many of Milwaukee's racing bits and were powerful machines. Springfield held the hope that its recently acquired Ace Four would provide an even more powerful response to the new Harley V-twins.

The Scout was still the largest selling motorcycle on the market, and Indian decided that the upgraded 101 made more economic sense than offering two large displacement models. With the Four now positioned at the top of the line, the 1000cc Chief was discontinued.

During this period, Jack Bauer was given the responsibility of developing a small car powered by the 1200cc Chief engine. The vehicle proved unsatisfactory, and another car with a 4-cylinder Continental engine was undertaken and a few protoypes were built. The small car project was finally abandoned, after considerable drain on the company resources.

Above: The 101 Scout was longer, lower and equipped with a front brake. The riding position was comfortable and the machine handled with ease and precision. A well balanced motorcycle.

1929 101 Scout
Owner/restorer – John Eagles
Orange, California

1929 FOUR

SPECIFICATIONS
ENGINE/DRIVETRAIN
Engine: IOE inline four
Displacement: 77ci (1265cc)
Bore & stroke: 2.75 x 3.25in
(69.8 x 82.5cc)
Horsepower: 30
Carburetor: Schebler
Transmission: 3-speed
Clutch: Wet multi-disc
Primary drive: Helical gear
Final drive: Chain
Brake: F. Internal expanding.
R. External contracting
Battery: 6-volt
Ignition: Splitdorf magneto

CHASSIS/SUSPENSION
Frame: Steel, double downtube
Suspension: Trailing link
girder/spring
Wheelbase: 59in (150cm)
Weight: 460lb (209kg)
Fuel capacity: 3.75gal (14.2lit)
Oil capacity: 3qts (2.84lit)
Tires: 25 x 3.85in
Top speed: 80mph (129km/h)
Color: Red
Number built: Approx. 500
Price: $435

FOUR (1929)

The transformation of Ace to Indian in more than just name began in 1929. With the intitial inventory of original Ace machines selling out, Springfield adapted the leaf-spring fork to a new single-downtube frame with a rear section based on the 101 Scout design. The new model also employed the Scout-style fuel tank.

In the spring, beginning with engine number EA-101, the Four was given an all-Indian frame with double front downtubes, and the model was designated 402. The wheelbase gained 1.5 inches (3.81cm) on the original Henderson model, and about 50 pounds (22.7kg) in weight. But it would gain more. Front brakes were twin-shoe internal expanding type and the rear a two-piece external contracting.

Indian replaced the Ace three-main bearing crankshaft with a five-main crank and fitted new cylinder heads and pistons. Valve springs and pushrods were still exposed, which allowed inhalation of dirt and caused premature valve wear. Displacement remained at 1265cc and the Four was rated at 30 horsepower. The high-pressure lubrication system developed by Arthur Lemon provided the engine more durability.

The Four was naturally more expensive to produce than the twins, and the price of $445 limited its market. The Indian Four was still a relatively compact sport-touring motorcycling, and had great appeal to the gentleman motorcyclist. The machine remained in this configuration for three years, as further modifications were postponed by the catastrophic disintegration of the American stock market.

Scout sales during the pre-crash period continued to grow, and the overhead-valve racing versions secured more high-performance publicity for Springfield. Harley-Davidson released its side-valve WL 750, which was accompanied by a limited number of overhead-valve engines to challenge Indians in hillclimbs.

Grass-track and speedway racing had generated increasing popularity in Australia and New Zealand. Since speedway found less appeal in the USA, and flat track dwindled with the onset of the Great Depression, many of the overhead-valve Indian and Harley racers went overseas. The racing engines were derived from the Prince, which was dropped from production in 1929, and few of these original racers remain in existence today. Harley-Davidson dropped their ohv 500 single the following year.

The next great racing confrontation between Springfield and Milwaukee would be conducted with 750cc side-valve V-twins. Motorcycle sales had reached their lowest point in 20 years, and the picture would get worse.

Bauer resigned as president of the company. Industrial shrinkage had left large portions of the factory vacant, and the owners still sought to put it to work manufacturing ancillary products. In 1929 they purchased the Hartford Outboard Motor Company, in the hope of utilizing the space and bolstering profits. When that project failed, a new group of stockholders made plans to build airplanes in Springfield, but that program never got off the ground.

Some years later a company report stated that the various attempts to diversify Springfield's product line in 1928 and 1929 had cost the company about $1.25 million in working capital. And then came the Great Depression.

Right: The oil pressure gauge, despite its lowly position hard by the brake pedal, was an important instrument on the Four. Oil leakage was a minor issue compared to overheating, which taxed the engine's lubrication system.

Right: The Indian Four gained about 75lb (34kg) over its Ace uncle. The acumen of Henderson's design, and the prime factor in its popularity with sport riders, was reflected in the horsepower-to-weight ratio. The earlier fours weighed under 400lb (181kg), and they were fast.

Above: The Ace engine ran aluminum pistons and forged connecting rods. The 3-main bearing crankshaft was superseded by a 5-main crank. The accessory pipe was called a "Zoomer."

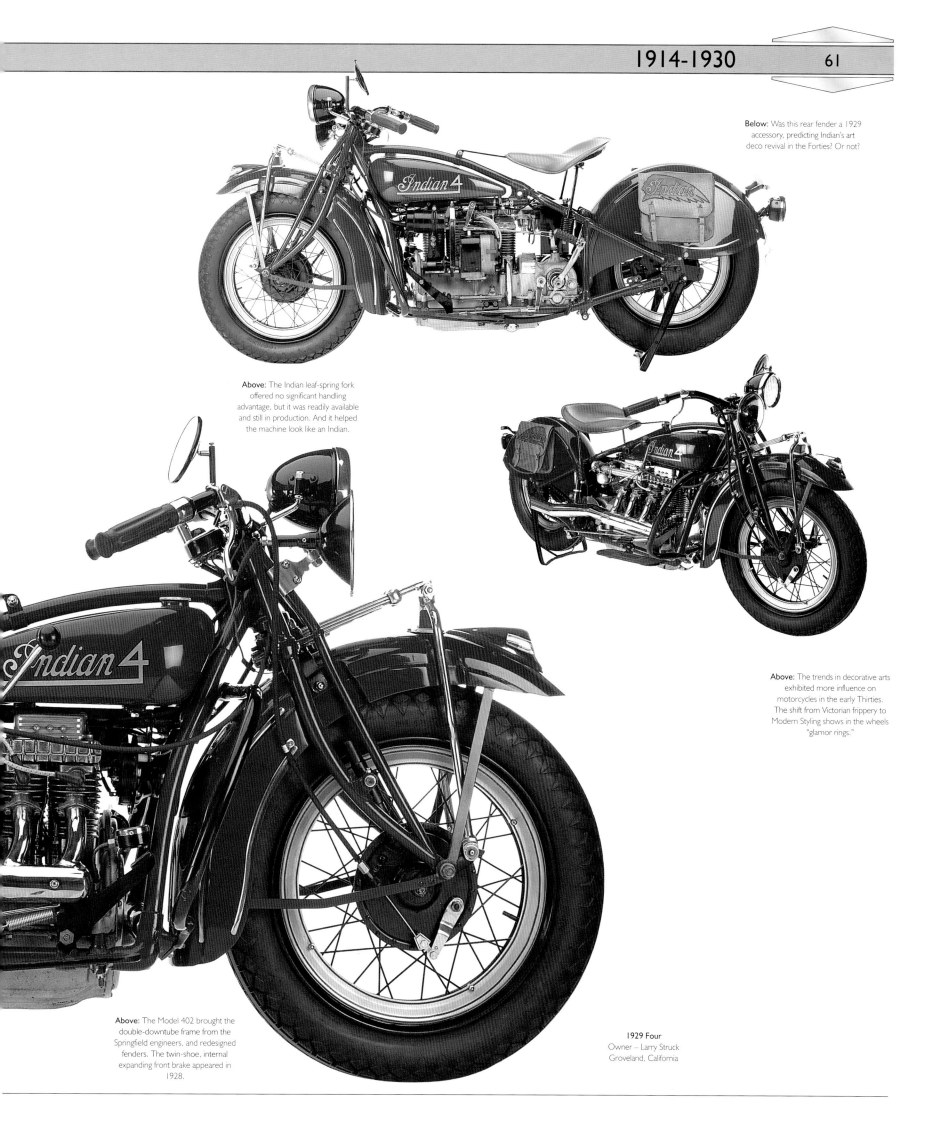

Below: Was this rear fender a 1929 accessory, predicting Indian's art deco revival in the Forties? Or not?

Above: The Indian leaf-spring fork offered no significant handling advantage, but it was readily available and still in production. And it helped the machine look like an Indian.

Above: The trends in decorative arts exhibited more influence on motorcycles in the early Thirties. The shift from Victorian frippery to Modern Styling shows in the wheels "glamor rings."

Above: The Model 402 brought the double-downtube frame from the Springfield engineers, and redesigned fenders. The twin-shoe, internal expanding front brake appeared in 1928.

1929 Four
Owner – Larry Struck
Groveland, California

FOUR (1930) AND CHIEF (1930)

1930 FOUR

SPECIFICATIONS
ENGINE/DRIVETRAIN
Engine: IOE inline four
Displacement: 77ci (1265cc)
Bore & stroke: 2.75 x 3.25in
(69.8 x 82.5cc)
Horsepower: 35
Carburetor: Schebler
Transmission: 3-speed
Clutch: Wet multi-disc
Primary drive: Helical gear
Final drive: Chain
Brake: F. Internal expanding.
R. External contracting
Battery: 6-volt
Ignition: Splitdorf magneto

CHASSIS/SUSPENSION
Frame: Steel, double downtube
Suspension: Trailing link
girder/spring
Wheelbase: 59in (150cm)
Weight: 460lb (209kg)
Fuel capacity: 3.75gal (14.2lit)
Oil capacity: 3qts (2.84lit)
Tires: 26 x 4.00in
Top speed: 80mph (129km/h)
Color: Red
Number built: Approx. 600
Price: $445

The wreckage of the stock market and the advent of the Great Depression had far-reaching effects on the motorcycle industry. In little more than a year, the Indian Motocycle Company had been owned by three different investment groups. The last, headed by one Norman Bolles, achieved new heights (or plumbed new depths) in the art of stock manipulaton.

When it was announced that the company had acquired the rights to build Sunbeam aircraft engines, and a number of stockholders realized that their shares were worth about one-third what they had paid for them, things began to unravel. Faced with lawsuits and possible prosecution, the owners cut a stock-trade deal with wealthy industrialist E. Paul duPont of Wilmington, Delaware. As majority shareholder, duPont hoped to employ the vacant factory space to build aircraft engines, but neither the company finances nor the national economy could support the plan.

The Arrow outboard motor, implemented by the previous regime, achieved little success in the market. Most Indian dealers were not interested in outboards, and the engine was dropped that summer. The Chief was fitted with a cast aluminum fuel tank for 1930, but it was replaced by a steel unit the following year. The recent periods of experimentation with non-motorcycle products, and the general management debacle, had caused serious quality control problems on the motorcycles.

As an amateur engineer and former motorcycle enthusiast, duPont approached his new role with considerable initiative. He immediately conducted his own comparison tests between the Chief and Harley-Davidson's VL, and found the Indian engine produced more vibration. The new owner took an active hand in

restoring the Indian name and reorganizing the production. He appointed Loren Hosley, former manager of duPont's car company, as the new production chief in Springfield.

Few changes were made to any of the existing models, but obvious cuts would have to be made in the production roster to turn the company around financially. One of these deletions, to the considerable dismay of many enthusiasts, was the 101 Scout. There arose a collective moan from sport riders around the country, saying nay, not the Scout. Get rid of that damn Four, why don't you, but leave us the Scout.

Below: The luggage rack, a standard accessory with the solo seat, hinted at the Four's practical side.

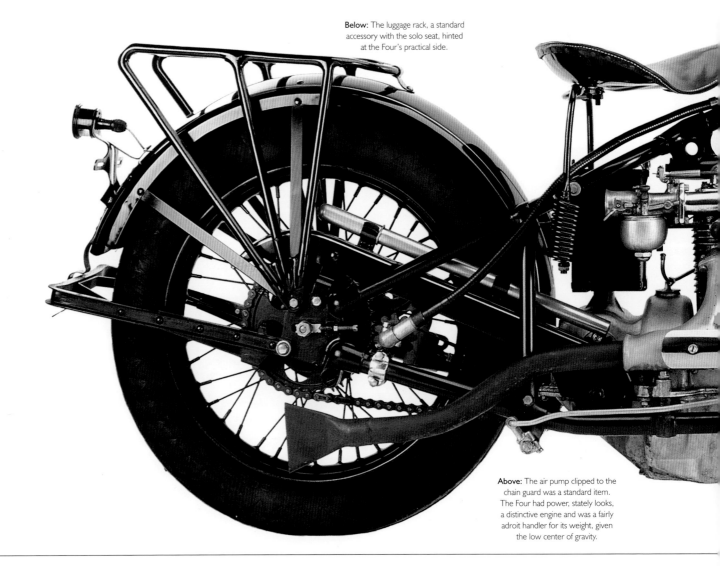

Right: The Indian Four went into 1930 without substantial modification in terms of appearance. Nor did it gain weight. The first generation of Indian Fours were not as fast as the Ace, but remained smooth runners.

Above: The air pump clipped to the chain guard was a standard item. The Four had power, stately looks, a distinctive engine and was a fairly adroit handler for its weight, given the low center of gravity.

Left: The transition to duPont ownership came not without problems with the machines. The Chief suffered excessive vibration and disintegrating engine components. For 1930 only, the Chief fuel tanks were cast aluminum.

1930 Chief
Owner – David Hansen
Ventura, California

Below: Low sport-style handlebars were popular on the Four. Still a relatively compact motorcycle, the seat height was only 27 inches (69cm) from the macadam.

'Twas not enough, however, to stay the hand of economic reformation, real or imagined. By his lights, duPont genuinely set out to see Indian restored to health with good products and sound management, and to again challenge Harley-Davidson. It might also reasonably be assumed that he relished the role of underdog for a change.

And to that task attached some real challenges. Indian production dropped to below 4,000 motorcycles for 1930, and the losses were nearly $750,000. Disaffiliated dealers had to be won back, and new dealers found. Contracts with suppliers stood in need of renegotiation. Then there was the depression. So, despite the general and often well-warranted mistrust of the rich and privileged, Indians fans stood nearly to a man, and said go E. Paul.

Above: Nickel-plated cylinders were prone to weathering, and most riders would eventually paint them black or silver. Harmonica-like boxes atop the heads have lids for manual rocker oiling.

1930 Four
Owner – Mort Wood
Sparks, Maryland

101 SCOUT (1931) AND *FACTORY HILLCLIMBER (1927)*

1931 101 SCOUT

SPECIFICATIONS
ENGINE/DRIVETRAIN
Engine: 42° side-valve V-twin
Displacement: 45ci (750cc)
Bore & stroke: 2.88 x 3.50in
(73.2 x 88.9mm)
Horsepower: 22
Carburetor: Schebler
Transmission: 3-speed
Clutch: Wet multi-disc
Primary drive: Helical gear
Final drive: Chain
Brake: F. Internal expanding.
R. External contracting
Battery: 6-volt
Ignition: Magneto

CHASSIS/SUSPENSION
Frame: Steel, twin downtube
Suspension: Leaf-spring fork
Wheelbase: 57in (144.8cm)
Weight: 370lb (168kg)
Fuel capacity: 2.75gal (10.4lit)
Oil capacity: 3qts (2.84lit)
Tires: 25 x 3.85in
Top speed: 75mph (121km/h)
Color: Red
Number built: Approx. 2,000
Price: $310

The 1931 and final 101 Scout was equipped with a new throttle-controlled oil pump, which matched oil delivery to the motorcycle's engine speed. Also new were the muffler, headlight and cadmium-plated spokes. The Scout was fitted with aluminum pistons, though cast iron jugs were optional. Indian also offered performance parts in the B-designated motors with different heads, valve springs and carburetor.

The Four also received new alloy pistons and a bigger clutch. The Chief got the same pistons and larger flywheels to minimize vibration, and all models had a new internal expanding rear brake. The Harley-Davidson Seventy-four, though it suffered early teething problems, made considerable power in smooth fashion. Indian engineers were charged with upgrading the Chief's performance for the following year. Unfortunately, Charles Franklin was unable to contribute to this process, having taken a leave of absence for health reasons.

Indian's business picked up markedly in 1931; new dealerships were established and credit restored with major suppliers. West coast distributor Hap Alzina and Kansas City dealer Al Crocker were instrumental in helping re-establish the factory's dealer network. Another young man who would subsequently become a feature of Indian folklore went to work for Crocker that year, fellow named Sam Pierce.

One curious event of 1931 was the arrival in Springfield of a Mr. Hewett, who set up his own shop in one corner of the factory. Instructions from management indicated that he was working on a special project and was not to be disturbed. Later a man in the advertising department was assigned to photograph Hewett's work, but told to keep it quiet. The mystery engineer left shortly thereafter and little more was said about his visit. About a year later Mr. Hewett's engine, a horizontally opposed side-valve four-cylinder, appeared in the nose of a new aircraft called the Piper Cub, designed by a Mr. Taylor of Ohio. The engine, designated the A-40, was built by the Continental Engine Company of Detroit, Michigan.

A more momentous story developed the same year, when the California Highway Patrol was ready to buy a fleet of 150 motorcycles. This caused ripples of corporate excitement in Springfield and Milwaukee, and bidding plans were promptly prepared. But it seems Ignaz Schwinn had circumvented the standard bid process and, through some subtle but devious chicanery, secured the contract for 150 Henderson Fours to prowl the California roadways. Naturally everyone at Indian and Harley-Davidson sputtered and fumed, threatening legal action, but nothing came of it. Some measure of revenge was taken, however, when four months later Schwinn announced his departure from the motorcycle business. Excelsior and Henderson were history.

The real shocker for Springfield came a few months later. According to undocumented legend, Walter Davidson surreptitiously tried to corner the police market with Such a Deal! Milwaukee would sell new VL Seventy-fours for $195 with the trade-in of any machine in service, regardless of brand or condition. The VL carried a retail price of $340. This scenario outraged both Springfield and Harley-Davidson's dealers, who were effectively cut out of the deal. The tactic caused so much flak that Davidson withdrew the offer before the end of the year. But what previously had the earmarks of a mostly good-natured rivalry between companies and riders, had now become a genuine pissing contest.

These anecdotes, it should be noted, are drawn from Harry Sucher's extensive history of Indian, *The Iron Redskin*.

Below: Despite its middleweight classification, the 101 Scout was not inexpensive to build. Money was tight.

Right: The final year for the 101 Scout, 1931, marked with sadness on the calendars of sporty bike fans everywhere. The last model had an easy-off rear wheel; the brake and sprocket remained on the motorcycle.

Below: Pennsylvania's Howard Mitzell was a champion hillclimber for over 25 years. The ohv 750cc was a favorite.

Left: Mitzell's tilt racer ran a reinforced Prince fork on a lowered keystone frame. Indian built two dozen of the overhead Forty-fives in 1926 and 1927. Al Crocker later made ohv conversion kits when Indian ran out of money for specialized engines.

1927 ohv 750
Owner – Tony Penachio
Millwood, New York

Left: The last 101 Scout was fitted with a cross-braced handlebar. The chrome-ringed headlight was a new feature, as was the Indian-face horn just below it. Despite its broad popularity among enthusiasts, the 101 Scout ran well behind the Chief in sales.

Above: The speedometer and fundamental instrument panel could be equipped with their own lights. The switch is for the headlight's high and low beam. A hand oil pump supplemented the engine's own.

1931 101 Scout
Owner – Edwin Aucott
Green Lane, Pennsylvania

Above: The muffler was a new item in 1931, and the wheels got cadmium-plated spokes. Is this not a handsome machine?

1932 SCOUT

SPECIFICATIONS
ENGINE/DRIVETRAIN
Engine: 42° side-valve V-twin
Displacement: 45ci (750cc)
Bore & stroke: 2.88 x 3.50in (73.2 x 88.9mm)
Horsepower: 22
Carburetor: Schebler
Transmission: 3-speed
Clutch: Wet multi-disc
Primary drive: Helical gear
Final drive: Chain
Brake: F & R. Drum
Battery: 6-volt
Ignition: Magneto

CHASSIS/SUSPENSION
Frame: Steel, twin downtube
Suspension: Leaf-spring fork
Wheelbase: 61in (155cm)
Weight: 430lb (195kg)
Fuel capacity: 3.75gal (14.2lit)
Oil capacity: 2.5qts (2.6lit)
Tires: 4.00 x 18
Top speed: 75mph (121km/h)
Colors: DuPont catalog
Number built: Approx. 900
Price: $295

203 SCOUT (1932) AND FOUR (1932)

By 1932 it was apparent that duPont's leadership had checked Indian's slide to oblivion. But the depression was growing more severe, and production costs had to be cut severely. So the new model news was not encouraging for dealers or sporting riders, because the 101 Scout was replaced by the model 203 Standard Scout, which was merely the 750 engine in a Chief frame. The model many riders considered the best Indian ever made was out of production.

Chassis design had been standardized to employ common parts among all three models. Even the Four was patterned on the common frame, but for the lower section to accommodate the long engine. Springfield did find another use for the Scout engine in the newly developed Dispatch Tow, a three-wheeled utility vehicle developed by Charles Franklin before his leave of absence. And the middleweight flathead was also enlisted in the development of a new model using components of the discontinued Prince.

The Standard Scout did still find favor with police departments for its smooth engine and reliability. And Chief fans were pleased to see the 1932 version produced less vibration and more trouble-free miles. Battery ignition was now standard on all models, with magneto optional. The lacquer paint of the previous year had proven unsatisfactory and was replaced by enamel, though the brand, not surprisingly, remained duPont Duco.

Indians were now heavier-duty motorcycles. In another industry irony, as Milwaukee had emulated Springfield in terms of racing designs, Indian now followed Harley for reliability. New forks, frames, clutches and stronger engines were designed to bring the motorcycles to the standards established by Milwaukee.

The new designs also altered the appearance of the Indian, which now had a larger and more rounded two-piece fuel tank that covered the top frame tube. The Chief generator was now fitted behind the rear cylinder and the circuit-breaker mounted at the front of the engine. Ignition was the wasted-spark style with both plugs firing every revolution, Harley-style

The new frame added more length to Four's wheelbase, which was now 61 inches (155cm), and the machine had gained

60 pounds (27kg). The engine was unchanged. Economic restrictions had effectively put new engine designs on hold, but had little impact on motorcycle styling, a less expensive enterprise. The Chief, Standard Scout and Four now displayed continuity of style, all attractive machines and each recognizably Indian.

The next attempt to complete the lineup, and hopefully compete with the Harley-Davidson single, was the Scout Pony. The model was built up from chassis components of the discontinued Prince, with power from a 500cc side-valve V-twin engine. A companion version, the Motoplane, ran a 750cc engine. Both were derived from the 101 Scout motor, but featured dry-sump oiling and chain-drive primary.

But the effects of the depression were settling in. Fewer than 3,000 motorcycles were produced for 1932, and the company lost $232,000. Plus, Springfield and motorcycle enthusiasts worldwide were saddened by the news that Charles Franklin died in October at the age of 46.

Left: The Chief, which had been the big Scout, now had an adopted stepson in the Scout, or Little Chief. Some riders would later upgrade the engine with stroker kits and Sport Scout heads and cylinders.

Right: The Scout name was still in evidence for the 1932 season, but the motorcycle was a Chief chassis with the 750cc Scout engine. This meant it was heavier, of course, and not quite so agile. But it was trustworthy and docile, a boon to former mounted policemen.

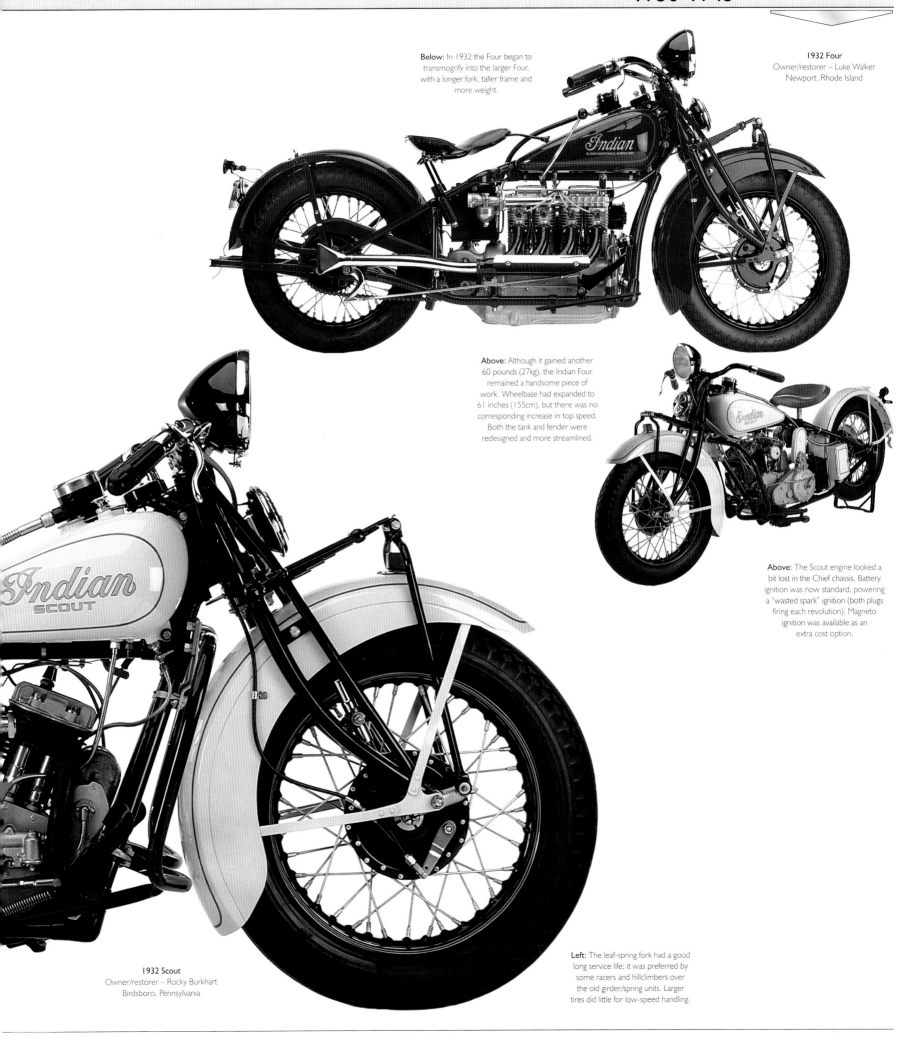

Below: In 1932 the Four began to transmogrify into the larger Four, with a longer fork, taller frame and more weight.

1932 Four
Owner/restorer – Luke Walker
Newport, Rhode Island

Above: Although it gained another 60 pounds (27kg), the Indian Four remained a handsome piece of work. Wheelbase had expanded to 61 inches (155cm), but there was no corresponding increase in top speed. Both the tank and fender were redesigned and more streamlined.

Above: The Scout engine looked a bit lost in the Chief chassis. Battery ignition was now standard, powering a "wasted spark" ignition (both plugs firing each revolution). Magneto ignition was available as an extra cost option.

1932 Scout
Owner/restorer – Rocky Burkhart
Birdsboro, Pennsylvania

Left: The leaf-spring fork had a good long service life; it was preferred by some racers and hillclimbers over the old girder/spring units. Larger tires did little for low-speed handling.

SPORT SCOUT (1934) AND FOUR (1933)

1934 SPORT SCOUT

SPECIFICATIONS
ENGINE/DRIVETRAIN
Engine: 42° side-valve V-twin
Displacement: 45ci (750cc)
Bore & stroke: 2.88 x 3.50in
(73.2 x 88.9mm)
Horsepower: 22
Carburetor: Schebler
Transmission: 3-speed
Clutch: Wet multi-disc
Primary drive: Triplex chain
Final drive: Chain
Brake: F & R. Drum
Battery: 6-volt
Ignition: Battery/coil

CHASSIS/SUSPENSION
Frame: Steel keystone
Suspension: Leading-link
truss/spring
Wheelbase: 56.5in (143.58cm)
Weight: 450lb (204kg)
Fuel capacity: 3.7gal (14lit)
Oil capacity: 2.5qts (2.37lit)
Tires: 18 x 4.00in
Top speed: 70mph (113km/h)
Colors: Red standard
Number built: Approx. 700
Price: $300

Period fashions aside, motorcycles became more attractive in the early 1930s. But never in the sport's history had so few people been able to afford one. While the machine's functional development was effectively stalled by cheap cars and devastating levels of unemployment, motorcycle styling reached the Art Deco phase. But pretty doesn't pay the bills, and the Indian Motocycle Company had reached the bottom of the barrel and couldn't meet its payroll. Loans were taken out to meet outstanding obligations, and employees were laid off. By 1933 the Depression had put Indian and Harley-Davidson under serious economic constraints.

The Motoplane was found to have frame problems exposed by the power of the 750cc engine. The model sold for $250, with the 500cc Pony priced at $225. The Harley-Davidson 350cc single, by comparison, sold for $195, and most dealers were discounting in the tough market. A decent used car cost about half the price of a new motorcycle. As an added aggravation, the wet-sump lubrication system in the Chief and Scout was prone to problems in regulating the flow of oil, and a number of oil pump designs were tested before the problem was sorted out.

In another move to control costs in materials and production, the primary gear drives in the Chief and Scout were replaced by duplex chains. The hope for economized racing drew together the management from Harley-Davidson and Indian with officers of the Motorcycle and Allied Trades Association and the American Motorcycle Association. The object of the gathering was to establish a racing formula using lightly modified production motorcycles for dirt-track, hillclimb and the newly popular TT scrambles racing.

They settled on a 750cc side-valve formula for dirt-track, since both Milwaukee and Springfield produced engines, with allowance for 500cc overhead-valve engines. The maximum compression ratio was 7.5:1 This mix would later create a large can of worms,

but the classification served American racing quite well for many years. The hillclimb and scrambles divisions were permitted use of 1300cc machines.

With the capitulation of Excelsior, hillclimb ace Gene Rhyne had joined the Indian team. Rhyne, the veteran Orrie Steele and a talented youngster named Howard Mitzell were the "slant artists" who would carry the Springfield banner.

But Springfield was now in such dire financial straits that appeals went out to the stockholders, who would have to see their holdings devalued in exchange for more shares and promissory notes from the company. The belt-tightening had reached the point that Indian stockholders were charged with helping salvage the company. The reorganization plan was finally approved in May. Springfield's motorcycle production fell to 1,667 machines, but cost-cutting had eliminated the deficit and the company showed a profit of $76,000 for 1933.

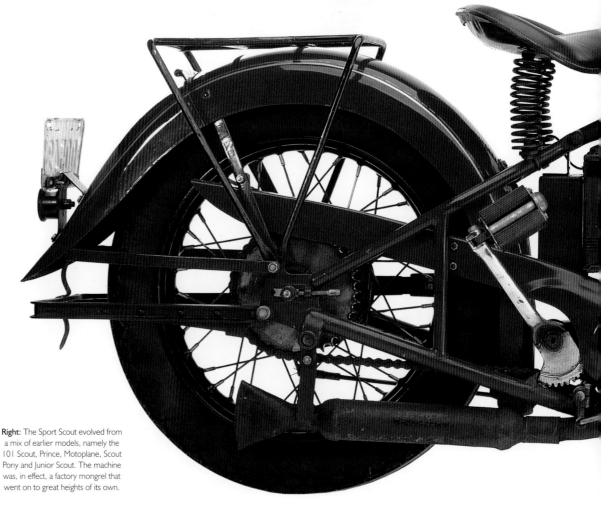

Right: The Sport Scout evolved from a mix of earlier models, namely the 101 Scout, Prince, Motoplane, Scout Pony and Junior Scout. The machine was, in effect, a factory mongrel that went on to great heights of its own.

Below: The Four underwent few revisions for 1933; more colors were added to the growing spectrum, and a chrome-plating package covered the most popular shiny bits.

Left: Sales of the Four were not living up to Springfield's expectations. Plans were underway for a new design that would first appear in 1935.

1933 Four
Owner – Jim Smith

Below: Cylinders heads and barrels were painted black, probably as another cost-saving move. The Sport Scout was heavier than the 101, and the keystone frame lacked the former's rigidity. The engine and transmission were solidly bolted together.

Left: It didn't take long for the hot rod gang to redraw the performance profile of the Sport Scout. A stroker kit with Chief flywheels brought the displacement to 57 cubic inches (935cc). Flared fenders indicate the dawn of another new styling era.

1934 Sport Scout
Owner – Mort Wood
Sparks, Maryland

DISPATCH TOW (1934) AND CHIEF (1934)

1934 DISPATCH TOW

SPECIFICATIONS
ENGINE/DRIVETRAIN
Engine: 42° side-valve V-twin
Displacement: 45ci (750cc)
Bore & stroke: 2.88 x 3.50in
(73.2 x 88.9mm)
Horsepower: 22
Carburetor: Schebler
Transmission: 3-speed
Clutch: Wet multi-disc
Primary drive: Chain
Final drive: Differential gear
Brake: F & R. Drum
Battery: 6-volt
Ignition: Magneto

CHASSIS/SUSPENSION
Frame: Steel, twin downtube
Suspension: Leaf-spring fork
Wheelbase: 57in (144.8cm)
Weight: 630lb (286kg)
Fuel capacity: 3.75gal (14.2lit)
Oil capacity: 2.5qts (2.37lit)
Tires: 25 x 3.85in
Top speed: 65mph (105km/h)
Colors: Red (2), blue (2), black,
cream
Number built: Unknown
Price: $375

The first Indian three-wheelers were powered by the 750cc side-valve engine from the Motoplane. The first rendition appeared in 1931 with the Scout engine and would see broad application in utility service, police work, sport riding and racing for many years. The certification of the Dispatch Tow was made the following year when Harley-Davidson introduced their own version. Tit for tat.

Milwaukee also redesigned their graphics and paint schemes to dress the Hogs up next to Indian's stylish designs and colors. With duPont's access to paint, Springfield was assured a colorful spectrum for the motorcycles. Harleys soon appeared in more colors, with new graphic designs on the fuel tanks and more elaborate striping. Indian offered 24 color combinations at no extra cost, and a choice of any color in the duPont catalog as an extra-cost option.

In 1934 both the Chief and Scout were fitted with a four-row primary drive chain, and both now had the dry sump lubrication system. The new valenced fenders followed the teardrop shape then appearing on automobiles. The larger fuel tanks were also new, and a 4-speed transmission was a $15 option on the Chief. Optional aluminum heads were available for both models. The battery/coil ignition was standard on the Chief, with the magneto a $25 option.

Both the Chief and Scout were offered in sidecar trim, which included an optional transmission with reverse gear. The Motoplane/Pony series was dropped for the development of another Prince-Scout hybrid that would be released later in the year, and christened the Sport Scout.

Indian's prospects improved in 1934 and production rose to 2,809 motorcycles. The management was sufficiently encouraged to undertake an overall update of the machines, intending to catch up with Harley-Davidson and be prepared for the inevitable reversal of the miserable economy. E. Paul hired Briggs Weaver to replace Charles Franklin as chief engineer. Weaver had previously served as an engineer on duPont's production of marine engines and automobiles.

Class C racing officially got underway with a limited number of events in 1934. Only two were national championship contests; the 200-mile national TT at Keene, New Hampshire went to Babe Tancrede on a Harley Seventy-four. The 6-hour Macon, Georgia race was won by Howard Almond on a Harley Forty-five. Joe Petrali on the Harley Peashooter was just beginning his domination of Class A dirt-track, and the 750cc hillclimb class. Indian was in the catch-up mode.

Right: The principal application for the new three-wheelers was the automobile repair business. One serviceman could pick-up a customer's car and tow the trike back to the shop. And vice-versa when the work was done.

Right: The Dispatch Tow, designed by Charles Franklin, was based on the 101 Scout chassis. In 1933 the trike adopted Sport Scout components.

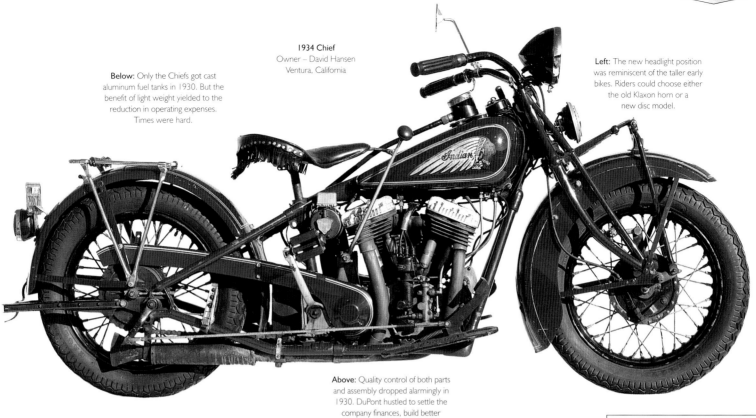

1934 Chief
Owner – David Hansen
Ventura, California

Below: Only the Chiefs got cast aluminum fuel tanks in 1930. But the benefit of light weight yielded to the reduction in operating expenses. Times were hard.

Left: The new headlight position was reminiscent of the taller early bikes. Riders could choose either the old Klaxon horn or a new disc model.

Above: Quality control of both parts and assembly dropped alarmingly in 1930. DuPont hustled to settle the company finances, build better engines and mollify irate dealers.

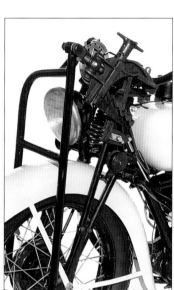

Above: The adjustable tow bar simply clamped to a car's rear bumper. But the system also made this a relatively easy motorcycle to steal.

Above: The Sport Scout engine received a compression reduction and lower gearing to handle the added weight. Dispatch Tow racing never caught on.

1934 Dispatch Tow
Owner – Mike Tomas
Riverside, California

CHIEF (1935) AND SPORT SCOUT (1935)

1935 CHIEF

SPECIFICATIONS
ENGINE/DRIVETRAIN
Engine: 42° side-valve V-twin
Displacement: 74ci (1200cc)
Bore & stroke: 3.25 x 4.44n
(82.5 x 112.7mm)
Horsepower: 34
Carburetor: Schebler
Transmission: 3 or 4-speed
Clutch: Wet multi-disc
Primary drive: 4-row chain
Final drive: Chain
Brake: F & R. Drum
Battery: 6-volt
Ignition: Circuit breaker
(magneto optional)

CHASSIS/SUSPENSION
Frame: Steel, twin downtube
Suspension: Leaf-spring fork
Wheelbase: 61in (155cm)
Weight: 490lb (222kg)
Fuel capacity: 3.75gal (14.2lit)
Oil capacity: 2.5qts (2.37lit)
Tires: 4.00 or 4.50 x 18
Top speed: 85mph (137km/h)
Colors: Red (2), blue (2),
green (2), yellow, silver, cream,
brown (2) and others
Number built: 3,715 (all
models)
Price: $340 (Y motor: $352)

Above: The original license
plate has stayed with the
motorcycle for over 62 years.
Registration is
probably overdue.

Right: The Chief tank and
fenders were redesigned in
1932, as more decorative
designs appeared on
automobiles. The motorcycle
market was fiercely contested
between Springfield and
Milwaukees. The machines
had to look smart.

Hard times had staggered both Indian and Harley-Davidson, but Springfield took the more devastating punch. The Sport Scout was late off the line, while Milwaukee had gained a loyal following with racing victories and by engineering a quick response to mechanical problems in the new bikes.

The Sport Scout suffered some characteristics of its parts-bin heritage. Fans of the 101 Scout were less than keen on the keystone frame, just didn't seem proper to use the engine as part of the frame. The machine ran close to 400 pounds (181kg), and what about those plates between the engine and gearbox? And the whole thing seemed to have an awful lot of pieces to it. Sure ain't no 101 Scout was the consensus.

But the Sport Scout was being sorted out. Indian had too much at stake to give up on the middleweight, a simple truth underscored by the reality that production was now running at less than 30 per cent of Milwaukee's output. The engineering staff on the Sport Scout consisted of Briggs Weaver, Erle Armstrong and Jimmy Hill, the latter two bringing both mechanical and racing experience to the enterprise.

The 750cc side-valve employed new cylinders, heads, a triplex chain primary drive and came standard with battery/coil ignition. The optional magneto was driven by sprocket off the primary chain, a system that would be abandoned the following year. The engine produced more power than the old 101, and could readily be stroked to 57 cubic inches (935cc) for more thrust. Eventually, as the parts supplies dwindled, even confirmed 101 fans would use Sport Scout engines in their machines.

The new model would also be vindicated on the racetracks, as the accomplishments of Ed Kretz, Rollie Free, Lester Hillbish and Woodsie Castonguay were entered in the record books. One popular conversion was to graft Sport Scout cylinders and aluminum heads to a 101 engine. Many riders still thought the cradle frame was both stronger and provided better handling than the later model's keystone frame.

The Chief was also revised with alloy cylinders and heads in 1935, the package designated the Y engine as opposed to the cast iron B version. The big twins had their own group of devoted supporters, more than a few of whom insisted that the Chief be faster than the Harley Seventy-four. The styling changed with the adoption of flared fenders like those on the Sport Scout. Riding a solo Chief, brothers Steve and Roger Whiting rode two-up to set a new transcontinental record of under five days.

In the Jacksonville, Florida national championship Class C race, Rody Rodenburg won the 200-miler on a Sport Scout. This event

Right: The new streamlining was
accentuated by the pinstriping. The
net effect made the motorcycle look
longer and lower, and suggested the
enticing appeal of Speed.

Below: This would be the final year
for screw-in gas and oil caps,
replaced by bayonet caps in 1936.

Above: In 1935 the Chief had a new
"snuffbox" circuit breaker ignition, or
optional magneto. Those who chose
the former often wished they hadn't.
The system was a bit fragile.

Below: The Sport Scout had started the trend to streamlined styling a year earlier. The model was also gaining popularity on the race track.

Below: The new "Y" motors appeared at mid-season in both the Chief and Sport Scout. Larger cylinders and aluminum heads allowed more power.

1935 Sport Scout
Owner – Mark Dooley
Anaheim, California

would evolve into the annual Daytona 200 national championship event. Woodsie Castonguay took the 100-mile championship race at Langhorne, Pennsylvania on a Sport Scout.

The Indian Motocycle Company was still in difficult financial waters, but production for 1935 was up to 3,715 machines. Rumors of national economic improvement were in the wind, and Springfield had reason to be pleased with the response to the new models. The next major project was a redesign of the Indian Four engine, which would produce results less pleasing. Milwaukee, in the meantime, was preparing the big news for 1936 with a 61-cubic inch (1000cc) overhead-valve V-twin. Hard times or not, the game was still afoot.

Below: The Indian headdress tank emblem first appeared in 1935. Three different striping treatments were offered on the tanks. This example has the standard panel.

Above: Corbin speedometers were offered in unlighted or lighted versions, as shown here. The tidy instrument panel now included the ignition switch.

1935 Chief
Owner – Mark Dooley
Anaheim, California

Left: Not all riders were captivated by the styling of the new fenders. The less deeply valenced mudguards would return as options a few years later, but only briefly. Art Deco prevailed.

1936 FOUR

SPECIFICATIONS
ENGINE/DRIVETRAIN
Engine: EOI inline four
Displacement: 77ci (1265cc)
Bore & stroke: 2.75 x 3.25in
(69.8 x 82.5cc)
Horsepower: 40
Carburetor: Marvel
Transmission: 3-speed
Clutch: Wet multi-disc
Primary drive: Helical gear
Final drive: Chain
Brake: F & R. Internal expanding
Battery: 6-volt
Ignition: Distributor

CHASSIS/SUSPENSION
Frame: Steel, double downtube
Suspension: Trailing link
girder/spring
Wheelbase: 61in (155cm)
Weight: 520lb (236kg)
Fuel capacity: 3.75gal (14.2lit)
Oil capacity: 3qts (2.84lit)
Tires: 26 x 4.00in
Top speed: 85mph (137km/h)
Colors: Red (2), blue (2),
green (2), yellow, silver, cream,
brown (2) and others
Number built: Approx. 600
Price: $410

Right: The high exhaust pipes
signaled the arrival of the
1935 Four, also known as the
"upside-down" four. Exhaust
valves moved to the top, with
intake valves underneath, for
reasons not yet entirely clear.

FOUR (1936) AND CHIEF (1936)

The 1936 Indian Four was, by historical consensus, a mistake. Although legions of Indian fans at the time didn't care much one way or the other. These riders had no use for a large, expensive motorcycle that weighed over 500 pounds (227kg). But to the smaller but no less dedicated number of four-cylinder enthusiasts, the "upside-down" four was a step in the wrong direction.

The nickname derived from the new valve arrangement on the 1936 engine. The exhaust valves were now atop the motor, which it was hoped would improve the cooling characteristics. New cylinder head fins were designed with the same objective. The intake valves had moved from the top to the side of the engine, which in theory would improve combustion, add horsepower and just be generally swell.

However, the engine was butt ugly, and carried a shield to keep the rider's right leg off the exhaust pipe. Compared to the earlier Ace design, with its graceful cast aluminum exhaust manifold, the upside down four looked more like an industrial workhorse engine. The Harley-Davidson 1000cc ohv V-twin Knucklehead, by comparison, was indisputably engineering with style. It looked like a chunk of airplane engine stuck between two wheels, and spoke smartly of heavy-duty horsepower. Score another win on the Milwaukee card.

On the other hand, even an upside-down four was better than no four at all, and Indian alone remained the American manufacturer of one. The inverted engine remained another year in production, modified with dual carburetors, but the four would then return to its original configuration. The two-year production amounted to some 1,600 machines.

The Sport Scout was treated to a larger oil pump, and now came dressed with the deeply skirted front fender of its Chief brethren. The Chief was fitted with an automotive-type distributor which replaced the wasted spark ignition. The Standard Scout was now designated the Scout 45. But the Sport Scout was generating the most orders, and more racers were setting the bikes up for competition.

The Los Angeles 45 Club held its spring meet at Muroc Dry Lake in April. Fred Ludlow turned the top speed, 128.57mph (206.9km/h), on a Sport Scout. Kenny Schofield rode his 101 Scout out from Hollywood, with his girlfriend on the back, and ran it through the traps at 107mph (172km/h). An Indian Chief ridden by Al Chasteen put up a run of 125mph (201km/h).

The Sport Scout posted its credentials across the board in 1936. Ed Kretz won the Savannah, Georgia 200-mile national and Lester Hillbish won the Langhorne, Pennsylvania 100-miler. The 200-mile roadrace national in New Hampshire went to Sport Scout rider Hanford Marshall.

So 1936 marked the renewed spirit of Indian in motorcycle competition, and the emergence of an exceptional racer in California's Ed Kretz, who would soon achieve the honorary title of "Ironman" for his skills and strength. Springfield produced just over 5,000 motorcycles for the year, and the profit picture continued to improve. The Indian Motocycle Company was not yet out of the woods, but could see the light at the tree line.

Below: This tank graphic was known as the arrow pattern. The left side of the Four engine was less tidy, dominated by the generator and distributor.

Above: The rationale for the overhead intake valves was better heat dissipation. Which in turn required a heat shield to avoid frying the rider's leg.

1936 Chief
Owner/restorer – Robin Markey
Etters, Pennsylvania

Above: Indian adopted the automotive-type distributor ignition in 1936. The system proved more trustworthy and reliable than the traditional wasted spark ignition.

Left: The Four continued its relatively lean profile, weighing in at around 520 pounds (236kg). The upside-downers were faster than the earlier models.

Above: Indian script cast into the timing cover first appeared on the Sport Scout. All models got more lubrication to the valve guides, and a stoplight switch was standard equipment.

Left: The new engine design, while it demonstrated improved performance, was a failure in terms of appearance. The older valve configuration made a more handsome engine, and would return in 1937.

1936 Four
Owner – Gene Calidonna
Seal Beach, California

SPORT SCOUT (1937), FOUR (1937) AND JUNIOR SCOUT (1937)

1937 SPORT SCOUT

SPECIFICATIONS
ENGINE/DRIVETRAIN
Engine: 42° side-valve V-twin
Displacement: 45ci (750cc)
Bore & stroke: 2.88 x 3.50in
(73.2 x 88.9mm)
Horsepower: 22
Carburetor: Schebler
Transmission: 3-speed
Clutch: Wet multi-disc
Primary drive: Triplex chain
Final drive: Chain
Brake: F & R. Drum
Battery: 6-volt
Ignition: Distributor or magneto

CHASSIS/SUSPENSION
Frame: Steel keystone
Suspension: Leading-link
truss/spring
Wheelbase: 56.5in (143.58cm)
Weight: 450lb (204kg)
Fuel capacity: 3.7gal (14lit)
Oil capacity: 2.5qts (2.37lit)
Tires: 18 x 4.00in
Top speed: 70mph (113km/h)
Colors: Red standard
Number built: 6,030 (all
models)
Price: $315

Above: The Indian head
design on the horn face was a
styling fixture until 1941.

Right: The Sport Scout was
fitted with a more deeply
valenced rear fender in '37,
and the chain guard grew
larger. The taillight lens was
new, and the exhaust pipes
and muffler were chromed.
Cadmium-plated wheels
were optional.

The recession rebound slowed somewhat in 1936, and few changes were made to the 1937 models. A problem with the Chief's ignition timing was rectified with new drive gears. The Scout Pony was now called the Junior Scout, having maintained its entry level popularity with a reduced priced. More women riders were attracted to the small machine, and some soon moved up to the Sport Scout. The gearshift lever on the Chief and Scout 45 was moved to the front of the tank, presumably for closer proximity to the handlebar. The new shift mechanism used a bellcrank linkage device that eliminated the positive feel of the earlier shifter. The change was less than popular, especially among the hot-rod riders.

While the civilian market showed no leaping gains in 1937, the racing community was sparked by the inaugural running of the Daytona 200 national championship event, and its winning by Ed Kretz on an Indian Sport Scout. Ed had only been riding for a few years, but he had an affinity for the sport. Following some good local results, he went to work for Floyd Clymer's Los Angeles dealership and was granted a factory racing Scout. His 1936 win at Savannah brought him national attention. A naturally talented rider, Kretz was also built like a bull-dog. Professional motorcyle racers of the earlier era were mostly small men, but the lighter machines of the era were easier to handle. The rough and

tumble combat of Class C racing was made to order for Kretz, whose physical strength prevailed in long races.

At the age of 26, Kretz was a newcomer to most of the 86 entries in the first Daytona 200. But he managed to take the lead on the second lap and proceed to lap the entire field on his way to victory. In 1938 he took a nasty crash in practice, but started the race with a sprained ankle and torn shoulder ligaments. He held the lead for three laps, faded somewhat and was eventually put out by a broken chain. In the 1939 event he was leading when his engine caught fire. Kretz was also leading at the half-way mark in 1940 when his engine expired.

Ed Kretz so dominated the sport in the late Thirties that fans automatically expected him to win. And most of his fellow racers

1937 Junior Scout
Owner – Peter Dunkel
Anaheim, California
Restored by Jerry Greer

Right: The Junior Scout, which
was formerly called the Scout
Pony, received many of the upgrades
awarded the other
models. The horn moved to the
top of the fork, above the new
sealed beam headlight.

1937 Sport Scout
Owner/restorer – Bob Stark
Perris, California

Below: The power of the Indian Four made it a natural choice for sidecar enthusiasts. The shift lever on all models was moved forward on the tank. The price, with sidecar and third-wheel brake, was $530.

1937 Four
Owner – Jim Smith

Below: The 1937 Four, second and final instalment of the upside-down engine, featured two Zenith carburetors. This was the fastest Four yet.

Left: The front fender of the Sport Scout was also more valenced to match the mudguards on the other models. But the Scout didn't get the interchangeable wheels and cast brake drums fitted to the Chief and Four.

Above: Options included the choice of a 3- or 4-speed transmission, and distributor or magneto ignition. The latter cost an extra $25.

concurred, that if his motorcycle didn't break, Ed would most likely win the race. Of course several of his competitors refused to consider Kretz unbeatable, which would mean relegating themselves to a lesser spot. The result was some intense motorcycle racing, and the coming of age for Class C competition. Stories are still told of the tussles among Kretz, Ben Campanale, Sam Arena, Jimmy Kelly and the Castonguay brothers.

Mid-way through the year a number of changes were made to the Four. The radial-fin cylinder heads were adopted to further improve engine cooling, and the exhaust-valve rocker arms were enclosed. New shields covered the exhaust and intake manifolds. At $675 the Four was not a volume seller, but plans for its revision and salvation were well underway.

Indian production rose to just over 6,000 machines for 1937, still running at about half the output of Harley-Davidson. And with the growth of Class C racing, more dealers gave support to local racers, and the top riders began traveling long distances to the major events. A new national championship series was emerging.

1938 FOUR

Specifications

Engine/Drivetrain
Engine: IOE inline four
Displacement: 77ci (1265cc)
Bore & stroke: 2.75 x 3.25in
(69.8 x 82.5cc)
Horsepower: 45
Carburetor: Schebler
Transmission: 3-speed
Clutch: Wet multi-disc
Primary drive: Helical gear
Final drive: Chain
Brake: F & R. Internal expanding
Battery: 6-volt
Ignition: Distributor

Chassis/Suspension
Frame: Steel, double downtube
Suspension: Trailing link
girder/spring
Wheelbase: 59in (150cm)
Weight: 540lb (245kg)
Fuel capacity: 3.75gal (14.2lit)
Oil capacity: 3qts (2.84lit)
Tires: 26 x 4.00in
Top speed: 95mph (153km/h)
Colors: Red (2), blue (2),
green (2), yellow, silver, cream,
brown (2) and others
Number built: Approx.300
Price: $425

For 1938 the Four returned to the original valve configuration, and won back some of the support lost by the upside-down model. The cylinders were now cast in pairs, which helped improve heat dissipation. Overheating had long been one of the Four's most troublesome problems.

Despite the improvements, many enthusiasts were more than a bit skeptical about the prudence of keeping the Four in the lineup. It cost significantly more to build, since few parts were interchangeable with the twins, and appealed to only a small segment of the market. The design was beginning to show its age, especially in the performance of the outdated clutch and gearbox.

But by damn if it wasn't a handsome motorcycle. And it was smooth, powerful and fast. So for those who could afford to buy and maintain one of these machines, it was well worth the premium to own the Cadillac of motorcycles. To the commited Four enthusiast, the V-twin was an agricultural engine by comparison. To the Sport Scout rider the Four was an unecessary exercise in weight, cost and complexity.

The new Chief and Sport Scout were both fitted with a stylish instrument panel on the tank, housing the speedometer, ammeter and ignition switch. The drive chain guard was enlarged to cover nearly the whole chain, and new cosmetic touches included elaborate pinstriping.

Speed records were still considered essential to publicize Indian's high-performance heritage. Indianapolis dealer Rollie Free ran a Sport Scout to 111mph (179km/h) at Daytona Beach,

Florida, and turned 109mph (175km/h) on a Chief. Later in the year, factory rider Fred Ludlow posted a 115mph (185km/h) run on a Sport Scout at Lake Bonneville in Utah, and pushed a Chief engine to 120mph (193km/h). The motors were built by Red Fenwicke and Pop Schunk. who worked for California distributor Hap Alzina. The cams came available the following year in the tweaked Bonneville engine.

Crusher Kretz was stronger than ever in 1938, and Class C had effectively replaced the old Class A professional racing. Harley-Davidson's Ben Campanale won the Daytona 200, and Milwaukee iron was ready to challenge the Sport Scout for racing glory. The Harley Forty-five began demonstrating a considerable power boost, owing to the tuning work of celebrated San Jose dealer Tom Sifton. The "Sifton Motor" became distinct from the factory version.

Kretz again won the Langhorne 100-mile national, and Woodsie and Frenchy Castonguay of Springfield both won national titles. In the inaugural Laconia, New Hampshire, 200-mile TT national, Ed Kretz was the winner and only six other riders finished. The event was nearly five hours long, and established Kretz with his lifelong nickname, Iron Man. Kretz also captured the Hollister TT and set a 10-mile speed record at the Springfield, Illinois mile.

The motorcycle market, however, was at a low ebb. Indian produced only 3,650 motorcycles and recorded a net loss of $12,000. Facing an uncertain future, Springfield made little more than cosmetic changes to the new models for the following year.

Below: In 1937, the luggage rack and set of saddlebags, in either black or tan, would set you back $13.

Below: A larger saddle arrived in 1938, and permitted some adjustment fore and aft. The year also saw the first application of a full color Indian head design on the tank.

1938 Four
Owner/restorer – Elmer Lower
Etters, Pennsylvania

Left: Perhaps the most famous, highest mileage, and winningest Sport Scout in the books belonged to Ironman Ed Kretz. A contender for 15 years, the racer was steadily upgraded. The frame was chromed when the bike was retired as a showpiece. Ed Kretz died in 1996.

1938 Sport Scout
Owner – Ed Kretz, Jr.
Monterey Park, California

1938 Chief
Owner/restorer – Mike Tomas
Riverside, California

Right: The headlight came back down in 1938, and the horn moved back to the top. The lamp was mounted to a new fork shield, the horn to the handlebar. The Chief sold for $385; $9 more for a 4-speed transmission.

Above: The new instrument panel was standard on the Chief, Four and Sport Scout. The ammeter on this Chief is a replacement item.

Above: Faithful fans of the Four were pleased to see the return of the right-side-up engine. New cylinders were cast in pairs rather than individually; the magneto was discontinued

Above: This was the first year for the 120mph speedometer, with or without the top speed hand, as on this Four's speedo. Red on gray was 1938 only.

CHIEF (1939), FOUR (1939) AND SPORT SCOUT (1939)

1939 CHIEF

SPECIFICATIONS
ENGINE/DRIVETRAIN
Engine: 42° side-valve V-twin
Displacement: 74ci (1200cc)
Bore & stroke: 3.25 x4.44in
(82.5 x 112.7mm)
Horsepower: 40
Carburetor: Schebler
Transmission: 3 or 4-speed
Clutch: Wet multi-disc
Primary drive: 4-row chain
Final drive: Chain
Brake: F & R. Drum
Battery: 6-volt
Ignition: Distributor (magneto
optional)

CHASSIS/SUSPENSION
Frame: Steel, twin downtube
Suspension: Leaf-spring fork
Wheelbase: 61in (155cm)
Weight: 520lb (236kg)
Fuel capacity: 3.75gal (14.2lit)
Oil capacity: 2.5qts (2.37lit)
Tires: 4.00 or 4.5 x 18
Top speed: 90mph (145km/h)
Colors: Red (2), blue (2),
green (2), yellow, silver, cream,
brown (2) and others, plus
metallic paint optional
Number built: 3,012 (all
models)
Price: $385

A number of small alterations appeared on the 1939 models, highlighted by the World's Fair paint scheme. Round air cleaners replaced the teardrop horn, and metallic paint was available as an option. The fork spring on the Sport Scout was tapered at each end rather than straight wound. The combustion chambers were modified for better high-rpm breathing. Development work on the new engines came largely from tuning work done by Indianapolis dealer Rollie Free and Jimmy Hill in Springfield. Flow testing on the heads was done at the Massachusetts Institute of Technology. The Chief got new pistons, rings and cams, and the Bonneville engines had high-performance cams and lifters.

New decorative touches included more chrome-plated parts such as the air cleaner, tailpipe and new rear bumper. Many of the small bits and fasteners formerly nickel-plated were now surfaced with cadmium. The only significant change to the Sport Scout chassis was a revised fork spring for a softer ride. By this time many Sport Scout enthusiasts were buying stroker kits with Chief flywheels, which brought displacement from 45 cubic inches (750cc) to 57 cubic inches (935cc). This provided a machine with the agile handling of a Scout and the highway touring speed of a Chief. For many riders, this was an altogether pleasant combination.

The rumors of war had been building for a couple years, and by 1939 had become something closer to eventualities. The recession-crippled motorcycle industry, however, was thrown a lifeline in the form of welcome potential military contracts. This time the army conducted a three-way competition to select the machines required for combat duty. The contestants were Indian, Harley-Davidson and Delco.

But prior to that face-off came orders from foreign allies for machines to supply forces with more immediate needs for equipment. One such order, for 5,000 Chiefs with sidecars, came from the government of France. Springfield was far from prepared to meet such a large order, which would outstrip Harley-Davidson production for the first time in many years.

The American racing scene was as yet unaffected by the shadows of war, and the traditional Indian vs. Harley wars continued in earnest. Ed Kretz and Harley's Ben Campanale battled for the lead at Daytona until an engine fire put Kretz in for emergency attention. Campy went on to win his second straight 200, followed by Ray Eddy on another Harley. Bill Anderson put his Indian in third place and was the only Springfield marque in the top ten. Fourth went to Canadian Brian Sparks on a 500cc Vincent HRD overhead-valve single. Sparks' brother Robert went on to win the 100-mile Langhorne national on a Norton International,

Below: Riders could choose the standard handlebar (shown) or the shorter and flatter sport bar.

Below: The fork assembly now contained three rebound leaves rather than two, and the spring angle increased slightly.

Right: Fork geometry was changed slightly on the Chief and Four in 1939, and another leaf was added to the spring. The headlight was larger, and the V pattern striping was optional.

Left: In 1939 the World's Fair paint scheme was optional on all models. Metallic paints came available the same year; this unrestored '39 features metallic blue and silver. The chromed exhaust manifold shield was new, and the magneto was back as an option.

1939 Four
Owner – Leon Blackman
Emmaus, Pennsylvania

1939 Sport Scout
Owner – Eric Vaughan
Monrovia, California

Above: The upswept tail pipe and rear bumper were offered on both the Sport Scout and Chief. The barrel-type fork spring was new.

the first British machine to win a championship Class C event. A harbinger of things to come.

At the 200-mile TT national in Chattanooga, Tennessee, the Sport Scout of Bob Hallowell was victorious over a field of 1000cc overheads and 1200cc side-valves. The Springfield, Illinois mile, which was becoming the premier dirt-track event of the season, went to Stanley Wittinski on a Sport Scout. Harley-Davidson, with the help of Tom Sifton, had overcome the Forty-five's performance deficit against the Sport Scout. Though still heavier, the Harley was more rugged throughout and normally prevailed in the longer distance races.

Indian production reached 8,883 machines, putting Springfield on an equal footing with Milwaukee. Both factories would soon turn their attentions to the contest for military contracts, and balancing civilian production with the demands of wartime requirements.

Left: A hinged rear fender remained standard issue on the Chief. In addition to metallic paints, numerous two-tone combinations were offered in 1939. Silver was a popular second color, as were combinations of maroon/orange and Chinese red/Indian red.

Above: New cylinders and heads arrived in 1939, the latter without the pent-roof combustion chambers used earlier. New lids improved high-rpm power.

1939 Chief
Owner/restorer – Bob Stark
Perris, California

SPORT SCOUT (1940), FOUR (1940) AND DISPATCH TOW (1939)

1940 SPORT SCOUT

SPECIFICATIONS
ENGINE/DRIVETRAIN
Engine: 42° side-valve V-twin
Displacement: 45ci (750cc)
Bore & stroke: 2.88 x 3.50in
(73.2 x 88.9mm)
Horsepower: 22
Carburetor: Schebler
Transmission: 3- or 4-speed
Clutch: Wet multi-disc
Primary drive: Triplex chain
Final drive: Chain
Brake: F & R. Drum
Battery: 6-volt
Ignition: Distributor or magneto

CHASSIS/SUSPENSION
Frame: Steel keystone
Suspension: Leading-link
truss/spring
Wheelbase: 58in (147cm)
Weight: 485lb (220kg)
Fuel capacity: 3.7gal (14lit)
Oil capacity: 2.5qts (2.37lit)
Tires: 4.50 x 18in
Top speed: 90mph (145km/h)
Colors: Red (2), blue (2),
green (2), yellow, silver, cream,
brown (2) and others
Number built: 10,431 (all
models)
Price: $390

Skirted fenders had first appeared on some European cars in the 1930s. The twin disciplines of streamlining and the flowing shapes of decorative art combined to cover more of the automobile's moving parts. The trend found application among some US car builders in the middle Thirties, the Chrysler Airflow the most notable example.

Despite the harmony of form and function in aerodynamic terms, the styles were too arty for most of the American audience. The designs faded in a few years, though most stateside manufacturers offered detachable fender skirts as options. Motorcycles, on the other hand, had always put their wheels in plain view. So the Indian models for 1940 came as something of a shock.

The first reaction from some riders was hey, why the hell did they cover up the wheels? Others took one look and said, now that is the most beautiful motorcycle we have ever seen. Springfield hedged the bet somewhat by offering optional open fenders for the Sport Scout in 1940, but after that the enclosures were standard on both models. Even the cylinder and head fins were given the streamlining treatment, and the kickstarter and drive chain were more enclosed.

And the rear wheel was no longer bolted directly to the frame. The new plunger suspension gave the wheel about two inches (5cm) of travel (in each direction) and further isolated rider from road. Some old timers thought this modern stuff had gone a bit too far, but motorcycle design had entered the next phase, where both styling and comfort had feature roles. The Sport Scout still featured a rigid frame.

The demand for military motorcycles put civilian production in a subordinate category, and the uncertainty of the impending war motivated a swell of orders from the public and service markets. The used bike market saw prices rise accordingly, and many dealers began putting together motorcycles from piles of leftover parts. In this pre-war shuffle, the numbers of modified motorcycles began increasing, with mix-and-match bikes an economic necessity. The hot rods, alley racers and bobbers (with trimmed fenders) would gain wide popularity after the war.

The mighty Four, on the other hand, was fast approaching the end of its lifespan. With the addition of skirted fenders, the new Four was a stately machine but a heavy one. Gassed up the big bike weighed more than 575 pounds (261kg), and with the prospects of wartime rationing on the horizon, the Henderson legacy reached its sunset. Production of the Fours gradually dwindled, with the last few built in 1942.

The 1940 model came with 4.50 x 18-inch tires, and 1941 saw the option of 5.00 x 16-inchers popularized by the fat rubber on the Harley Seventy-four. The larger tires did nothing to improve the Four's handling, and reduced its already limited ground clearance. But many riders liked the looks.

Indian and Harley-Davidson split the racing wins about evenly in 1940. Ed Kretz won his third Langhorne 100-miler, and Melvin Rhoades' win at Springfield was the fourth in a row for Indian. Riding a 1200cc Chief with plunger suspension, Ted Edwards won two TT nationals.

The total production was just over 10,000 machines, including military models, and Springfield enjoyed a welcome period of financial health.

Right: Indian's full fender skirts caused something of a sensation in 1940. The lines seemed evenly drawn between those who loved the new look and those who hated it. Standard unskirted fenders remained available as options for 1940 only.

Below: The Sport Scout and Thirty-fifty, Models 640 and 540, combined skirted fenders and the rigid rear frame section. The Chief and Four were both awarded the plunger suspension.

Below: The gracefully streamlined cylinder heads appeared in 1940, and the ignition coil moved to below the seat. The teardrop tank emblem was also new.

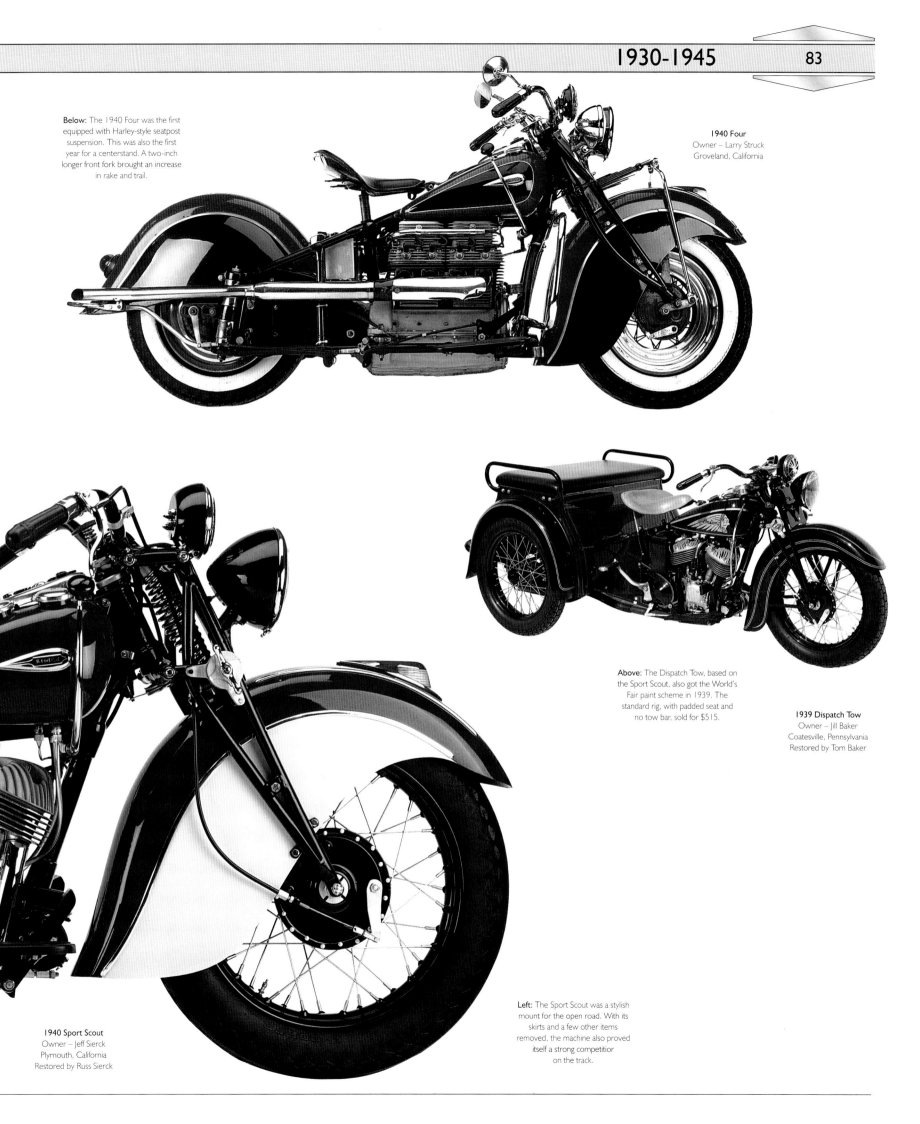

Below: The 1940 Four was the first equipped with Harley-style seatpost suspension. This was also the first year for a centerstand. A two-inch longer front fork brought an increase in rake and trail.

1940 Four
Owner – Larry Struck
Groveland, California

Above: The Dispatch Tow, based on the Sport Scout, also got the World's Fair paint scheme in 1939. The standard rig, with padded seat and no tow bar, sold for $515.

1939 Dispatch Tow
Owner – Jill Baker
Coatesville, Pennsylvania
Restored by Tom Baker

Left: The Sport Scout was a stylish mount for the open road. With its skirts and a few other items removed, the machine also proved itself a strong competition on the track.

1940 Sport Scout
Owner – Jeff Sierck
Plymouth, California
Restored by Russ Sierck

CHIEF (1941), SPORT SCOUT (1940) AND FOUR (1941)

1941 CHIEF

SPECIFICATIONS
ENGINE/DRIVETRAIN
Engine: 42° side-valve V-twin
Displacement: 74ci (1200cc)
Bore & stroke: 3.25 x 4.44in
(82.5 x 112.7mm)
Horsepower: 40
Carburetor: Schebler
Transmission: 3- or 4-speed
Clutch: Wet multi-disc
Primary drive: 4-row chain
Final drive: Chain
Brake: F & R. Drum
Battery: 6-volt
Ignition: Distributor (magneto
optional)

CHASSIS/SUSPENSION
Frame: Steel, twin downtube
Suspension: F. Leaf-spring.
R. Plunger
Wheelbase: 62in (157cm)
Weight: 745lb (338kg) (with
sidecar)
Fuel capacity: 3.5gal (13.25lit)
Oil capacity: 2.5qts (2.37lit)
Tires: 4.50 x 18in
Top speed: 75mph (121km/h)
Colors: Red (2), blue (2),
green (2), yellow, silver, cream,
brown (2) and others
Number built: 8,739 (all
models)
Price: $579 (with sidecar)

With military production the top priority, few changes were made to the civilian models for 1941. The Sport Scout now had the plunger frame and both it and the Chief were fitted with 16-inch wheels. Skirted fenders were standard on both models, and the open fenders were no longer offered for the Scout. Unskirted fenders remained available on the 500cc Junior Scout.

Widespread moodiness attended this fattening-up of the Sport Scout, which now topped 500 pounds (227kg) and looked virtually identical to the Chief. One alternative was to install a stroker kit for more power to carry the added weight down the road. Another was simply to buy a Chief. Or a Harley Forty-five. None of these options held great appeal for the confirmed Scout enthusiast. All of which provided more incentive for the shade tree engineers to build their own motorcycles from bits and pieces.

The Four could still be had with 18-inch wheels until the existing inventory was gone, when sixteens became the only option. Few civilian Fours were being sold by 1941, most of the production undertaken was to fill orders from law enforcement agencies. The Four was also handicapped by its high price, which had risen to $1,100. No civilian orders were taken for 1942 Fours, and that would be its final year in production.

According to Harry Sucher's historical research, the final lot of 2,200 French military Chiefs was completed in late March of 1940. The machines were loaded aboard the freighter SS *Hanseatic Star*, chartered by the Swedish Export Line, and departed for France on April 12th. The ship never made port in Le Havre, and was pre-

1941 Chief
Owner – Bob Mercer
San Jose, California

Above: The Chief also had seatpost suspension rather than external springs. Military models were fitted with wide-clearance, unskirted fenders.

Right: The sidecar design changed just before World War II. The older style, shown here, gave way to the more streamlined version on the the far right. The sidecar chassis were redesigned in the process.

Above: The sidecar added $120 to the price of a new Chief. An optional brake for the third wheel was an additional $10. The US sidecar market was modest; most went to export and commercial use.

1940 Sport Scout
Owner/restorer – Bob Stark
Perris, California

Left: This 1940 Sport Scout sports the 1941 tank trim. Military versions would soon take over production.

Above: The short, full-coverage chain and kickstart cover was used only in 1940. Tires were 4.00 x 18in. The Sport Scout had gained nearly 100 pounds (45kg) since its inception in 1934.

Below: 1940 was the last year for the Indian head horn face design. The new horn in 1941 featured Indian in block letters, above a sealed-beam headlight.

Above: Art Deco styling extended to the sidecar in 1941. Chrome-plated headlights were new, saddle padding was thicker and chrome strips were added to the gas tank. The mighty Four, with sidecar, sold for $635.

1941 Four
Owner – Jeff Gilbert
Los Angeles, California

Above: Standard tires were 4.50 x 18in; in 1941, the 5.00 x 16in rims were made available as options. For gearbox with reverse, add $13.50.

sumed to have been sunk by German submarines. The Nazi blitzkrieg had now turned to western Europe and France was occupied in a matter of weeks. The *Hanseatic Star* may well have been lost at sea with all hands, though it may have been diverted to another Allied country, and the motorcycles eventually used against the Germans. By some accounts, she was sunk by enemy action off the Irish coast.

Both Indian and Harley-Davidson were cranking out more motorcycles for the US Army and Allied forces overseas. Most of the Indians sold to Allied forces were the 500cc 640A models, followed by the 750cc 640B, which was later redesignated the Model 741.

Indian racers racked up nine Class C national victories in 1941, compared to four for Harley-Davidson. The most significant omen appeared at Daytona, when Canadian Billy Mathews won the 200-miler on a Manx Norton. Harley-Davidson's new WR factory racer filled out most of the next nine positions. Indian experimented with a new big-base version of the Sport Scout, but with little success. The Daytona race was suspended by the war and would not resume until 1947.

1940 POLICE CHIEF

SPECIFICATIONS
ENGINE/DRIVETRAIN
Engine: 42° side-valve V-twin
Displacement: 74ci (1200cc)
Bore & stroke: 3.25 x 4.44in
(82.5 x 112.7mm)
Horsepower: 40
Carburetor: Schebler
Transmission: 3- or 4-speed
Clutch: Wet multi-disc
Primary drive: 4-row chain
Final drive: Chain
Brake: F & R. Drum
Battery: 6-volt
Ignition: Distributor (magneto
optional)

CHASSIS/SUSPENSION
Frame: Steel, twin downtube
Suspension: F. Leaf-spring.
R. Plunger
Wheelbase: 62in (157cm)
Weight: 625lb (283.5kg)
Fuel capacity: 3.5gal (13.25lit)
Oil capacity: 2.5qts (2.37lit)
Tires: 4.50 x 18in
Top speed: 75mph (121km/h)
Colors: White, black/white,
black/silver
Number built: Unknown
Price: Fleet $ negotiable

POLICE CHIEF (1940), THIRTY-FIFTY (1941) AND FOUR (1941)

The 1940-41 models would be the last civilian motorcycles produced in any great numbers until 1946. Motorcycle dealers effectively had their supply cut off for the war years, and many went out of business. Others were able to survive repairing and selling used machines, lawn mowers, bicycles, washing machines or whatever they could find.

Both Indian and Harley-Davidson factories were permitted under the regulations of government contracts to allot a percentage of their output for civilian law enforcement agencies. So there remained between Milwaukee and Springfield a continuing mix of politics and marketing.

The sidecar was restyled and featured a more streamlined shape with art deco trim. Indian also retained the Dispatch Tow, available with either standard or large body, and sidevans in open and closed configurations. Springfield maintained its courtship with the police, offering the Chief and Four with either 18-inch or 16-inch wheels. The police Indian was heralded as the "The Pride of the Force," and touted as the best thing since the Tommy Gun.

"Only Indian has the Miracle SPRING FRAME. It's new, *sensational*! Spring Frame floats you over the roughest roads as though they were smooth concrete – gets you there and gets action *fast*! Your Indian grips the road, under perfect control. You get away faster, brake better. Spring Frame, brilliant new styling, and many other features make the 1940 Indians the world's outstanding police motorcycles."

The police models could be ordered with radio equipment, siren, heavy duty luggage rack and pannier boxes. The rumors and innuendo regarding Indian and Harley-Davidson indulging in various forms of graft, corruption, special favors and backroom deals to secure sales are largely true.

The advent of World War II effectively closed the first chapter in the American formula of production-based motorcycle racing. While British and European manufacturers had continued the

tradition of factory competition specials, and would maintain their efforts following the war, the Yanks stuck with modified road bikes. Class C racing, born of economic necessity and despite rules manipulated by Milwaukee, would evolve into a framework of great national competition. And eventually emerge as an essential arena for manufacturers from Britain and Japan.

Class A professional racing was thus consigned to history. When organized racing resumed once more after the war, the American national championship series combined dirt-track ovals, TT scrambles and road-racing circuits. For more than 30 years the program would offer thrilling competition and a training ground for international stars of the future.

Above: Know where Motorola got its name? Offenders might outrun the patrolman, but not the radio. The battery-pack was carried in the left rear pannier box.

1940 Police Chief
Owner/restorer – Bob Stark
Perris, California

Right: Indians were always popular with the nation's peace officers. This police model saw active duty with the California Highway Patrol in the Forties. Competition between Springfield and Milwaukee for police fleet contracts was intense for 50 years.

1941 Thirty-fifty
Owner/restorer – Robin Markey
Etters, Pennsylvania

Below: The little twin had full fenders only in 1940. In its final civilian year the skirts on the Thirty-fifty were gone and the teardrop tank emblem added.

Left: A sealed beam headlight and new horn also graced the 500cc roadster. Early-style clincher rims remained until the end.

Right: The 5.00 x 16in tire was optional on the Four in 1941. The fork was slightly wider to accommodate fenders that were likewise. This fuel tank is not fitted with the chrome strips that were standard for that year.

1941 Four
Owner – Peter Dunkel
Anaheim, California

Above: In its police uniform, radio, battery, siren, lights and cold-weather windshield, the Chief easily topped 600lb (272kg). But the overall image spoke strongly of authority, mission and woe to the criminal miscreants.

Above: Four-cylinder power had not progressed apace with the machine's increased weight, now 575lb (261kg).

ARMY CHIEF (1941), DISPATCH TOW (1941) AND SPORT SCOUT (1941)

1941 MILITARY CHIEF

SPECIFICATIONS
ENGINE/DRIVETRAIN
Engine: 42° side-valve V-twin
Displacement: 74ci (1200cc)
Bore & stroke: 3.25 x 4.44in (82.5 x 112.7mm)
Horsepower: 40
Carburetor: Linkert
Transmission: 3- or 4-speed
Clutch: Wet multi-disc
Primary drive: 4-row chain
Final drive: Chain
Brake: F & R. Drum
Battery: 6-volt
Ignition: Distributor (magneto optional)

CHASSIS/SUSPENSION
Frame: Steel, twin downtube
Suspension: F. Leaf-spring. R. Plunger
Wheelbase: 62in (157cm)
Weight: 550lb (249.5kg)
Fuel capacity: 3.5gal (13.25lit)
Oil capacity: 2.5qts (2.37lit)
Tires: 4.50 x 18in
Top speed: 75mph (121km/h)
Color: Olive drab
Number built: Approx. 3,000
Price: Unknown

Springfield did not come out on top in the competition for military contracts with the US War Department. That distinction went to Harley-Davidson, although Indian did devote nearly all its efforts to producing machines for the US Army and the Allied forces.

Milwaukee was simply in a much better position after the depression to supply military hardware. The plant in Springfield had fallen to five per cent of its production capacity in the 1930s, and had done well to survive at all. By the time the nation began gearing up for war in 1939, Indian no longer had the tooling or personnel to move quickly and effectively as a military supplier.

The French order for 5,000 Chiefs was a godsend, in effect, and allowed Indian to regenerate its production capacity more quickly than would have otherwise been possible. In retrospect it may have also injected a false sense of security, though by most accounts E. Paul duPont had lost much of his enthusiasm for motorcycle manufacturing. The owner had taken an active interest in his first decade, but the death of plant manager Joe Hosely in 1941 and the impending war had diluted his involvement. Although the war meant a return to profits, duPont began thinking of selling the company.

The factory, meanwhile, was well occupied with producing military machines and developing new ones. The M1 model, a 221cc side-valve single, was called the Extra Light Solo. The ostensible purpose for the small bike was to create a machine small and light enough to be dropped by parachute (crated), then put immediately into action. No records have been found to show how many Solos were actually built, or if they were ever dropped from planes successfully.

The 841, a much larger motorcycle by comparison, was commissioned by someone in the war department with an abiding preference for shaft-drive machines. It had been noted that during

German military campaigns in the North African desert, the BMW motorcycles performed well. With Harley-Davidson at work on a BMW copy, the decision came to give Indian a shot at a shaftie of their own. With the arrival of the versatile Willys Jeep, both projects were promptly abandoned.

With Sport Scouts out of the civilian pipeline, racers searched about for interim alternatives. Many of the popular 101 Scouts were modified for racing, with the most popular addition being Sport Scout cylinders and heads. A number of these machines were plenty fast, and a few dozen still appear in vintage races.

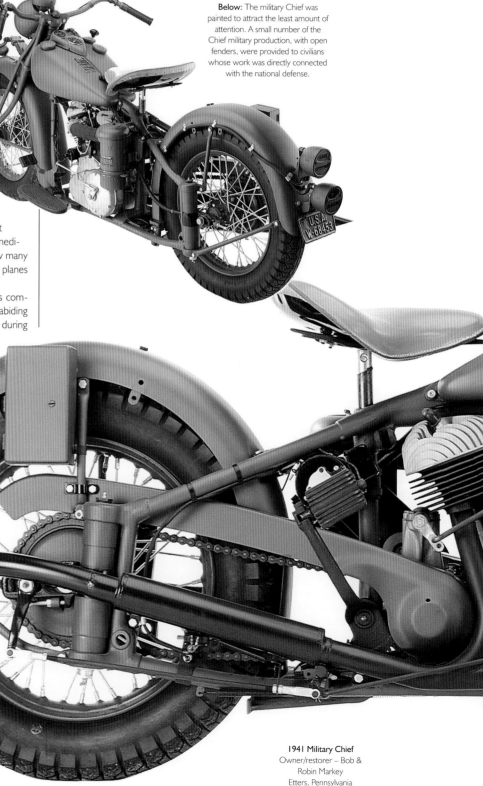

Below: The military Chief was painted to attract the least amount of attention. A small number of the Chief military production, with open fenders, were provided to civilians whose work was directly connected with the national defense.

Right: The first large batch of military Chiefs was built to fill an order for the French army. Indian founded a training school for military motorcycle mechanics in 1939. Both Indian and Harley-Davidson built machines for allied armed forces well before the US was drawn into the war.

1941 Military Chief
Owner/restorer – Bob & Robin Markey
Etters, Pennsylvania

Left: The Indian head tank emblem appeared on 1942 models. In racing trim, the Sport Scout continued its winning ways in national competition, as Harley-Davidson struggled to catch up. Then the events of World War II put racing on hold.

1941 Sport Scout
Owner/restorer – Bob Stark
Perris, California

Above: Suspension came to the rear wheel of the Sport Scout in 1941, adding even more weight to the roadster's profile. Still, stroked to 944cc, the former middleweight could go smartly down the road.

1941 Dispatch Tow
Owner – Jeff Gilbert
Los Angeles, California

Above: The Dispatch Tow remained a solid member on the Indian roster, popular with both law enforcement and commercial clients. The price with the standard body and tow bar, $570.

Left: Most of the Chiefs on military duty were attached to sidecars. Most units prefered the lighter 640 and 741 models for dispatch work.

Above: How many Chiefs saw action in France is unknown. They did not seem to delay the Germans.

Left: Although the military version of the Chief had a minor US Army role, production for allied forces pushed Springfield above Milwaukee's output for the first time in many years.

640B (1942), CHIEF (1942) AND SPORT SCOUT (1942)

1942 640B

SPECIFICATIONS
ENGINE/DRIVETRAIN
Engine: 42° side-valve V-twin
Displacement: 45ci (750cc)
Bore & stroke: 2.88 x 3.50in
(73.2 x 88.9mm)
Horsepower: 22
Carburetor: Linkert
Transmission: 3- or 4-speed
Clutch: Wet multi-disc
Primary drive: Triplex chain
Final drive: Chain
Brake: F & R. Drum
Battery: 6-volt
Ignition: Distributor or magneto

CHASSIS/SUSPENSION
Frame: Steel keystone
Suspension: Leading-link
truss/spring fork
Wheelbase: 58in (147cm)
Weight: 485lb (220kg)
Fuel capacity: 3.7gal (14lit)
Oil capacity: 2.5qts (2.37lit)
Tires: 4.00 x 18in
Top speed: 75mph (121km/h)
Color: Olive drab
Number built: Classified
Price: Unknown

With the USA now commited to World War II, civilian motor-cycles were in short supply. This would be the final year of production for the Four, nearly all of which went for police duty, and only a handful of the Junior Scouts were built for the '42 model year. By February the government called a halt to production of civilian vehicles, and, as a result, no factory catalog was printed for 1942.

This year marked the first appearance of the Indian head tank logo with block-style lettering, which would carry over to the 1946 models without the underlining trim strip. Most of the Chief production for 1942 was also earmarked for police use, though a limited number of civilian models were made. Materials shortages imposed by the war were apparent early on; when the supply of chromed parts was exhausted, the ensuing parts were painted.

The 1941 colors remained available for the early '42 models, although Police silver was replaced by gray.

Although Springfield manufactured 16,647 motorcycles for 1942, no records have turned up showing how many were non-military machines. Nearly all of the 16,456 1943 models were marked for war duty.

By the spring of 1942 the federal government had imposed gasoline rationing in the eastern states, expanding the restrictions nationwide in December. The national speed limit was reduced to 40mph (64km/h) and later to 35 (56km/h), in an

1942 Chief
Owner/restorer – John Dufilie
North Stonington, Connecticut

Right: Fully rigged for field duty, this 640 includes basic accommodations for rider and one passenger. The American army used mostly the Harley-Davidson counterpart, the 750cc WLA, for both dispatch and reconnaissance. Motorcycles were rarely used intentionally in combat.

1942 640B
Owner/restorer – Bob & Robin Markey
Etters, Pennsylvania

attempt to conserve both fuel and rubber during the war.

The 741 was a hybrid military version of the Junior and Sport Scout, now called the Thirty-fifty for its 30.5 cubic inches (500cc), and the 640 designated the army version of the 750cc Sport Scout. Motor numbers on the smaller engine were prefaced by the letters GD, while the 750cc military models were marked FD. The original prototype for Indian's military middleweight was labeled the 641, based on the Junior Scout. This was the final year of civilian production for the Four, Sport Scout and Thirty-fifty.

Indian racing star Ed Kretz, who was now 31 years old, tested the prototype 841 shaft-drive military models in Springfield. As a military motorcycle instructor, Kretz taught novice recruits how to ride and repair the machines from both Indian and Harley-Davidson. He became expert in the operation and maintenance of

the 841, and ran training sessions in the Arizona and Utah deserts.

Military mechanics were trained in Springfield by Indian veteran Erle Armstrong, who was later joined by Jimmy Hill and Jack Neiss. The school was later moved to Springfield College and more instructors hired to accommodate the increasing numbers of trainees. The Indian Motorcycle Company was now part of the USA war machine.

Below: This Sport Scout, formerly in the collection of actor Steve McQueen, had been identified as a 1942 model. But it appears to have bits from earlier years. Note the Harley seat. Steve was something of an iconoclast.

1942 Sport Scout
Owner – Otis Chandler
Ojai, California

Left: Very few civilian models of the Chief were produced in 1942. The Indian head tank emblem carried over after the war, but the chrome strips were discontinued. This color scheme is Indian red/Fallon brown.

Left: Rifle scabbards were made for both the M1 carbine and the Thompson submachine gun. Both weapons had certain advantages.

Above: The Sport Scout engine, slightly detuned, proved itself worthy in military situations where speed was less important than durability.

Left: An entrenching tool was included just in case the rider found himself in sudden need of a foxhole, or decided to bury the motorcycle.

741 (1942), 841 (1944) AND CHIEF (1944)

Above: The 841 instrument panel included green and red warning lights for the generator and oil pressure.

During the heaviest demands of the war years, 1942-43, Springfield produced more than 33,000 motorcycles. Harley-Davidson manufactured some 55,000 in the same period. Indian profits for 1942 were above one million dollars.

The 841 project was quite a departure for engineers in Springfield. The principal design target, as with Milwaukee's BMW clone, was to produce a motorcycle engine virtually immune from overheating. Indian built a 90-degree 750cc side-valve V-twin set transverse in the frame, a design popularized 20 years later by Moto Guzzi. The 841 was a long, heavy motorcycle with foot-shift 4-speed transmission, shaft drive, spring frame and new front fork.

The prototype handled reasonably well, and the power was adequate for a top speed of almost 75mph (121km/h). The heads and cylinders were based on the Sport Scout, the oil tank fitte-

Right: The shaft-drive 841 was built in response to a government contract. The fork design would appear on the Chief after the war.

snugly below the seat and the battery below that. The 841 was, despite its weight of 550lb (250kg), fairly easy to ride. The new fork, a girder-type with twin pivot arms on each side, and springs on either side of a hydraulic shock absorber, provided better handling than the leaf-spring fork. The fork would later be employed on the Chief models after the war.

Historian Harry Sucher puts 841 production at 10,826, and reports that most were sold as war surplus for $500 in 1944. Some retained their military dress, but most were converted for civilian use with skirted fenders and glossy paint.

Indian founder George Hendee died in 1943 at the age of 77. Later in the

1944 841
Owner/restorer – Bob Stark
Perris, California

Right: The 500cc 741 was used widely by allied military forces in World War II. In spite of its marginal horsepower (about 5), the Thirty-fifty was easy on fuel and not too difficult to handle in extreme conditions. It was not particularly well suited for retreat.

1942 741
Owner/restorer – Bob & Robin Markey
Etters, Pennsylvania

year Indian was awarded the Army-Navy Production Award, and both Oscar Hedstrom and Cannonball Baker were present for the ceremony. Early in 1944, Chief Engineer Briggs Weaver left Springfield to join the Torque Manufacturing Company of Connecticut. His prototype work there would lead to the production of a new line of Indian motorcycles after the war.

As the war wound down, and military contracts were canceled, Springfield found itself with some 4,000 military motorcycles and the spare parts to build many thousands more. Nearly all of this inventory was sold to dealers, parts suppliers and a few individuals with either prescient foresight or dumb luck. These parts effectively ensured that Indian motorcycles would remain on the road long after their official production had ceased.

But the Sport Scout was now gone, ditto for the Four. Shortly after the war ended, E. Paul duPont sold the Indian Motocycle Company to Ralph Rogers, head of a large manufacturing conglomerate. Though his goal, to build cars, airplanes and motorcycles in Springfield hadn't been achieved, duPont is credited with sustaining Indian during the depression years. Mr duPont died in

1950. Ralph Rogers, age 36, brought to Indian a successful history of industrial management and financing. Rogers was convinced that Indian could thrive once again with its traditional models supplemented by new lightweights in the European style. Unfortunately, his efforts would ultimately prove too little too late.

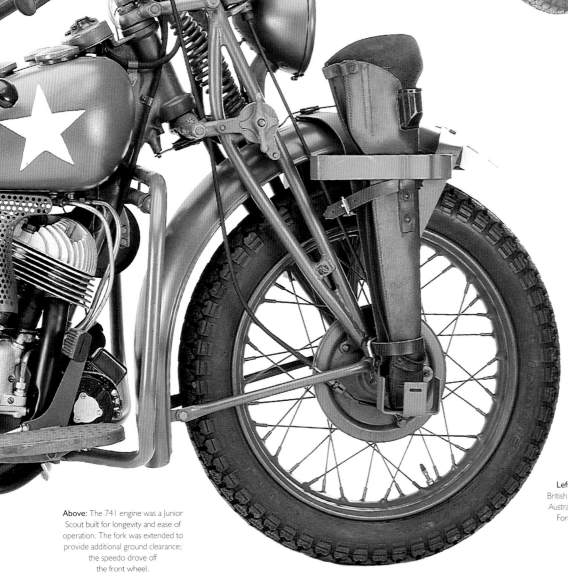

1944 Chief
Owner – Mike Tomas
Riverside, California

Above: An ammunition box and rifle scabbard were mounted on either side of the front fender. The fork design, which dates back to the Prince of 1926, also found wide application on racing bikes. Some racers first honed their skills during wartime, often under considerable pressure.

Left: The 741 was used by the British, Canadian, Polish, Russian and Australian armies. And the Royal Air Force, but only on the ground.

Above: The 741 engine was a Junior Scout built for longevity and ease of operation. The fork was extended to provide additional ground clearance; the speedo drove off the front wheel.

1946 CHIEF

SPECIFICATIONS

ENGINE/DRIVETRAIN
Engine: 42° side-valve V-twin
Displacement: 74ci (1200cc)
Bore & stroke: 3.25 x 4.44in
(82.5 x 112.7mm)
Horsepower: 40
Carburetor: Linkert
Transmission: 3- or 4-speed
Clutch: Wet multi-disc
Primary drive: 4-row chain
Final drive: Chain
Brake: F & R. Drum
Battery: 6-volt
Ignition: Distributor (magneto optional)

CHASSIS/SUSPENSION
Frame: Steel, twin downtube
Suspension: F. Leaf-spring.
R. Plunger
Wheelbase: 61in (155cm)
Weight: 560lb (254kg)
Fuel capacity: 3.5gal (13.25lit)
Oil capacity: 2.5qts (2.37lit)
Tires: 4.50 x 18in/5.00 x 16in
Top speed: 85mph (137km/h)
Colors: Black, red, blue
Number built: 6,974
Price: $540

Right: As the only model in Springfield's post-war lineup, the Chief had to carry the company fortunes. The Indian head tank emblem and girder/coil fork derived from the military 841 were both new. Skirted fenders gained wider appreciation.

CHIEF (1946-47)

Ralph Rogers, like duPont before him, was new to the motorcycle business. But he had extensive experience in industrial management and marketing, and was instrumental in the success of Cummins diesel engines. Rogers developed a keen interest in motorcycles, learned to ride and researched the market thoroughly. He was convinced that a new market for lightweight motorcycles would emerge after the war, and that British-style singles and twins would find the widest appeal.

In 1945 Rogers bought the Torque Engineering Company, which had undertaken the design and manufacture of lightweight motorcycles under the direction of former Indian engineer Briggs Weaver. Later in the year, with a $4 million loan from the Atlas Corporation of New York, he also acquired the Indian Motocycle Company. In 1946 the two companies were consolidated in the old East Springfield factory. Some equipment was moved from the State Street plant, but most of the tooling was well beyond its service life and was scrapped. Many old Powerplus components and complete factory racing machines were sold off at bargain prices to dealers and local enthusiasts.

Indian's uncertain future in 1945 left the Chief as the only model offered for 1946. The single modification to the pre-war design was the adoption of the military 841 fork, a girder/spring unit with a hydraulic shock absorber. The new front suspension gave more than double the wheel travel of the old leaf-spring unit, providing both smoother ride and better handling. The first 1946 models were available only with black paint.

Following the four-year motorcycle shortage imposed by the war, and the return to civilian life of thousands of young men whose first riding experiences were in the military, the demand for new machines was high. Harley-Davidson, unaffected by shifting ownership, was in a superior position to capitalize on the booming post-war motorcycle market. Milwaukee's product roster included the 750 and 1200cc flatheads and 1000 and 1200cc overhead-valve Knuckleheads. And the effects of post-war inflation wouldn't kick in until 1947, when motorcycle prices jumped 30 per cent.

Springfield, meanwhile, was in a serious scramble to outfit a new plant, develop a new line of lightweights, reassure dealers and

Below: Saddlebags and whitewall tires were among the accessories gaining more popularity after the war. Folks were keen to get dressed up.

1946 Chief
Owner – Trev Deeley Museum
Vancouver, British Columbia

1946 Chief
Owner/restorer – Bob Stark
Perris, California

1946 Chief
Owner – Douglas Allen
California

Below: Not all riders liked the subdued tank emblem, preferring the colorful Chief war bonnet graphic.

Above: The new front fork more than doubled the wheel travel on the Chief. Combined with softer springs in the plunger suspension at the rear, this meant a smoother ride.

Above: The 841-style horn was mounted between the frame tubes. The first run of post-war Chiefs were available only with black paint. Red and blue were offered later in the year.

Left: During the production year, Indian switched from 4.00 x 18in to 5.00 x 16in tires. The new fork featured a hydraulic shock absorber between dual coil springs.

convince riders that Indian was back on the road to glory. Rogers embarked on a national tour of dealerships, hoping both to upgrade their marketing skills and sell them on the new line of lightweight machines. British motorcycles were establishing a foothold in the marketplace, and the advantages of foot-shift, hand-clutch and less weight showed notable appeal.

Many of the dealers were more than a bit skeptical about Rogers' plans, and some were resistant to his modern approach to motorcycle marketing. But most Indian dealers were willing to do whatever was necessary to regain a greater share of the market, and were impressed by Rogers' enthusiasm and commitment. By far the most common refrain, however, from both dealers and riders, was the call to resume production of the Sport Scout. Rogers indicated that both new Scouts and Chiefs would be forthcoming, but that the first order of business was development of the vertical singles and twins.

No disadvantage was apparent among Indian racers in 1946, since they won nearly every event of the first full season of racing in five years. Ed Kretz continued his domination with a record-setting victory at the 100-mile Laconia, New Hampshire, road-race, knocking 31 seconds off the previous time. The Iron Man would have lowered the record further, but threw a chain on the 37th lap and had to push his machine into the pits for a replacement.

1947 CHIEF

SPECIFICATIONS
ENGINE/DRIVETRAIN
Engine: 42° side-valve V-twin
Displacement: 74ci (1200cc)
Bore & stroke: 3.25 x 4.44in
(82.5 x 112.7mm)
Horsepower: 40
Carburetor: Schebler
Transmission: 3- or 4-speed
Clutch: Wet multi-disc
Primary drive: 4-row chain
Final drive: Chain
Brake: F & R. Drum
Battery: 6-volt
Ignition: Distributor (magneto
optional)

CHASSIS/SUSPENSION
Frame: Steel, twin downtube
Suspension: F. Leaf-spring.
R. Plunger
Wheelbase: 61in (155cm)
Weight: 560lb (254kg)
Fuel capacity: 3.5gal (13.25lit)
Oil capacity: 2.5qts (2.37lit)
Tires: 5.00 x 16in/4.50 x 18in
Top speed: 85mph (137km/h)
Colors: Black, red, blue, white
Number built: 11,849
Price: $475

CHIEF (1947)

Even though Springfield struggled to assemble new production lines and motorcycles, the company had managed to turn out nearly 7,000 Chiefs in 1946. Harley-Davidson production more than doubled that. The reorganization process continued into 1947, and the Chief remained the only Indian offered for sale.

Production costs for the lightweight machines had almost doubled the original projections, and Indian was again strapped for cash. Faced with mounting inflation and cost overruns, Ralph Rogers merged Indian with the Hill Diesel Engine Company, in which he was the majority stockholder. The move allowed Springfield some temporary financial relief, pending more extensive reorganization

later in the year. Rogers also undertook the planning of a vigorous national advertising campaign, and once again visited Indian dealers to promote the new models.

Few modifications were made to the Chief for 1947. The Indian head tank emblem was replaced by script lettering, and the front fender light incorporated an Indian head lens. The front fork links were extended by a half inch, and 5.00 x 16-inch tires became standard with 4.50 x 18s available as options. A longer sidestand was fitted farther forward, and the chainguard had an open cutout for the kickstart mechanism.

The Chiefs sold well, but Springfield was still losing ground to inflation and development costs on the lightweights. In July, Rogers moved to merge Indian with his companies in the air-conditioning business, and borrowed another $1.5 million to support the continuing reorganization.

Matters took another turn for the worse when early test

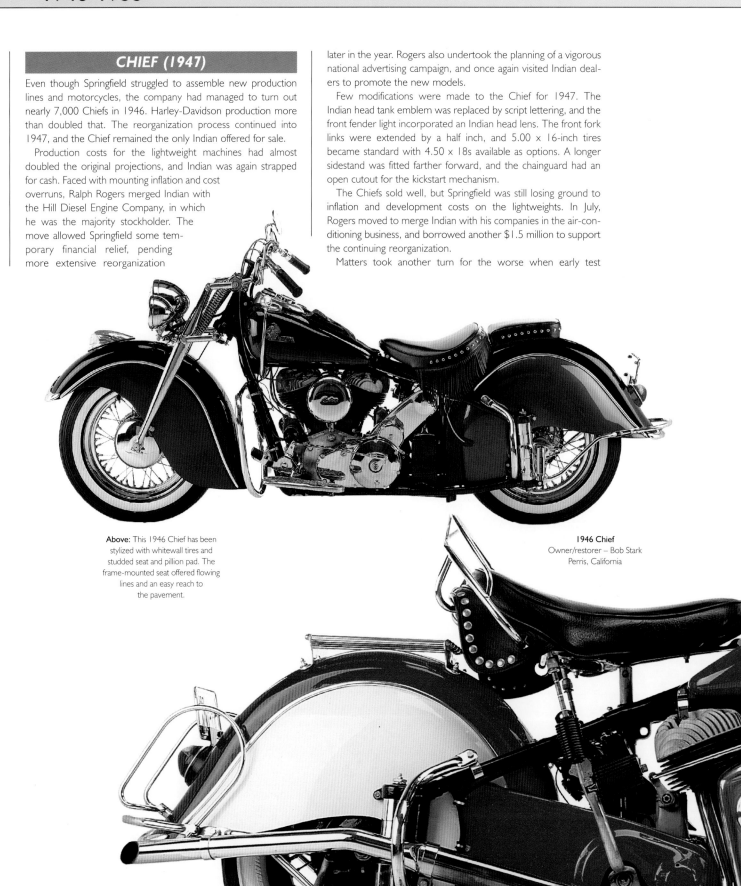

Above: This 1946 Chief has been stylized with whitewall tires and studded seat and pillion pad. The frame-mounted seat offered flowing lines and an easy reach to the pavement.

1946 Chief
Owner/restorer – Bob Stark
Perris, California

Right: Wartime shortages were no longer problems for manufacturers in 1947. Two-tone paint options were offered once again, and the roster of accessories reflected the trend toward full-dress motorcycles. The Chum-Me seat and windshield were among the most popular.

1947 Chief
Owner/restorer – Bob Stark
Perris, California

Right: Chromed front and rear safety guards (aka crash bars) were popular additions, and often prevented expensive paint and repair jobs.

1947 Chief
Owner/restorer – Bob Stark
Perris, California

Above: The Chief was again the only model in 1947. The sidecar rig, with upgraded suspension, is a fiberglass reproduction by Champion Sidecars, Huntington Beach, California.

Left: The windshield was mounted to the upper accessory bar, the spotlights to the lower one. The Indian head front fender light was first offered in 1947.

Above: Indian script replaced the Indian head tank emblem. The center engine cowling was first used on 1952 models, but is often retrofit for styling.

Left: 5.00 x 16in tires became standard equipment in 1947, though the 4.50 x 18in skins remained optional. New fork links were a half-inch longer.

on the new vertical singles and twins turned up significant problems. The most problematic was a new four-cylinder design that didn't reach production. The prototype singles and twins were fitted with girder/spring forks and keystone frames, but when they reached production the bikes had telescopic forks and cradle-loop frames. A number of problems were addressed before the new machines faced final assembly, but several key weaknesses went unresolved in the rush to market the new lightweights. Disgruntled dealers once again issued the call for a new version of the Sport Scout.

Once again, the racing community managed to uphold the Indian tradition with wins in the key races. The Daytona 200, run for the first time since the war began, was won by Johnny Spiegelhoff on one of the pre-war big-base Sport Scout prototypes, and Ted Edwards was second on another Scout. Edwards finished second in the 1947 Laconia 100, a race dominated by the increasingly competitive Harley-Davidson WR. Harley's Jimmy Chann took the national title at the Springfield Mile, his first of three in a row.

Perhaps the most noteworthy result came at California's rugged Greenhorn Enduro, a timed two-day event covering some 500 miles (800km) of desert and mountain trails. Max Bubeck was the victor on his specially modified 1939 Indian Four. Fifty years later, Mad Max remains a desert rat and a leading exponent of the four-cylinder machines.

MODEL 648 SCOUT (1948) AND CHIEF (1948)

1948 BIG-BASE SCOUT

SPECIFICATIONS
ENGINE/DRIVETRAIN
Engine: 42° side-valve V-twin
Displacement: 45ci (750cc)
Bore & stroke: 2.88 x 3.50in
(73.2 x 88.9mm)
Horsepower: 40-45
Carburetor: 1.25 Linkert
Transmission: 3- or 4-speed
Clutch: Wet multi-disc
Primary drive: Triplex chain
Final drive: Chain
Brake: F & R. Drum
Ignition: Edison-Splitdorf
magneto

CHASSIS/SUSPENSION
Frame: Steel keystone
Suspension: Leading-link
truss/spring
Wheelbase: 58in (147cm)
Weight: 325lb (147kg)
Fuel capacity: 3.7gal (14lit)
Oil capacity: 2.5qts (2.37lit)
Tires: 4.00 x 18in
Top speed: 115mph (185km/h)
Colors: Red, black, blue, green
Number built: 50
Price: $750

In the two years following the war, motorcycle registrations in the United States had more than doubled. Quite a number of these machines were made in Great Britain, and were equipped with foot-shift and hand-clutch, unlike the standard Indian or Harley-Davidson. Naturally, Ralph Rogers figured that the new British-style lightweights from Indian would capture a healthy share of the new market.

Indian dealers were less certain. Beyond the teething problems of the new models, they were also at a displacement disadvantage against most of the imports. Plus, both the new single and twin would have to be priced about 20 per cent higher than originally planned. And they wouldn't be ready until the middle of the year.

So, for the first half of 1948, the Indian Chief was once again the only model offered by Springfield. A number of changes were made to the big twin, including new crankcases and a gear-driven aluminum oil pump. The later models featured a rectangular-section frame brace under the seat, and the shift lever mount on the front downtube switched from a casting to a welded tube.

The generator was now equipped with an automotive-type voltage regulator, and a warning light replaced the ammeter on the instrument panel. The new Stewart-Warner speedometer was driven by the front wheel, and a new horn was fitted between the front down-tubes. Narrower, sport-style handlebars were available as options, and the Chief was fitted with only 5.00 × 16-inch tires. The color

choices for 1948 were Indian red, sea foam blue, deluxe black and prairie green.

In spite of Springfield's financial difficulties, the commitment to a strong racing presence had not yielded to the grip of economics. But the 648 Daytona would be the last of the Sport Scouts. Its prototypes had been developed for the Daytona race before the war, and Johnny Spiegelhoff's race-winner in 1947 was one of what would be called the big-base Scouts. To satisfy AMA rules, Indian built 50 of the engines for the 1948 race.

The 648 was a high-compression Bonneville 750 engine with stronger crankcases, domed pistons, steel racing flywheels and the Chief's aluminum oil pump. The oversize cases housed a cast-in oil sump at the lower rear and oil scrapers which combined to improve crankcase breathing. The gear-driven Edison-Splitdorf magneto mounted vertically above the oil pump, which featured flexible, side-mounted feed and return lines. The front fork was adapted from the 741 military model.

Included in the $750 price were a smaller gas tank, selection of sprockets and foot pegs to replace the footboards for racing. Springfield even offered a set of racing guidelines for Daytona.

Floyd Emde, like Spiegelhoff another former Harley racer, put his 648 on the front row in 1948, and at the end became the first rider to lead the Daytona 200 from start to finish. This would be Indian's final victory in the famous race.

Above: The fork and some rear frame sections were provided by the 741 military model. The flywheels, cylinders and heads came from the 841. The Daytona Scout was a child of war.

Right: Although the competition Sport Scout was designated 648, the first prototypes were actually built and raced before the war. One of the 50 post-war examples was ridden to victory by Floyd Emde at Daytona Beach, Florida in 1948.

1948 Big-base Scout
Owner – Jim Smith

Right: John Polovic, an ace mechanic at Charles Stark's Indian shop in Akron, Ohio, created the Rainbow paint scheme in 1942. Factory reps were impressed, but the cost for such detail work was too high for production bikes.

Below: The Chum-Me seat featured ajustable collets to set suspension according to the load.

1948 Chief
Owner/restorer – Bob Stark
Perris, California

Above: The Chief engine got a new aluminum oil pump in 1948, which was also used on the Daytona Scout. A new voltage regulator was fitted to the generator. The kickstand moved forward on the frame.

Above: The original Stewart-Warner speedometer has been replaced by a 1952 Corbin instrument. The new speedometer was driven by the front wheel. The 45-degree offset ammeter was used in 1947. Mix and match is all part of the custom game.

Above: The magneto, formerly at the rear of the primary drive, moved to the oil pump. Steel flywheels, domed pistons and improved breathing capacity made the Daytona good for 115mph (185km/h).

Left: The front fender, lifted from the Junior Scout, was trimmed for racing duty. The wheels and brake drums were Sport Scout items, with 741 backing plates. Bill Tuman, Ernie Beckman and Bobby Hill raced the bikes successfully into the mid-Fifties.

1949 ARROW AND SCOUT

SPECIFICATIONS
ENGINE/DRIVETRAIN
Engine: ohv vertical single/twin
Displacement: 13ci (220cc).
Twin 27ci (440cc)
Bore & stroke: 2.38 x 3.00in
(60.5 x 76.2mm)
Horsepower: 10/20
Carburetor: Linkert or Amal
Transmission: 4-speed
Clutch: Wet multi-disc ·
Primary drive: Triplex chain
Final drive: Chain
Brake: F & R. Drum
Battery: 6-volt
Ignition: Magneto

CHASSIS/SUSPENSION
Frame: Steel keystone
Suspension: F. Telescopic fork.
R. Plunger (optional on Arrow)
Wheelbase: 51in (129.5cm)
Weight: 260/295lb (118/134kg)
Fuel capacity: 2.5gal (9.46lit)
Oil capacity: 1.5qts (1.42lit)
Tires: 3.25 x 18in
Top speed: 55/75mph
(88.5/121km/h)
Colors: Blue, red, yellow,
turquoise
Number built: Approx.
11,000 total
Price: $250/$350

Right: The 220cc Arrow,
which debuted in 1949, was
expected to launch a new era
in American lightweight
motorcycles. But the machine
was not properly sorted out
before it reached the dealers'
showrooms, and the results
were grim.

ARROW (1949) AND SCOUT (1949)

The long-awaited lightweight "verticals" finally appeared in mid-1948 as 1949 models. The 220cc Arrow single and 440cc Scout twin had been in development for four years, at an investment cost of some $6.5 million according to Ralph Rogers. Many Indian fans were of the opinion that it was money wasted. A considerable portion of the funding, as it turned out, had come from the pocket of Rogers himself.

The rationale behind these machines was fairly simple, and looked convincing on the surface. The influx of British and European motorcycles pointed the way to a future of lighter motorcycles, sporting bikes with hand-clutch, foot-shift and easy handling. The prognostication proved true, but the first Indian verticals fell short of the performance and reliability demands of

new market. And by the time Springfield was able to resolve the problems, it was already too late. And two other determining factors, one a decision within the Indian organization and another beyond Springfield's control, would combine to cripple the company beyond repair.

Later history, in the form of Honda, would verify Rogers' approach to motorcycle marketing, but in Indian's case the products did not fulfill the promises of the advertising campaign. National sports and movie celebrities were hired to tout the joys

Left: The new Scout, and the Arrow, were designed by Briggs Weaver, who had headed engineering at duPont's automobile company. Weaver's earlier projects included the Sport Scout and Indian's military models. New Scout styling derived from British designs.

1949 Scout
Owner/restorer – Bob Stark
Perris, California

1949 Scout
Owner/restorer – Bob Stark
Perris, California

1949 Arrow
Owner – Trev Deeley Museum
Vancouver, British Columbia

Right: The Arrow, shown here in Sunshine yellow, was a handsome lightweight. With about 10 horsepower and 260lb (118kg), the motorcycle was easy to handle. But numerous early production problems saddled the bikes with a bad reputation.

Left: The Arrow and Scout were offered with accessory groups that included saddlebags, luggage rack and spotlights. Advertising featured prominent sports and movie celebrities touting the machines' user-friendly nature and economical operation.

Above: Shabby production control plagued the early Arrow engines. The plunger rear suspension was available as an option.

Left: The 3.25 x 18in tires were an oddball size in the American market. The original spoke pattern proved too weak to withstand much abuse.

of the new easy riding machines, but the realities of slipshod production and assembly effectively doomed the verticals to oblivion. The early machines suffered from difficult starting, oil leakage, weak wheels and poor ignitions. Indian was forced into an expensive scramble to fix the problems, and in the process made the fateful decision to discontinue production of the Chief.

Several prototype Chiefs, featuring telescopic forks, hand-shift and foot-clutch had already been built. But Springfield had invested so much time and money in the new lightweights, they could hardly afford to let the project fail. And with a financial situation now in peril, and a shortage of products for a growing market, Rogers went to England to negotiate for more capital and the import of British motorcycles. He cut a deal with John Brockhouse, who invested $1.5 million dollars and sent one of his own engineers to Springfield. Rogers also hired veteran engineer Arthur Constantine, who had worked for Harley-Davidson and Excelsior. The moves didn't sit well with Briggs Weaver, who shortly resigned.

The last crippling economic blow came in the fall, when the British government devalued the pound by nearly 30 per cent. The move made British motorcycles about 20 per cent cheaper in the States, and effectively put Indian's revival in the dumpster.

CHIEF (1950) AND WARRIOR/WARRIOR TT (1950)

1950 CHIEF

SPECIFICATIONS
ENGINE/DRIVETRAIN
Engine: 42° side-valve V-twin
Displacement: 80ci (1300cc)
Bore & stroke: 3.25 x 4.81in (82.5 x 122.2mm)
Horsepower: 40
Carburetor: Linkert
Transmission: 3- or 4-speed
Clutch: Wet multi-disc
Primary drive: 4-row chain
Final drive: Chain
Brake: F & R. Drum
Battery: 6-volt
Ignition: Distributor

CHASSIS/SUSPENSION
Frame: Steel, twin downtube
Suspension: F. Telescopic fork.
R. Plunger
Wheelbase: 62in (157.5cm)
Weight: 560lb (254kg)
Fuel capacity: 3.5gal (13.25lit)
Oil capacity: 2.5qts (2.37lit)
Tires: 5.00 x 16in
Top speed: 95mph (153km/h)
Colors: Red, black, blue, yellow, turquoise
Number built: Approx. 1,600
Price: $750

Above: Lower slipper brackets on the rear suspension were shortened on the 1950 Chief to increase ground clearance by one inch. 5.00 x 16in tires were now the only rubber fitted.

Right: The Chief returned in 1950, and not a moment too soon. When Springfield dropped the big twin in 1949, more than a few riders threw in the towel and shifted their allegiance to Harley-Davidson, and suffered the scorn of their Indian pals.

Ralph Rogers, under pressure from lenders, dealers and John Brockhouse, resigned as president of the Indian Motocycle Company in January of 1950. The company was divided into two components; manufacturing would be conducted by an Atlas subsidiary, the Titeflex Corporation, manufacturer of aircraft components. The second entity, the Indian Sales Corporation, controlled by John Brockhouse, would distribute Indian, Norton, Matchless, Royal Enfield, AJS and Vincent motorcycles in the United States.

Following a chorus of complaints from dealers in 1949, and the defection of many riders to Harley-Davidson, Springfield had resumed production of the Chief for 1950. Several of the components fitted to the 1949 prototypes were found on the new production models, foremost among them a telescopic front fork. The conversion to hand-clutch and foot-shift was not satisfactorily sorted out, and did not reach production.

The big twin engine also got bigger, with an additional ⅜-inch (9.5mm) stroke bringing displacement to 1300cc, or Eighty cubes in American measurement. A Torque Evener compensating sprocket was added to cushion the primary drive, which necessitated a bulge in the primary cover. The front fender was slightly smaller than earlier skirted coverings, and the footboards were

fitted with aluminum extenders for passenger footrests. The return of the Chief was a sign of encouragement to Indian dealers and riders, and Springfield assured the public that Indian was again on the road to recovery.

Most of the problems with the lightweights had been addressed and resolved for 1950. The frames were painted black, rather than matching the bodywork, and the horn moved from under

Below: The Chief was now fitted standard with right-hand throttle and left-hand shift. Indian script on the tank had a red or black background.

Below: The Chum-Me seat and optional luggage rack returned unchanged from earlier models. Some Chiefs had a rear-wheel-drive speedometer.

Above: The Chief made the jump from 1200 to 1300cc with an increase in stroke. According to the engine number, this is the first Chief off the line in 1950.

1950 Warrior TT
Owner/restorer – Bob Stark
Perris, California

Left: The Warrior TT was purpose-built for scrambles and enduro competition. The 500cc twin had longer suspension front and rear.

Above: Ed Kretz helped with testing on the prototype competition model. The TT came too late to help restore Indian's prospects, but Joe Gee rode one to win the 1951 Jack Pine enduro.

Below: The street version of the Warrior was built in 1950 and 1951. Despite the added power and reliability of the 500cc models, the vertical twins went quickly to history. Shame.

1950 Warrior
Owner/restorer – Bob Stark
Perris, California

1950 Chief
Owner – Bob Mercer
San Jose, California

to the front of the frame. Leftover 1949 models were sold at discount, and a new version of the twin was introduced as the 500cc Warrior. The displacement increase was intended to put Indian on more competitve footing with the British models, but the American twins remained at a price disadvantage.

The new twin was also offered in an off-road version called the Warrior TT, which featured high pipes, longer fork and revised rear springs. The TT was no match for the British bikes, or the old Sport Scouts, in professional dirt-track events, but had some success in amateur scrambles. Max Bubeck won California's Cactus Derby enduro on a Warrior in 1950, and 12 years later would win the rugged Greenhorn 500 on an extensively modified version.

On the National scene, Springfield's former glory was fading fast. Ed Kretz had switched to Triumph, and the only Indian in the Daytona results was Jimmy Kelly in 17th place. But Bobby Hill and Bill Tuman were mounting a comeback in dirt-track racing, and would soon record Indian's final victories by reclaiming the national title from Harley-Davidson.

CHIEF (1951) AND SCOUT-WARRIOR (1949-51)

1951 CHIEF

SPECIFICATIONS
ENGINE/DRIVETRAIN
Engine: 42° side-valve V-twin
Displacement: 80ci (1300cc)
Bore & stroke: 3.25 x 4.81in
(82.5 x 122.2mm)
Horsepower: 40
Carburetor: Linkert
Transmission: 3- or 4-speed
Clutch: Wet multi-disc
Primary drive: 4-row chain
Final drive: Chain
Brake: F & R. Drum
Battery: 6-volt
Ignition: Distributor (magneto optional)

CHASSIS/SUSPENSION
Frame: Steel, twin downtube
Suspension: F. Telescopic fork.
R. Plunger
Wheelbase: 62in (157.5cm)
Weight: 560lb (254kg)
Fuel capacity: 4.7gal (17.8lit)
Oil capacity: 2.5qts (2.37lit)
Tires: 5.00 x 16in
Top speed: 95mph (153km/h)
Colors: Red, black, blue, yellow
Number built: Approx. 900
Price: $850

Above: Speedometer styles switched part way through the year in 1951. Earlier models featured this face with Indian head and arrow needle. The later unit had a black face with Indian script.

Right: Few styling changings were made on the 1951 Chief. This example is fitted with the 1952 engine and fork panels. The front and rear wheels remained interchangeable; overall gear ratio on the Eighty was 3.73:1.

The Chief was little changed for 1951. Some later models were fitted with rear-wheel-drive Corbin speedometers, apparently leftover stock. Most were equipped with the front-drive Stewart-Warner units used previously. As in 1950, the Chief was again standard with right-hand throttle control to conform with the lightweights' pattern.

Engine numbers were changed in 1951, with digits (101-up) preceded by the solo letter C, rather than the three letters used in prior years. Big twin serial numbers followed the old system, with a 3 followed by the year and production number (351-101-up).

Neither the Arrow nor Scout were in the model lineup for 1951. The Warrior and Warrior TT were still offered, with the road model featuring two-tone paint and a new tank decal. A new model from Brockhouse Engineering in England made its first appearance in 1951. The Brave, a 250cc side-valve met with little success in the States, despite its light weight and relatively low price of $300.

Springfield was obviously fighting a losing battle in the general marketplace, but privateer racers kept the Indian name in the news with strong results in major national events. Most of the top riders had switched to British marques for road-racing, but stuck with the venerable Sport Scout for dirt-track competition. Foremost among these were Bobby Hill, Bill Tuman and Ernie Beckman.

Ohio's Bobby Hill recaptured the National Championship for Indian by winning the Springfield Mile in 1951, breaking a string of Harley-Davidson victories. Hill also won the Milwaukee Mile national, a sweet victory in Harley's back yard. In 1952, aided by the tuning wizardy of machinist Dick Gross, Hill went on to win five national championship races. In the Dodge City 200 he rode a Norton, but the Sport Scout took the checkers at Richmond,

Springfield, Syracuse and Indianapolis. Few in attendance could have known that these would be the final racing showdowns between Indian and Harley-Davidson. But they could hardly have asked for greater closing acts.

At Richmond, Virginia the frontrunners were the Indians of Hill and Beckman, Jimmy Chann on the Harley and Norton-mounted Dick Klamfoth. Hill and Chann, both of Columbus, Ohio, broke free at mid-race and put on a show that had the crowd on its feet. Chann had the advantage coming off the turns, but Hill would regain the lead on the straightaway. The battle see-sawed back and forth, but Hill edged away on the final lap to win.

The following year, at the Milwaukee Mile National, Hill brought the crowd of 10,000 to its feet with another remarkable ride. Two rising stars from California, Al Gunter on a BSA and Joe Leonard on Harley, had taken the early lead and drawn away. Hill had made a lousy start and was running eighth after three laps, then began picking up places at a serious rate. With two and a half laps remaining, and the crowd cheering him on, Hill passed Gunter and Leonard on the back straight and pulled away.

At Springfield, Hill was leading when his motor soured, and the race became another epic barnburner between Gunter, Leonard, Harley-mounted Don Hawley and Bill Tuman on the Indian, who took the win. In 1953, at Williams Grove, Pennsylvania, Ernie Beckman and Bobby Hill finished 1-2, and drew the final curtain on 40 years of racing between Indian and Harley-Davidson.

Below: In addition to the traditional Chum-Me seat, riders now had the option of a bench seat.

Below: Adjustments to the rear suspension springs balanced wheel movement with the action of the telescopic fork.

Above: The Chief engine remained unchanged for 1951. Throttle jockeys would have the engine stroked to displace 97 cubic inches (1600cc), which put top speed over 120mph (193km/h).

Right: Both the Arrow and Scout were gone in 1951, with the Warrior the only remaining overhead-valve model on the Springfield roster. Many dealers were left with a number of early verticals that were sold at cost.

Below: This 1949 Scout has been modified with a 1951 Warrior paint scheme on the tank. A handful of 1952 Warriors were built, but then production was suspended.

1949 Scout
Owner/restorer – Bob Stark
Perris, California

Left: Most riders found the telescopic fork a welcome addition to the Indian Chief. The hydraulics provided both improved ride, roadholding and a more contemporary look.

Above: The fork panel behind the headlight was introduced in 1952. Clubman, Sportsman and Roadmaster models offered different groups of accessories.

1951 Chief
Owner/restorer – Bob Stark
Perris, California

CHIEF (1953) AND BRAVE (1951)

By 1952 the Titeflex Corporation was under pressure from financiers to tighten up Indian's balance sheets. Design and engineering work was well underway on a new version of the Warrior and a prototype with a Sport Scout engine in the Warrior chassis, but both projects were canceled. Later in the year the production of Warriors was suspended entirely, when management decided to cut its losses and devote all manufacturing to the Chief.

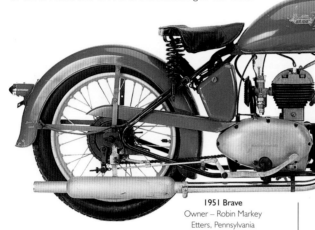

1951 Brave
Owner – Robin Markey
Etters, Pennsylvania

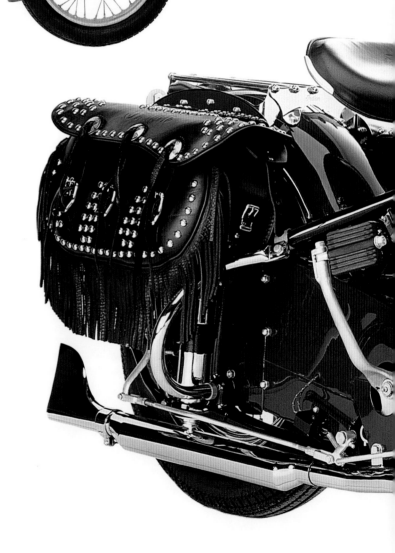

Left: The British-built Brave replaced the domestic lightweights in 1951. The 250cc four-stroke single had a 3-speed transmission, telescopic fork and no rear suspension. Though it weighed less than 250 pounds (113kg), the Brave attracted little interest.

The rear-wheel-drive speedometer, adopted on the later 1951 Chiefs, was used on all the 1952 models. The front fender was trimmed slightly, and the upper fork legs were finished in chrome. Behind the headlight a new panel fit between the fork tubes, and featured a winged insignia at the top and Roadmaster script at the bottom. The dimmer switch shifted from the handlebar to the left footboard, and the horn moved to the top of the front downtubes.

The fuel tank was more tapered at the rear and carried a new decal behind the nameplate, featuring a winged design incorporating a circle enclosing the word "Eighty" to designate cubic inches. Customers could order either low-rise or Western-style handlebars. The bars now had external cables for throttle, choke and spark advance.

Another new feature was the bench-style version of the Chum-Me-Seat, available as an option. The foam rubber cushion extended over the rear of the tank, and a large grab rail surrounded the rear of the seat. The shift pattern was reversed to put higher gears forward, giving the rider more leg room when carrying a passenger.

Engine internals were unchanged, but a number of revisions were made to the hardware. An Amal carburetor replaced the Linkert unit, and a lower exhaust pipe was fitted with a Warrior-type muffler and fishtail tip. A new bodywork panel was inserted between the exhaust pipes, covering the oil pump, distributor and camcase.

The lightweight Brave, imported from England, was offered from 1951 through 1953. Widely mistaken for a two-stroke, the engine was actually a 250cc four-stroke flathead. Valve adjustment was achieved by removing the single bolt holding a flat plate on the right side of the engine. The wet sump cases also included a 3-speed Albion transmission, shifted by foot and clutched by hand. Horsepower was rated at 2.6.

The Brave, fitted with telescopic fork, sprung seat and rigid rear wheel, weighed only 250 pounds (113kg) ready to go, and cost about $300. Few American riders showed interest in the little single, but California racer Del Branson became an early fan of lightweights. With a few modifications, he rode a Brave to a second place in the Big Bear run and a first in the Moose Page Memorial Hare 'n Hound. Just goes to show.

1953 Chief
Owner/restorer – Elmer Lower
Etters, Pennsylvania

1953 CHIEF

SPECIFICATIONS
ENGINE/DRIVETRAIN
Engine: 42° side-valve V-twin
Displacement: 80ci (1300cc)
Bore & stroke: 3.25 x 4.81in (82.5 x 122.2mm)
Horsepower: 40
Carburetor: Linkert or Amal
Transmission: 3- or 4-speed
Clutch: Wet multi-disc
Primary drive: 4-row chain
Final drive: Chain
Brake: F & R. Drum
Battery: 6-volt
Ignition: Distributor (magneto optional)

CHASSIS/SUSPENSION
Frame: Steel, twin downtube
Suspension: F. Telescopic fork. R. Plunger
Wheelbase: 62in (157.5cm)
Weight: 560lb (254kg)
Fuel capacity: 3.5gal (13.25lit)
Oil capacity: 2.5qts (2.37lit)
Tires: 4.75 x 16in
Top speed: 95mph (153km/h)
Colors: Red, black, blue, yellow, green (2), scarlet, tangerine, metallic blue, brown, olive drab
Number built: Approx. 1,300 (1952/53)
Price: $960

Above: Age requirements for antique license plates vary from state to state. The Antique Motorcycle Club of America has chapters throughout the country.

Right: The first of the last of the Indian Chiefs appeared in 1952. Except for a few minor details, the '52 and '53 models were the same. Year identification is often difficult because reproduction parts are often retrofit to earlier models.

Above: The final Indian tank emblem incorporated a stylized wing in the background, with the "Eighty" designation to show the healthy supply of cubic inches.

Left: Upper fork legs were chromed on the final renditions of the Chief. Spotlights, windshield, saddlebags and luggage rack remained popular options. The horn was moved up to a bracket in front of the fuel tank.

Above: Cylinder heads were slightly modified on the final Chiefs. The exhaust system also changed to clear the engine cover. The straight pipe had a Warrior-style muffler and fishtail tip.

1953 CHIEF

SPECIFICATIONS
ENGINE/DRIVETRAIN
Engine: 42° side-valve V-twin
Displacement: 80ci (1300cc)
Bore & stroke: 3.25 x 4.81in
(82.5 x 122.2mm)
Horsepower: 40
Carburetor: Linkert or Amal
Transmission: 3- or 4-speed
Clutch: Wet multi-disc
Primary drive: 4-row chain
Final drive: Chain
Brake: F & R. Drum
Battery: 6-volt
Ignition: Distributor (magneto
optional)

CHASSIS/SUSPENSION
Frame: Steel, twin downtube
Suspension: F. Telescopic fork.
R. Plunger
Wheelbase: 62in (157.5cm)
Weight: 560lb (254kg)
Fuel capacity: 4.7gal (17.8lit)
Oil capacity: 2.5qts (2.37lit)
Tires: 4.75 x 16in
Top speed: 95mph (153km/h)
Colors: Red, black, blue, yellow,
green (2), scarlet, tangerine,
metallic blue, brown, olive drab
Number built: Approx. 1,200
Price: $960

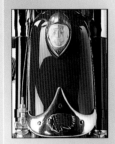

Above: Chief's warbonnet
imagery adorned the front
fender. Speedometer drives
shifted between the front
and rear wheel.

Right: Raised aluminum
footrests for the passenger
first appeared on the 1950
Chief. The right rear mounting
bracket was revised in 1952.
Tires switched to 4.75 x 16in
to compensate for the added
length of the front fork.

CHIEF (1953)

The 1953 Chief, last of the breed, was little changed from the previous year. The kick-start lever was slightly longer, and the front fender mounted a bit lower to avoid getting dinged by the horn. Color availability remained the same.

The Dunlop 4.75 x 16-inch tires, also fitted a year before, made the Chief a bit more agile at low speeds. Although Harley-Davidson introduced the option of foot-shift in 1952, Springfield was not moved to follow suit. Harley's big twin was still without rear suspension, and Indian touted the combination of comfort and safety offered by the sprung frame. And Milwaukee's Panhead was still a piddling 1200cc engine, compared to the Chief's mighty 1300cc powerplant.

"Full eighty cubic inches packed with power, the Chief engine is the biggest and huskiest ever housed in a motorcycle frame. Each of its mighty barrels develops as much power as most other motorcycle engines, and together they spell GO!!"

But the end was now at hand. Firm production numbers from Indian's last few years have not turned up. The most highly educated guesses put the numbers between 500 and 700 Chiefs in 1952 and a like number for 1953. Barely an echo of the glory years. As the final survivor of the Springfield tribe's protracted death, the late-model Chief has become the prominent symbol of the Indian marque. Numerous abortive attempts to revive the name have all been based on the final Chief. The ensuing badge-engineered models from England, one of which would carry the Chief name, were derived from different bloodlines altogether.

These were perhaps the most American of motorcycles. To the uninitiated, Indians and Harley-Davidson were indistinguishable, both just big V-twin-powered machines with few differences. Indian enthusiasts, you may be sure, do not feel that way. The Indian, after all, came first. And the marque always displayed some indefinable element of distinction, some unique sign of character or personality. Not, in other words, just another motorcycle.

Of course all genuine enthusiasts feel the same way about their favorite rides. Indian riders simply display their allegiance with a bit more intensity, hold the banner a little higher, and demonstrate the unwavering devotion of the true believer.

Indian, after all, was America's Pioneer Motorcycle for more than fifty years. And will remain so forever. Amen.

Left: The 1948-1951 speedometer
with its Indian head design and
arrow-style needle, is the most
popular. The trip meter was absent
after 1947.

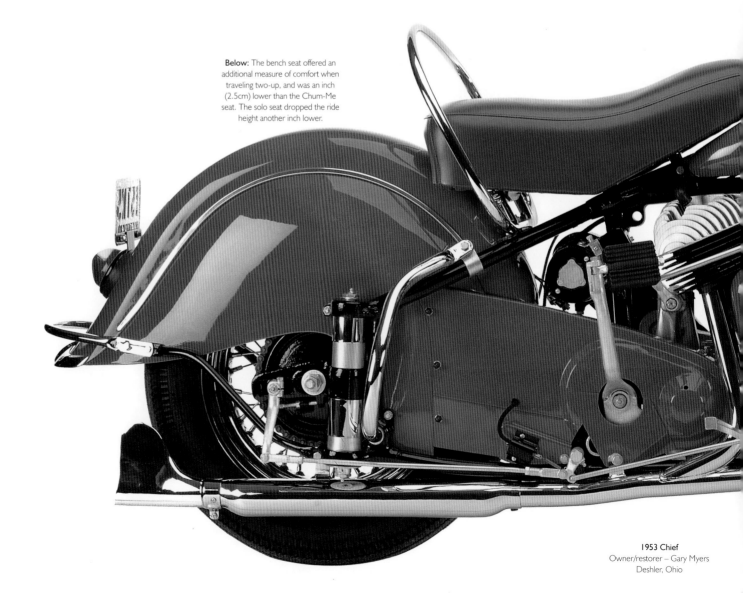

Below: The bench seat offered an
additional measure of comfort when
traveling two-up, and was an inch
(2.5cm) lower than the Chum-Me
seat. The solo seat dropped the ride
height another inch lower.

1953 Chief
Owner/restorer – Gary Myers
Deshler, Ohio

1951-53 Chief
Owner – Trev Deeley Museum
Vancouver, British Columbia

Left: A low handlebar and solo seat were favored by sporting riders. Enthusiasts who had no need of large saddlebags tended to prefer the high-pipe exhaust system.

Above: This Chief displays a combination of components from 1951 to 1953 models. The front fender and exhaust system represent earlier issue, the tank logo and engine cover came later.

Above: With the solo saddle, the Indian Eighty displays the graceful form of its skirted fenders to best advantage. Many found this the best-looking motorcycle ever built. And still do.

Left: On a 1300cc V-twin with a big soft saddle, a friend and an open road, you may just have the closest thing yet to heaven on earth. Tangerine dreams.

SINGLE (1908) AND THOR (1908)

The first modified motorcycle was probably the first motorcycle sold. Two-wheelers have always attracted tinkerers, and a personalized machine is simply more satisfying than a bone stock production model. Two activities that also followed close on the heels of the first commercial bikes were racing and stunt riding. Bicycle racing had led directly to the development of motorcycles, so competition was a natural corollary. And daredevil stunts were inevitable sideshow entertainments.

A young lady named C' Dora, from Europe, was one of the first stunt riders to thrill American audiences with her perfomance in the "Globe of Death." This hollow ball of latticed steel featured two riders looping the globe's circumference, one vertically and the other horizontally, their paths crossing twice each lap. Very few of the performers were female, so C' Dora's feats naturally drew attention.

Indian boasted in 1909 that only four performers in the world had looped the "Globe of Death" on motorcycles, that all had used Indians and none had been injured. C' Dora had brought along a European motorcylce for her first American appearance, but according to the Indian advertisement, "got an Indian as soon as she could. IT NEVER FAILS HER."

Young C' Dora appeared astride this machine on the cover of *The Motocycle News* in April 1909. As the text modestly stated, "Other performers have been using the INDIAN for over two years, both in this country and abroad, and to its reliability they owe their lives."

Above: C'Dora's machine was originally fitted with battery and coil ignition. The later magneto version proved the advantage of adding lightness.

Right: Rear frame bracing was no doubt added for strength, to withstand the centrifugal force imposed by circulating rapidly within the "Globe of Death."

Right: Motorcycling was barely even a commercial enterprise before it became a daredevil sport. Death-defying stunts were titillating.

Above: As Indian advertised: "RISKING YOUR LIFE is Serious Business, and the Show Performers who do it cannot afford to make mistakes in selecting their apparatus."

Right: The Aurora Automatic Machinery Company, located just outside Chicago, Illinois, built Indian engines from 1902 to 1907. The company also built its own brand, called the Thor.

Left: The Thor engine owed a considerable engineering debt to Indian's Oscar Hedstrom. The brand enjoyed some commercial success in the midwest, and mounted an ambitious racing program. A Thor twin was second in the 1914 Dodge City 300-mile race.

THOR

The Thor was produced by the Aurora Automatic Machinery Company, which built Indian engines from 1902 to 1907. The Illinois company paid Indian a royalty to reproduce the Hedstrom motor for other manufacturers, and also built their own machines using various names.

As the motorcycle market expanded quickly, this arrangement strained both Aurora's manufacturing capabilities and its relationship with Springfield. Oscar Hedstrom was not particularly keen on having derivatives of his engine used in other motorcycles, since he had no control over the quality of units not destined for Indian. Plus, Aurora was increasingly unable to meet Springfield's production schedule for engine and carburetor castings. Both problems were solved in 1907 when Hendee and Hedstrom expanded the Springfield facilities to include a forge and foundry, where Indian would build their own engines.

Thor did achieve some racing success under the guidance of tuner Bill Ottaway. The machines were popular in midwestern enduros, and gained national notice in 1914 when Thor rider Bill Brier finished second to Indian's Glen Boyd in the premier Dodge City 300-miler. The same year, Ottaway left Thor to become the supervisor of the new racing department at Harley-Davidson.

1908 C'Dora Special
Owner – Tom Hensley
Highland Park, California
Restored by Steve Huntzinger

TWIN (1913), TWIN (1915) AND POWERPLUS (1916)

The 1913 Indian motorcycles carried the luggage of Historical Significance. Not only was this Springfield's high water mark for total production (31,950), it was the first year for the revolutionary cradle-spring frame. And it was also the year that Harley-Davidson, their hand forced by Indian, decided to form a factory racing team. Plus, Oscar Hedstrom retired in 1913.

Naturally the 1913 singles and twins are serious collectibles, and many have been restored to their original condition. And, in some cases, to "better" than their original condition. Over-restored is the current term. But others are simply well maintained and ridden, even modified to be ridden more handily in modern traffic. Which is the case with John Eagles' 1913 twin shown here.

Eagles has restored quite a few motorcycles for himself and others, but he also enjoys riding the older machines. Riders in 1913 had their choice of either a single speed or a 2-speed transmission, and in 1915 Indian introduced their first 3-speed gearbox. Eagles chose a 1917 3-speed transmission to make his vintage twin more suitable for the open road. "It helps you keep up with traffic," John says.

Max Bubeck is another fan of old Indians, and, at the age of 80, may well hold the overall mileage record. In 1993 he rode the 1915 twin shown here from San Diego, California to New York City, attempting to retrace the 1914 run by Cannonball Baker. Max had only two serious problems on the journey, valve dome gaskets and the Kansas Highway Patrol. The gaskets began burning out early on, and kept failing at intervals all the way across the country. Repairs were made each time.

Below: Ken Smith's 1916 Powerplus with sidecar shows the patina of maturity. The sidecar ride is quite comfortable. There is nothing disgraceful about old age.

1916 Powerplus
Owner – Ken Smith
Philadelphia, Pennsylvania

Right: One benefit for fans of early Indians, whether they are collectors, riders or both, is the number of motorcycles in existence. In 1913, Indian produced nearly 32,000 machines.

1913 Twin
Owner/restorer – John Eagles
Orange, California

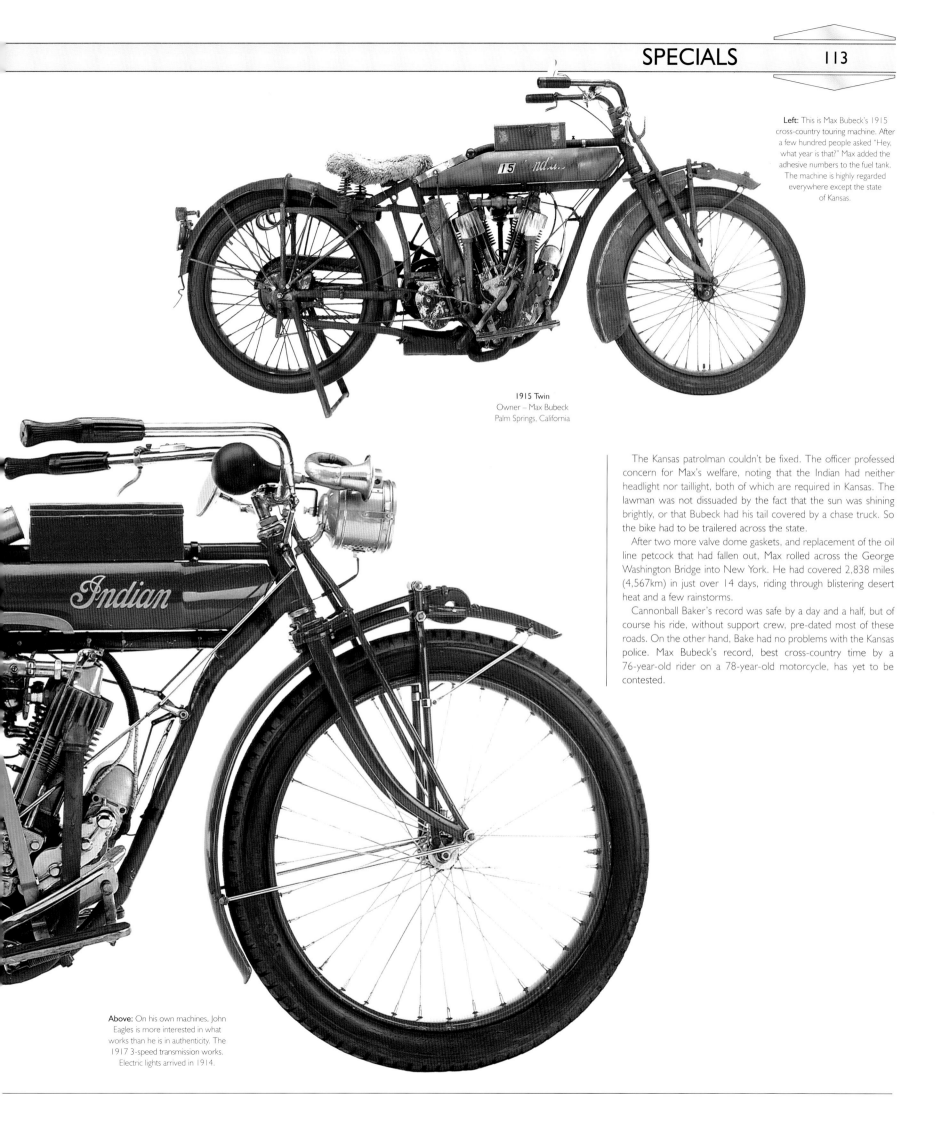

Left: This is Max Bubeck's 1915 cross-country touring machine. After a few hundred people asked "Hey, what year is that?" Max added the adhesive numbers to the fuel tank. The machine is highly regarded everywhere except the state of Kansas.

1915 Twin
Owner – Max Bubeck
Palm Springs, California

The Kansas patrolman couldn't be fixed. The officer professed concern for Max's welfare, noting that the Indian had neither headlight nor taillight, both of which are required in Kansas. The lawman was not dissuaded by the fact that the sun was shining brightly, or that Bubeck had his tail covered by a chase truck. So the bike had to be trailered across the state.

After two more valve dome gaskets, and replacement of the oil line petcock that had fallen out, Max rolled across the George Washington Bridge into New York. He had covered 2,838 miles (4,567km) in just over 14 days, riding through blistering desert heat and a few rainstorms.

Cannonball Baker's record was safe by a day and a half, but of course his ride, without support crew, pre-dated most of these roads. On the other hand, Bake had no problems with the Kansas police. Max Bubeck's record, best cross-country time by a 76-year-old rider on a 78-year-old motorcycle, has yet to be contested.

Above: On his own machines, John Eagles is more interested in what works than he is in authenticity. The 1917 3-speed transmission works. Electric lights arrived in 1914.

SCOUTS (1928 AND 1929)

The 101 Scout, one of the highlights in Indian's fractured history, was produced for only four years, 1928 to 1931. But it became Springfield's most durable sport bike and racer, dominating the dirt tracks for the final 25 years of factory-supported racing. Even though the 101 would be supplanted by the Sport Scout, the early version was favored for its cradle frame and neutral handling,

The Great Depression of the 1930s constrained both the manufacturing and racing of high-performance engines, but a number of racing motors from the late Twenties still appeared at major events. The twin-carburetor Altoona motor powered Jim Davis to several national titles in 1928, and many of the older 750cc overhead-valve engines were successful in hillclimbs.

The Scout model had gone largely unchanged since its inception in 1920. The competition from Harley-Davidson had grown steadily throughout the decade, and Indian recognized the need for a new middleweight in the lineup. The result was the 101 Scout, the final design by Charles Franklin and one that secured his place at the forefront of motorcycle engineering.

The 101 was longer than its predecessor, by about three inches (7.62cm), and shorter at the seat by nearly the same amount. The front fork provided both more rake and trail, and the engine bolted more solidly to the frame. The 101 Scout was easier to start, ride and stop, since it had a front brake. An exceptionally well-balanced motorcycle, which naturally made it quite popular with racers. On the debit side were its increase in weight and decrease in ground clearance. Buyers could choose the 600 or 750cc engine, and mosted opted for the latter.

Unfortunately, development of the 101 Scout coincided with another disastrous period of muddled management and severe financial drainage in Springfield. The model would be lost in the reorganization shuffle under the ownership of E. Paul DuPont, and ultimately replaced by the Sport Scout in 1934.

By historical coincidence, it was 1931, final year for the 101 Scout, when young Sammy Pierce went to work as a mechanic for the Indian dealer in Kansas City. Sam would later become known as "Mr. Indian," and mount a yeoman effort to save the company in its final days. He also built some interesting motorcycles, one of which was the "Harley Eater" shown here.

Left: In order to fit the engine with two carburetors, Pierce used two Sport Scout rear cylinders, the front one turned 180 degrees. Equipped with hand clutch and foot shift, the machine was built for the 20-mile national championship at the Sacramento Mile.

Below: Pierce called his product the American Indian. One model was the Super Scout, and the custom example shown here was affectionately called the "Harley Eater."

Right: In the Sixties, the unofficial western branch of Indian motorcycles was the shop of Sam Pierce in San Gabriel, California.

1928 Super Scout
Owner – Tom Hensley
Highland Park, California

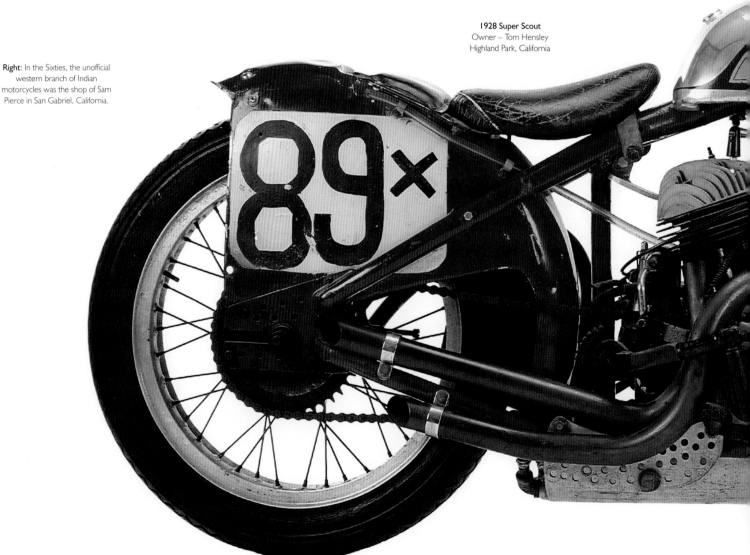

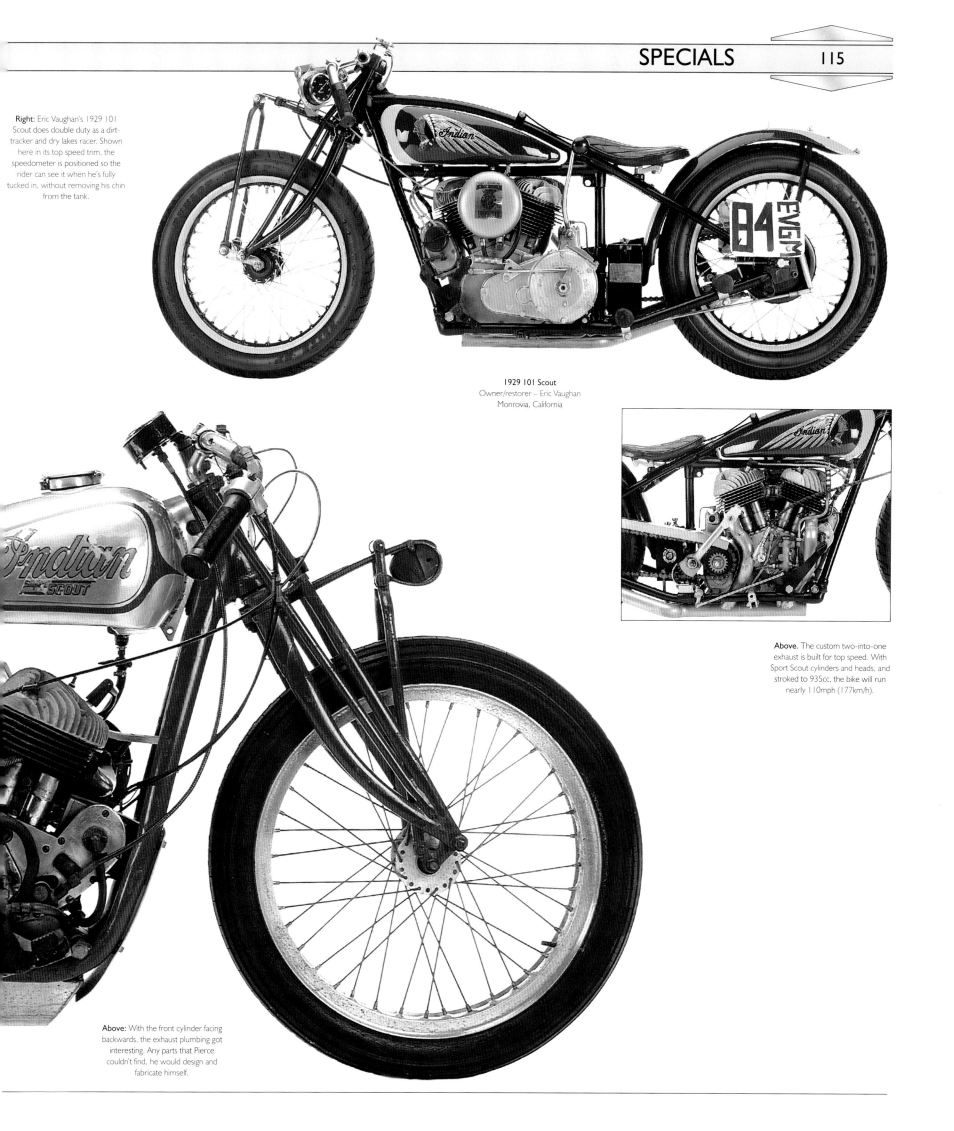

Right: Eric Vaughan's 1929 101 Scout does double duty as a dirt-tracker and dry lakes racer. Shown here in its top speed trim, the speedometer is positioned so the rider can see it when he's fully tucked in, without removing his chin from the tank.

1929 101 Scout
Owner/restorer – Eric Vaughan
Monrovia, California

Above. The custom two-into-one exhaust is built for top speed. With Sport Scout cylinders and heads, and stroked to 935cc, the bike will run nearly 110mph (177km/h).

Above: With the front cylinder facing backwards, the exhaust plumbing got interesting. Any parts that Pierce couldn't find, he would design and fabricate himself.

HILLCLIMBER (1936), CROCKER (1936) AND SPORT SCOUT (1936-41)

Professional racing virtually dried up in the Depression years, but that didn't keep people from enjoying some motorized competition. Hillclimbing was the form least affected by the crippled economy. Since it required only a steep hill and little expense in terms of organization, slant racing against the clock combined the elements of motorized excitement and community picnic.

Both Indian and Harley-Davidson recognized that hillclimb was the most cost-effective way to support competition and generate publicity for their products. Indian boasted a formidable team in Orrie Steele, former Excelsior star Gene Rhyne and young Howard Mitzell. Among the most potent machines from both factories were special overhead-valve 750s with dual exhaust ports. These high-compression engines ran on alcohol and developed upwards of 50 horsepower. Smartly up the hill they flew.

Speedway racing, popular in Europe and Australia, also enjoyed stateside popularity in the early Thirties. Al Crocker, a Los Angeles Indian dealer, and his foreman Paul Bigsby built several speedway frames with converted ohv Scout engines. Later they built their own overhead-valve engines, which were raced by future international stars Jack and Cordy Milne. When his engine was outpowered by the JAP British motors, Crocker moved on to his next goal, building a special high-performance V-twin for the road.

The 45-degree ohv twin was designed with stout cylinders capable of displacing from 1000 to 1500cc. The engine was carried by plates bolted to the frame, which had the transmission case cast as an integral unit. The heavy-duty 3-speed gears were said to be capable of handling 200 horsepower. The girder fork carried double compression and rebound springs, friction damper and steering damper. With aluminum castings throughout, the Crocker V-twin weighed in at just under 500 pounds (227kg).

The Crocker was fast, hell-for-strong and ruggedly handsome. But it was simply too expensive to build as a machine-shop motorcycle, and to buy in a Depression economy. Only about 100 of the V-twins were made, nearly half of which now remain in the hands of collectors. Crocker's creation presaged the superbike era that was still a few decades away.

Below: Sport Scout racers adopt minor variations in handlebars, footpeg and seat positions, suspension and wheels. Small adjustments become an evolutionary process.

1936-41 Sport Scout
Owner – Dodge Brothers Racing
Granada Hills, California

Below: This Sport Scout was raced in the Forties and Fifties by Harry Pelton. The Dodge family keeps the tradition alive today.

Above: The game of mix and match continues today in vintage racing. This is a 1937 Sport Scout Bonneville engine, with 1941 cylinders and heads, in a 1936 frame.

Right: What we have here is a motorcycle designed to go uphill in a hell of a hurry. The chains and sprocket indicate serious purpose.

1936 750cc Hillclimber
Owner – Max Bubeck
Palm Springs, California
Restored by Brad Wilmarth

1936 1000cc Crocker
Owner/restorer – Chuck Vernon
La Mirada, California

Below: The Crocker V-twin employed aluminum for the fuel tanks, footboards, generator drive case, instrument panel and taillight.

Left: The production fork, based on the Sport Scout unit, featured compression and damping springs. This early version has a single spring.

Above: Al Crocker married Gertrude Hasha, the widow of former factory racer Eddie Hasha. They moved to Los Angeles and operated the Indian distributorship from 1928 to 1934.

Below: Since the object was to get up the hill in the most hurry with the least fuss, and weight, the small Junior Scout fuel tank was light and out of the way. The chains helped also.

Left: Lightness was also among the most desirable qualities in a front end, so the Junior Scout fork served the purpose well. Suspension travel was less important, since the front wheel was usually skimming the bumps or aviating above them.

Above: The Edison magneto is visible below the seat. Harold Mathewson piloted this slant slingshot for more than 20 years.

FOUR (1939), CHOUT (1929/46) AND SPORT SCOUT (1940)

By 1939 most of the economic damage of the Depression had been repaired, and Springfield was rejuvenated by the French government's order for 5,000 military motorcycles. Indian now offered metallic paint schemes, and the first of the big base Sport Scouts were put in the hands of top racers for testing.

Indian had discontinued the magneto-equipped Four in 1938, offering only a battery ignition model. The magneto was reinstated in 1939, which would be the last year for the non-skirted fenders.

Max Bubeck probably has more time and miles on Indian Fours than any man alive. He has owned the bike shown here for nearly 60 years, and in the first 14 years he put 122,000 miles (196,335km) on it. In 1947, when the Greenhorn Enduro resumed after World War II, Max won the two-day event on his Four. In 1948 he rode a "Chout," (Chief engine in a Scout frame), to a speed of 135.58mph (218.19km/h), which was the highest speed yet recorded on an unstreamlined Indian.

Bubeck parked the Four when Indian manufactured the vertical twins, which he rode in enduros for nearly 15 years. In 1986 he restored the Four to use as a highway machine, and has since used it to cross the United States three times. The motorcycle has now logged more than 165,000 miles (265,535km), including enduros, all recorded by the original owner.

The secrets to the longevity of Bubeck's Four are his modifications to the engine's lubrication system.

When Max bought this bike, at the age of 22, from Floyd Clymer, the first thing he did was take the engine apart. The Indian crankshaft had oil passages from only three of the five main bearings. Bubeck drilled the crank so that all the rods were fed directly, and made breathers for the intake valve covers to improve top end oiling. Later he changed the poured babbit rod bearings to more durable inserts.

The final upgrades that made Max's Four a reliable long-distance, high-speed motorcycle were the addition of an oil filter and oil cooler. In 1990 Bubeck and Larry Struck became partners in the Indian "4" Experience, which specializes in the complete modernization of the venerable engine.

1940 Sport Scout
Owner – Team Bergstrom
San Mateo, California

Below: Newcomers to vintage racing often express surprise at the number of Sport Scouts on the track. And that so many of them look so good. And go so fast.

Above: Longest trip: 9,000 miles (14,500km) in 1989, California to Massachussets and back on the scenic route. Bubeck was inducted into the Indian Hall of Fame.

1929/46 Chout
Owner – Dodge Brothers Racing
Granada Hills, California

Right: This is the motorcycle version of a muscle car. The 1946 1200cc Chief engine in a 1929 101 Scout frame is nicknamed a Chout. This one is raced by Andy Dodge, who is respectful of its power-to-weight ratio.

Above: The Chout's gearshift lever is tucked out of the way at the bottom edge of the fuel tank. The original magneto postition at the base of the front cylinder is left vacant.

Left: This is the motorcycle Max Bubeck rode to victory in the 1947 Greenhorn Enduro. He later finished eighth in the Cactus Derby and came fifth in the 1948 Greenhorn. Max parked the Four in 1953, and it sat idle for the next 33 years.

Above: The Chout has been streamlined and lightened by removing most of the cylinder fins. A high-performance Joe Hunt magneto replaces the distributor used on road models.

Above: Bubeck revived his trusty Four in 1986 for the first of three cross-country trips. The oil cooler was originally a refrigerator condenser coil.

1939 Four
Owner/restorer – Max Bubeck
Palm Springs, California

SPORT SCOUT RACERS (1940)

Even though sporting riders lamented the passing of the 101 Scout, its successor proved to be an outstanding racing bike. Harley-Davidson was understandably relieved by the demise of the 101, which outsold Milwaukee's flathead Forty-five. And when the Sport Scout was first introduced in 1934, it appeared more the product of parts-bin economics than of high performance design and engineering.

The Sport Scout did derive from a succession of less successful machines: the Standard Scout of 1932 was simply a Scout engine in a Chief frame; the 600cc Scout Pony of the same year utilized the keystone frame of the earlier Prince, and the Motoplane, offered only in 1933, was a 750cc version of the Scout Pony, and the motor proved too much for the frame.

But the Sport Scout transmission bolted directly to the engine, unlike the earlier models' plate connectors. And although it was some 20 pounds (9kg) heavier than the 101, the Sport Scout soon started winning races. Ed Kretz won the 200-mile National Championship event at Savannah, Georgia in 1936, and veteran Fred Ludlow set the top speed of 128.57mph (206.9km/h) at California's Muroc Dry Lake, against much larger engines. Kretz went on to win the inaugural Daytona 200 the following year.

As independent tuners squeezed more power from the Sport Scout engine, Milwaukee set to work upgrading the performance of their 750. Class C racing had become the premier racing division in the national championship series, and only Indian and Harley were in the game.

For 20 years the Sport Scout set the pace for American dirt-track. Number 1K, shown here, has been broadsliding the dirt ovals for more than 50 years. Built originally by Indian dealer Bob

Mullaney, it was later acquired by southern California enthusiast Dean Hensley, who steadily refined it over the years. Assisted by restoration expert Steve Huntzinger, Hensley built a thoroughly modern version of the 1940 Sport Scout. Stronger engine mounting plates subdue frame flex, a steering damper minimizes head shake and a small White Power gas shock helps keep the front wheel planted.

The engine features oil scrapers, double-action oil pump and vented gearbox. The wheels are 18-inch aluminum Akronts laced to Barnes hubs, with a quick-change sprocket at the rear. Tom Hensley, Dean's brother, still races it in vintage events.

Left: Flywheel scrapers, a scavenger oil pump and well-vented cases help the old Forty-five develop good power. Note the vent tube at rear of the gearbox. The air cleaner cover is open at the back for healthy inhalation. All good for about 40 horsepower.

Below: The racing motorcycles of the Forties and Fifties rarely looked this good. But meticulous restoration is a tribute to the original builders. And now the bikes are even faster.

Right: Number 1k is one-third of the Three K Racing Team. Mike Tomas of Kiwi Indian owns 2k, and 3k belongs to Ed Kretz, Jr. The threesome presents a forceful appearance at vintage racing events.

1940 Sport Scout
Owner – Tom Hensley
Highland Park, California
Restored by Steve Huntzinger

Right: The skirted fenders of 1940 created a backlash, resulting in "bobbers" with shorter fenders at both ends. The full bob featured stubby, unskirted fenders.

1940 Sport Scout
Owner/restorer – Marv Baker
Vallejo, Callifornia

Above: With its dual fishtail exhaust pipes and high bars, this is a genuine alley racer of the Forties. Except for the Volkswagen generator.

1940 Sport Scout
Owner/restorer – Bob Shirey
Sacramento, California

Above: "I was in that race too. Would'a finished first but, Throttle stuck, Chain broke, Plug fouled, Bottle fatigue, Bit by snake, Hungry, Sleepy, etc." Business card of Bob "Last Place" Shirey.

Above: Hensley's hauler has been upgraded with contemporary suspension components, and a steering damper to subdue headshake at high speeds on the long tracks.

Left: Dirt-track tires have changed little over the years, nor have dirt-track surfaces. Wheels, on the other hand, are both lighter and stronger.

SPORT SCOUTS (1940-48)

Indian and Harley-Davidson followed similar paths of motorcycle development, although Milwaukee did most of the following. Neither company was keen to design and build completely new models with any regularity, a high-risk proposition even in markets more stable than motorcycling. So American motorcycles developed in a modular fashion; engines had first priority, then frames, suspension, brakes and so forth. Components were fashioned piecemeal. No one could afford to throw out the old designs and start with a clean sheet of paper.

Economy of manufacture was essential to survival, but it also ensured that American motorcycles would remain on the road well beyond their natural service lives. Given their incremental

Below: Bobbers began to proliferate shortly after World War II. The trend was toward lighter, sportier motorcycles that emulated the stripped versions on the racetracks.

1940 Sport Scout
Owner/restorer – Bob Stark
Perris, California

development, and broad interchangeability of components, Indians and Harleys became the Tinkertoys and Legos of motorcycling.

Some purists might argue that Robin Markey's green Scout hybrid is an affront to the true spirit of mix-and-match motorcycles. But as an expert restorer of traditional classic bikes, he wouldn't care. Markey calls it The Toy.

The engine, originally a big-base Sport Scout, has been extensively modified for optimum power. (Robin won't publish his trade secrets.) The oil pump is an earlier cast-iron unit. The main frame section is 1940 Sport Scout, while the rear section is 1937 tubing. A 1949 Scout provided the front fork assembly and fender, with the bobbed rear mudguard derived from a '36 Sport Scout. A 640 military model donated the chain guard.

Markey cut down the Sport Scout fuel/oil tanks, and fabricated the exhaust pipes and battery box. The saddle, pillion and taillight are all Bates items, and the handlebar and risers are from Flanders. For running gear and controls, Robin dug into the Honda parts bin. (His father, Bob, is a long-time Indian and Honda dealer.) A 1965 Honda 160 provided the front wheel and brake, while the rear hoop and double-leading-shoe stopper are from a 1966 Super Hawk. The brake pedal, shift lever, footpegs and clutch lever are also Honda CB77.

Knowing his bitsa would ruffle the war bonnets of Indian traditionalists, Markey went the whole way and painted it a metallic green used on the Honda del Sol cars. Absolutely outrageous; but after all, it's his toy.

Above: A handful of big-base Sport Scouts were built before the war. The bike was developed to deal with threat of Harley-Davidson's 750cc racer.

1948 Big-base Scout
Owner/restorer – Mike Parti
North Hollywood, California

Above: Rider Johnny Spiegelhoff rode one of the first big-base racers to victory in the 1947 Daytona 200. Indian then built 50 bikes to meet AMA regulations.

Above: The Indian head fender ornament appeared on the Sport Scout from 1934 through 1937.

Above: Markey's Green Meanie is not your average Indian Forty-five. Beneath the glitzy exterior beats the heart of a genuine racing engine. Sportster riders have been humiliated.

1940-71 Super Scout
Owner/creator – Robin Markey
Etters, Pennsylvania

841 (1941) AND 741 (1941)

Combat historians are fond of the military models produced by both Harley-Davidson and Indian. Curiously enough, the two most collectible models are those that never made it to the front lines: Harley's XA opposed twin and the 841 V-twin from Indian, both shaft-drive machines.

Only about 1,000 of each model were built, and both were significant engineering departures for their respective builders. The Harley was a virtual copy of the BMW boxer twin, but the Indian featured a transverse 90-degree V-twin in the style later popularized by Italian manufacturer Moto-Guzzi. Then company owner E. Paul duPont contributed some of the design and engineering for the 841.

This motorcycle was significantly different from any Indian product before or since, the only shaft-drive machine the com-pany produced and the first foot-shift model. The cylinders and

Left: The headdress tank graphic and pin striping complete the non-military transmogrification of the 841. This was the most popular design among Indian fans, and was often revived to replace the metal nameplates used after the war.

Below: Dressed in civilian garb, with skirted fenders and chromium trim, the 841 is an elegant piece.

Left: The fork developed for the military model became the basis of the post-war Chief front end. The wheels and brakes also made the transition to peacetime. The 841 never did see active duty in its army uniform.

1941 841
Owner – Dean Rigsby
Stockton, California
Restored by Ted Williams

heads were adapted from the Sport Scout, but the girder/spring/shock fork assembly was unique to the 841. This front end, in slightly narrower and longer form, was fitted to the Chief after the war. Both the Harley XA and the 841 weighed nearly 550 pounds (249kg).

A complete registry of the surviving 841s has yet to be com-piled, and some collectors have expressed doubt that the total production ever reached 1,000. Historian Harry Sucher puts the total at 1,056. Many of the remaining examples have been modified for civilian use, some using the Chief skirted fenders as the model shown here. Educated guesstimates have posted the number of complete 841s extant at between 300 and 400.

The 741, of course, was built in far greater numbers and many were shipped to allied military forces overseas. The British forces preferred the 741 for its fuel economy. Indian built some 45,000 military models between 1939 and 1944. Examples of both the 640 and 741 still turn up occasionally in European barns and warehouses.

Thousands of military Harleys and Indians were sold off as sur-plus in 1944, and most were converted to civilian configuration. Springfield also found itself the owner of a huge stockpile of spare parts when the war ended, which were also sold in lots at bargain prices. This sizeable inventory, later complemented by the parts left over at the end in 1953, kept Indian riders in spares for decades thereafter.

Above: Most of the engine components derived from the Sport Scout, including the cylinders and heads. The 841 was Springfield's first application of a foot-shift transmission.

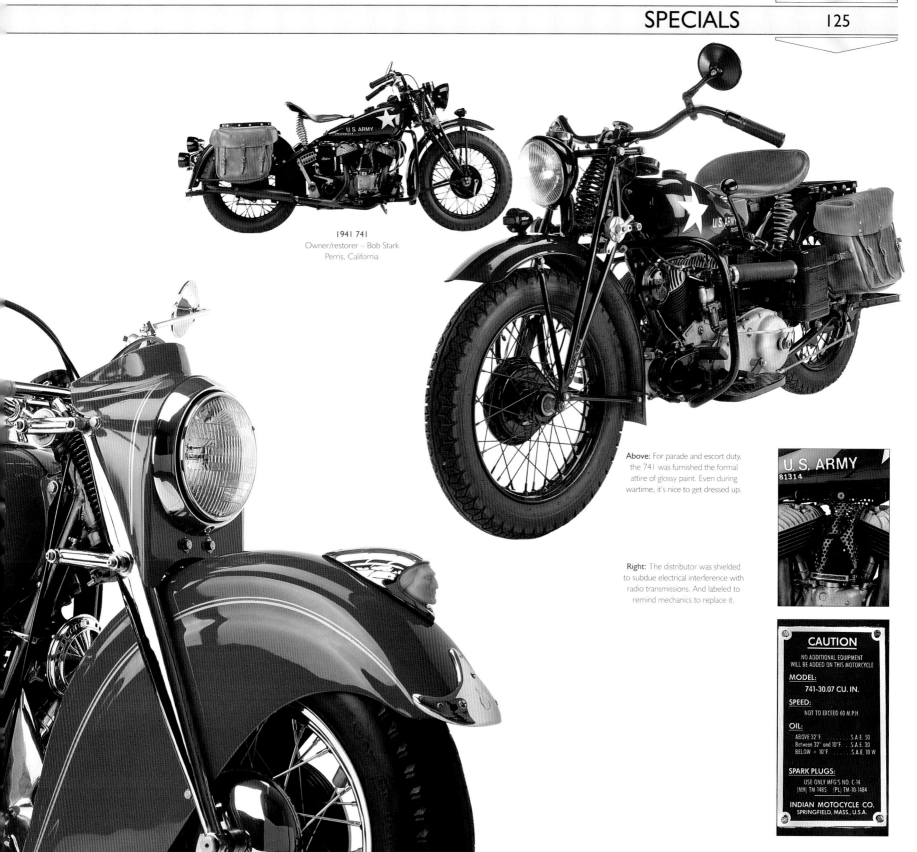

1941 741
Owner/restorer – Bob Stark
Perris, California

Above: For parade and escort duty,
the 741 was furnished the formal
attire of glossy paint. Even during
wartime, it's nice to get dressed up.

Right: The distributor was shielded
to subdue electrical interference with
radio transmissions. And labeled to
remind mechanics to replace it.

U.S. ARMY
81314

CAUTION
NO ADDITIONAL EQUIPMENT
WILL BE ADDED ON THIS MOTORCYCLE

MODEL:
741-30.07 CU. IN.

SPEED:
NOT TO EXCEED 60 M.P.H.

OIL:
ABOVE 32°F. . . . . S.A.E. 50
Between 32° and 10°F. . . S.A.E. 30
BELOW + 10°F . . . . S.A.E. 10 W

SPARK PLUGS:
USE ONLY MFG'S NO. C-14
(MM) TM-1485   (PL) TM-10-1484

INDIAN MOTOCYCLE CO.
SPRINGFIELD, MASS., U.S.A.

Above: In full military gear, the 741
would be straining its milk to reach
much more than 60mph (97km/h).
The warning probably served the
the survivability quotient of both
rider and machine.

Left: Most of the thousand-some
841s were eventually transformed
into standard machines. The design
was well suited to commercial
service, and the bike was unique
among Indians.

CHIEF (1948) AND SCOUT (1949)

In 1951, when Bob Stark first saw this Indian Chief, it was sitting a used car lot in Akron, Ohio. Although his father Charles was the local Indian dealer, young Bob could only afford a Cushman scooter at the time. And the car dealer wasn't interested in a trade-in. The price on the Chief was $450.

Charles agreed to let Bob buy the bike, when he saved up the money. About a month later, having scraped together $425, Bob went by to check on his bike as he did nearly every day. The Chief was gone. Bob was crestfallen, and more than a bit pissed off.

A year later an ad in the paper was offering a 1948 Chief for $325. Bob was the first one there, surprised to find that it was not only the same bike, but that it had only 65 more miles (105km) on the odometer than it had a year before. Bob handed over the cash, promising himself, and the Chief, that after their long-unrequited relationship he would never sell the motorcycle.

Forty-six years later the odometer has turned from 1,825 to 232,000 miles, and the name on the registration remains the same. The Chief has gained some accessories over the years, including the tail trunk, windshield and telescopic fork. Bob has

gained a little weight as well, but together they are fat and happy.

Some folks thought Max Bubeck was crazy for riding an Indian Four in the desert for ten years. And when he switched to the 1949 Scout, and rode that for the next 20 years, they still thought he was crazy. When he finally switched to Hodaka they figured he'd gone completely round the bend. But he kept on winning.

The Scout, affectionately known as Old Blue, has been through several incarnations over the years. Max took the displacement out to 500cc early on, and later built a stout two-into-one exhaust system. In 1955 he adapted an aftermarket swingarm for Triumph, and gave Blue and himself a more comfortable ride. With six inches (15cm) of travel in front and four (10cm) in the rear, the desert rocks seemed to shrink a bit. That was the same year Bubeck's mentor, Frank Chase, won the Greenhorn Enduro with a Chief engine in an 841 frame.

In 1962, Max and Old Blue won the Greenhorn, marking one of the last major victories for Indian. Contemporary skeptics tend to think that enduros were much easier in those days, but it ain't so. Out of 170 entries, only 23 riders finished the '62 Greenhorn. Bubeck, at age 45, won it on a motorcycle many people thought was obsolete the day it came out.

1948 Chief
Owner/restorer – Bob Stark
Perris, California

Below: The tail trunk is called a Scoot Boot, originally built as a boating accessory in the Fifties. It makes a perfect suitcase/toolbox/cooler for motorcycle touring, and is one of the few examples still on the road.

Below: With fringed Chum-Me seat, rear bumpers, saddlebags and windshield, Bob's "life-timer" is ready for the open road. In the 21st century it should turn a quarter-million miles.

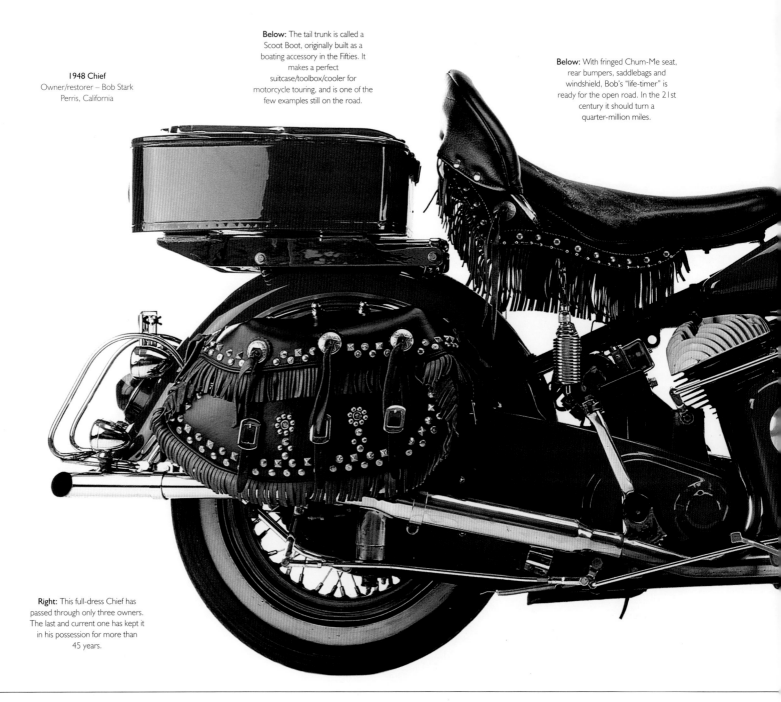

Right: This full-dress Chief has passed through only three owners. The last and current one has kept it in his possession for more than 45 years.

Below: Bubeck's pucker-bush bomber started life as a 1949 Scout and eventually grew to 500cc. A Corbin speedo is mounted on the ignition switch plate. The license plate on this original desert sled reads "TWIN JUN."

1949 Scout
Owner/modifier – Max Bubeck
Palm Springs, California

1949 Scout
Owner – Trev Deeley Museum
Vancouver, British Columbia

Above: This lightly customized 1949 Scout represents the motorcycle styling trends that took hold in the Fifties. And shows what might have been.

Above: Stark's '48 Chief has been modernized with components from the 1952 models; a telescopic fork, engine cowling and tank emblem. And more horse-pressure in the motor.

Above: The design flaws in the vertical twin were minor, and could have been resolved. But the shortcuts on sourced parts, final assembly and testing proved fatal.

PIERCE P-61 (1951), ARROW (1949) AND CHIEF (1951)

Sam Pierce became one of the enduring legends in the history of Indian motorcycles, not only for his brand loyalty, but for his inventive nature and his sense of humor. Young Sammy started as a mechanic for Al Crocker's Kansas City dealership in 1931, and after World War II he opened his own shop near Los Angeles.

Like Rollie Free, Pierce made a lifetime sport of aggravating Harley-Davidson riders, dealers and the factory. He had once raced one of the Milwaukee bikes, but after a serious crash he landed in the hospital with both legs broken. When his sponsor took the bike back and didn't bother to inquire after Sam's condition, Harley-hating became his favorite

hobby. He would later mount a display case in his shop labeled "H-D Parts Dept.," which contained seven gauges of baling wire.

Sam Pierce was a motorcycle racer, car dealer, custom car builder, machinist and racing sponsor. His most famous rider was Ed Kretz, who later took over Sam's shop in Monterey Park, California. For nearly 20 years after Indian's official demise, Pierce was building and selling Indian motorcycles. He bought the parts inventories of numerous dealerships around the country, and made several attempts to revive the production of Indians. His 1951 prototype, the American Rocket pictured here, was Pierce's first example of what he hoped would be the next Indian.

Below: Bob Stark's Starklite Indian racing team, a rag-tag bunch of volunteers, campaigns a full stable of 1949 Arrow singles. Which are faster than one might think.

Left: While the Arrow showed little success in the motorcycle market of its day, the lightweight single was a fundamentally sound machine. Agile handling is a plus on the track.

1949 Arrow
Owner/restorer – Bob Stark
Perris, California

Right: The P-61 frame and fuel tanks first saw service with the Indian 841. The taillight was, of all things, a Harley-Davidson item.

Above: The racing-style high/low exhaust system was an interesting feature. Chain adjustment was by eccentrics on the rear axle.

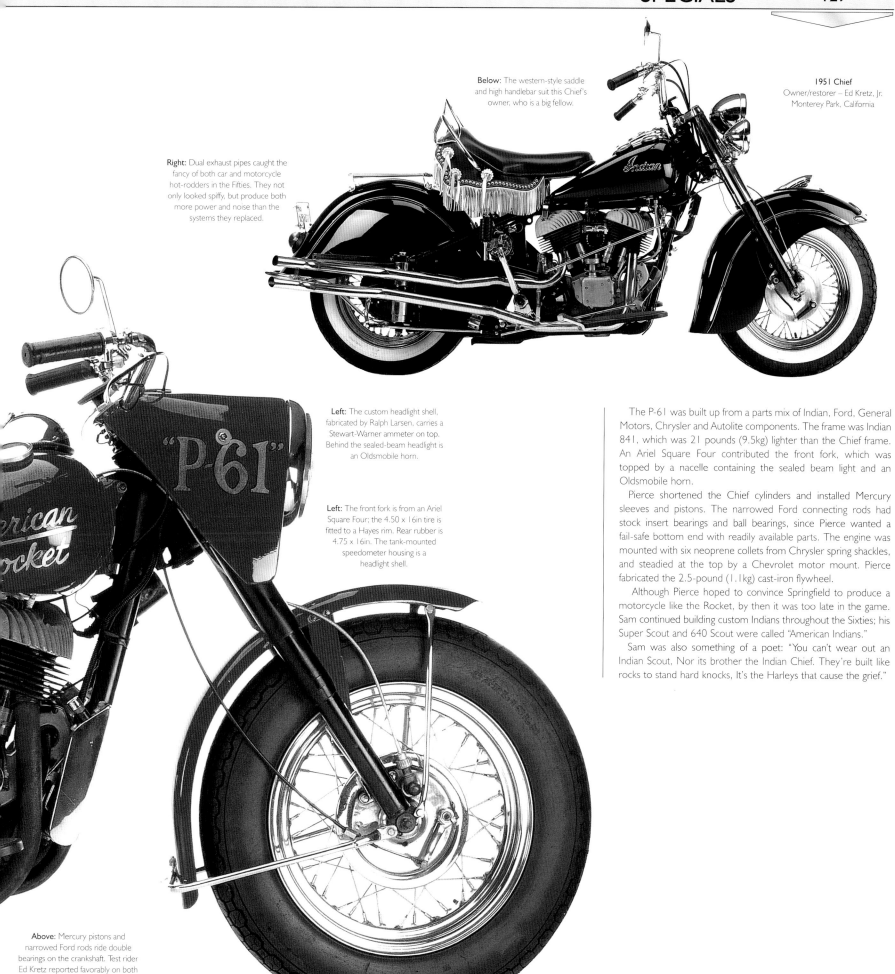

Below: The western-style saddle and high handlebar suit this Chief's owner, who is a big fellow.

Right: Dual exhaust pipes caught the fancy of both car and motorcycle hot-rodders in the Fifties. They not only looked spiffy, but produce both more power and noise than the systems they replaced.

1951 Chief
Owner/restorer – Ed Kretz, Jr.
Monterey Park, California

Left: The custom headlight shell, fabricated by Ralph Larsen, carries a Stewart-Warner ammeter on top. Behind the sealed-beam headlight is an Oldsmobile horn.

Left: The front fork is from an Ariel Square Four; the 4.50 x 16in tire is fitted to a Hayes rim. Rear rubber is 4.75 x 16in. The tank-mounted speedometer housing is a headlight shell.

The P-61 was built up from a parts mix of Indian, Ford, General Motors, Chrysler and Autolite components. The frame was Indian 841, which was 21 pounds (9.5kg) lighter than the Chief frame. An Ariel Square Four contributed the front fork, which was topped by a nacelle containing the sealed beam light and an Oldsmobile horn.

Pierce shortened the Chief cylinders and installed Mercury sleeves and pistons. The narrowed Ford connecting rods had stock insert bearings and ball bearings, since Pierce wanted a fail-safe bottom end with readily available parts. The engine was mounted with six neoprene collets from Chrysler spring shackles, and steadied at the top by a Chevrolet motor mount. Pierce fabricated the 2.5-pound (1.1kg) cast-iron flywheel.

Although Pierce hoped to convince Springfield to produce a motorcycle like the Rocket, by then it was too late in the game. Sam continued building custom Indians throughout the Sixties; his Super Scout and 640 Scout were called "American Indians."

Sam was also something of a poet: "You can't wear out an Indian Scout, Nor its brother the Indian Chief. They're built like rocks to stand hard knocks, It's the Harleys that cause the grief."

Above: Mercury pistons and narrowed Ford rods ride double bearings on the crankshaft. Test rider Ed Kretz reported favorably on both the power and handling of the P-61.

1951 Pierce P-61
Owner – Louis Fisher
Monrovia, California

ROYAL ENFIELD INDIANS (1963-64)

The British chapter in Indian history is not a favorite among traditional fans of the Springfield marque. Many enthusiasts held the consensus that Brockhouse Engineering Ltd. was not interested in assisting with Indian's survival, but merely in gaining a delearship network and a foothold in the American market.

As a result, the British Royal Enfields that arrived with Indian badges were generally dismissed by those faithful to the long-standing traditions of motorcycles in the Springfield manner. Some of the true believers even managed to take the British invasion as a

Below: This 250 is a sporty version of the motorcycle below. With smaller fenders, no electrics and a 5-speed transmission, it scoots.

Left: Despite being cute and nimble, the Royal Enfield lightweights captured little of the American imagination. Their best seller was the 750cc Interceptor twin, which was introduced in 1962.

1964 Royal Enfield 250
Owner/restorer – Bob Stark
Perris, California

Right: By the Sixties the Royal Enfields were marketed under their own name. These singles carry Indian tank badges just out of nostalgia.

Right: The relationship between Indian and Royal Enfield lasted five years, from 1954 to 1959. The transition from American to British was not smooth.

1963 Royal Enfield 250
Owner – Bob Stark
Perris, California

personal affront, even though the business decisions were simply matters of economics.

The Royal Enfield arrangement lasted from 1954 through 1959, although some dealers would attach Indian nameplates to British models that came in later years. The Enfield slogan, "Made Like a Gun," seemed to have little in the way of persuasive effect on American buyers. The motorcycles had little in common with Indian styling or engineering, and were lightweights by comparison.

In terms of racing, Enfield was at a disadvantage against the machines from Norton, Triumph, BSA and Matchless, which by this time had been firmly established in American competition.

There were exceptions, of course, such as the Royal Enfield 500cc single tuned by Shell Thuet and ridden by Eliot Schultz on the Ascot half-mile dirt-track. But the machines were not destined to achieve any significant results on the national racing calendar.

By 1962, the Royal Enfield vertical twin had grown to 750cc and was named the Interceptor. It would achieve the company's best results in the stateside market, but was still overshadowed by the other British makes. Financial difficulties finally overtook the company in 1968 and production was suspended.

Ironically, the Enfield badge did survive as an Indian motorcycle, meaning as made in India. The 500cc Enfield Bullet, basically the same engine used in the Americanized Woodsman and Westerner over 40 years ago, is still manufactured in Madras, India. The pushrod single, rated at 22 horsepower, has a top speed of about 80mph (129km/h). The machine was developed from the 350cc version, the standard motorcycle of the Indian armed forces.

Left: During their period as Indian-badged machines, the Royal Enfields carried Americanized model names. The standard road version of the 250 was called the Hounds Arrow. The lighter sport model (upper left) was known as the Fire Arrow.

Below: American riders did discover one thing with the advent of British machines; that motorcycles could actually have good brakes.

Above: By this time the movement to overhead-valve engines with foot-shift and hand-clutch was well underway. The British influence was pervasive for the next decade.

MUNRO SPECIAL (1920-67)

Bert Munro was a man on a mission. On top of that, he was from New Zealand. No one has ever come up with a rational explanation for Bert's desire to make a 1920 Indian go 200 miles an hour (322km/h). But he must have had one that satisfied himself.

Munro found a helpmate in Sam Pierce, who provided the Kiwi speed demon with technical assistance and a place to build his streamliner. Bert began his project back in the 1920s, when the top speed of his then new 600cc Scout was 54mph (87km/h). He resolved to make the motorcycle faster, and every year thereafter he managed to bump the velocity a bit. In the 1960s, a grandfather by then, Bert announced to friends and family that he was going to run the bike at the Bonneville salt flats in Utah.

In 1962 the Scout engine had grown to 850cc, was fitted with overhead valves, and clocked 162mph (261km/h) at Bonneville. The following year a broken connecting rod stymied the attempt, but in 1964 Munro ran his homemade rocket up to 184mph (296km/h). By 1966 he had enlarged the engine to 920cc, but the top speed dropped to 168 (270km/h). Once again Bert rebuilt the engine, with displacement up to 950cc.

Munro's streamliner became a monument to his dedication and persistence. The special pistons were sand-cast, in the sand of a New Zealand beach. Bert designed the four-cam valve system and the 17-plate clutch. The connecting rods were carved from the axle of a Caterpillar tractor.

At Bonneville Speed Week, in 1967, Bert Munro established the class record with a two-way average of 183.58mph (295.44km/h). And in his qualifying run he set the record for the fastest speed ever recorded with an Indian, 190.07mph (305.88km/h). The streamliner was then retired.

Dean Hensley, moto-historian and avid Indian enthusiast, acquired the machine some years later. His friend Steve Huntzinger restored the streamliner to the condition exhibited here, and it was displayed on a platform in Dean's dining room. There it remains today, now in the care of Dean's brother Tom.

As a strong supporter of vintage motorcycling, Dean Hensley's contagious enthusiasm made him a popular figure throughout the sporting community. Unfortunately, Dean died in a 1992 traffic accident. Hundreds of friends were on hand for his funeral, which included the full-throttle salute of 21 Indian motorcycles at his graveside. The funeral service was followed by an old-fashioned wake, an event of which, all in attendance agreed, Dean would have fully approved.

Above: A four-cam system of Munro's own design operated the overhead valves. The designer/builder also made his own sand-cast pistons, in the sand of a New Zealand beach.

Right: With half its aerodynamic shell removed, the Munro Special is revealed as compact assemblage of old and new bits and pieces. The streamliner represents more than forty years of patient development.

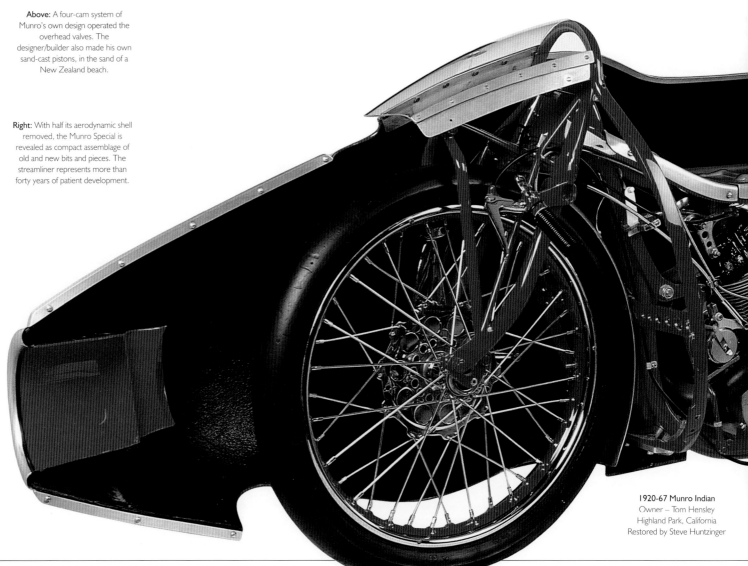

1920-67 Munro Indian
Owner – Tom Hensley
Highland Park, California
Restored by Steve Huntzinger

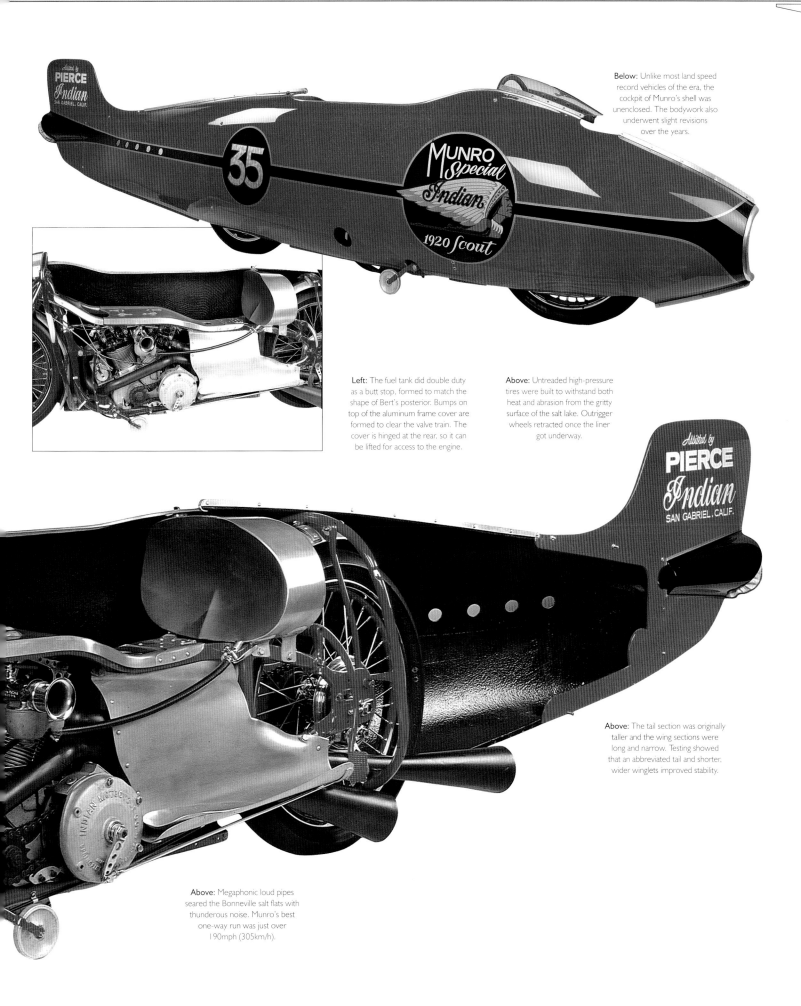

Below: Unlike most land speed record vehicles of the era, the cockpit of Munro's shell was unenclosed. The bodywork also underwent slight revisions over the years.

Left: The fuel tank did double duty as a butt stop, formed to match the shape of Bert's posterior. Bumps on top of the aluminum frame cover are formed to clear the valve train. The cover is hinged at the rear, so it can be lifted for access to the engine.

Above: Untreaded high-pressure tires were built to withstand both heat and abrasion from the gritty surface of the salt lake. Outrigger wheels retracted once the liner got underway.

Above: The tail section was originally taller and the wing sections were long and narrow. Testing showed that an abbreviated tail and shorter, wider winglets improved stability.

Above: Megaphonic loud pipes seared the Bonneville salt flats with thunderous noise. Munro's best one-way run was just over 190mph (305km/h).

APACHE (1957), TRAILBLAZER (1958) AND BRAVE (1953)

1957 APACHE

SPECIFICATIONS

ENGINE/DRIVETRAIN
Engine: OHV vertical twin
Displacement: 42ci (693cc)
Bore & stroke: 2.75 x 3.54in (70 x 90mm)
Horsepower: 43
Carburetor: Amal
Transmission: 4-speed
Primary drive: Chain
Final drive: Chain
Brakes: F & R. Drum
Battery: 6-volt
Ignition: Coil/points

CHASSIS/SUSPENSION
Frame: Steel, double downtube
Suspension: F. Telescopic forks. R. Hydraulic shocks
Wheelbase: 54in (137.2cm)
Weight: 390lb (177kg)
Fuel capacity: 3.5gal (13.25lit)
Oil capacity: 2qts (1.89lit)
Tires: F. 3.50 x 19in. R. 4.00 x 18in
Top speed: 110mph (177km/h)
Color: Fire red
Number imported: 457
Price: $995

American motorcycling had changed markedly after World War II. The trickle of British and European machines before the war grew in a few years to a steady flow. The lighter overhead-valve British singles were winning races long the province of Indian and Harley-Davidson, and were soon followed by even more road-worthy vertical twins. Many Indian dealers switched to BSA, Triumph, Ariel and Velocette in the early Fifties.

With the absence of the Indian Sport Scout, and the generally disappointing performance of the Harley-Davidson K model, the British middleweights found an eager audience among American riders. With the Warrior discontinued in 1952, leftover vertical twin engines were used in the Patrol model, a 3-wheeler hybrid of the Warrior and old Dispatch Tow. The Patrol, designed to retain some of Indian's police market, featured electric start and hydraulic brakes. The British-made Brave was last offered in 1953, but had little impact on the market in the USA or England.

In the final years, the Chief and Warrior shared showroom space with machines by Royal Enfield, AJS, Matchless, Norton and Vincent. The US distribution rights to most of the British motor-cycles were subsequently sold to other companies. In 1954, Indian dealers were supplied with Royal Enfield Meteor 700 twins and Ensign 150 singles. Even though the dealers and most riders had known of Springfield's financial problems for some time, the final suspension of production still came as a shock. After 52 years in business, it just didn't seem possible. But with each economic shift – the depression, World War II, Korea – and accompanying changes of management, Indian had steadily lost ground.

The Titeflex Corporation, a subsidiary of early Indian investor the Atlas Company, had sold nearly all the old Springfield tooling and parts, most of which were eventually purchased by Chicago dealer Ed Nichols. The parts supply was substantial, and was the

source for many diehard Indian dealers for years thereafter. A number of Indian shop owners made the ultimate sacrifice and switched to Harley-Davidson, while others banked on the most promising British makes of Triumph or BSA. In the late Fifties, some dealers would sign on with a fledgling Japanese company named Honda.

For 1955 the Royal Enfields were re-badged as Indians and given Americanized names. The 250cc Clipper became the Fire Arrow, the 500cc Bullet single was called the Woodsman and the 500cc twin the Tomahawk. The 700cc Meteor was offered as the Trailblazer or sportier Apache, and later as the Chief.

Above: The Apache was the sport version of the Royal Enfield twin, known in England as the Super Meteor 700.

Right: The Royal Enfield machines from Great Britain became Indian's primary models in 1955. The Indian Sales group also acted as the American distributor for Norton, Matchless, AJS and Vincent motorcycles.

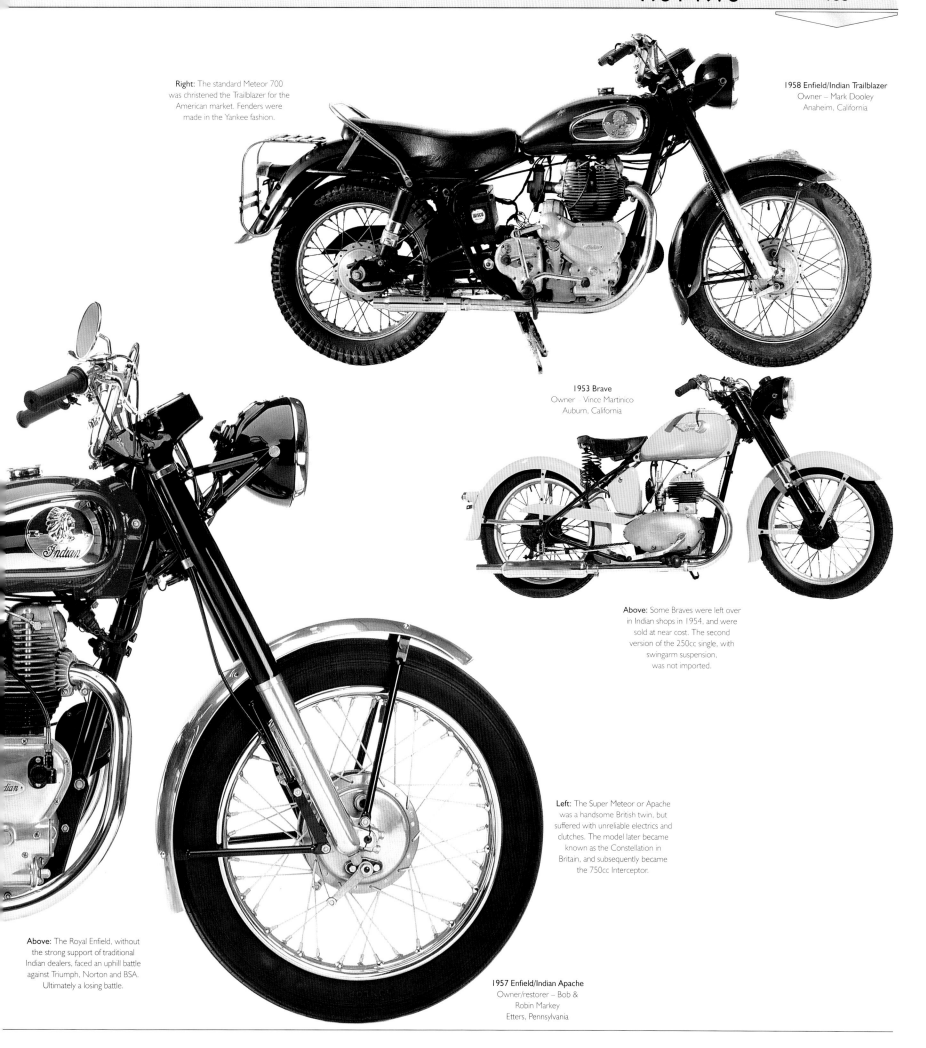

Right: The standard Meteor 700 was christened the Trailblazer for the American market. Fenders were made in the Yankee fashion.

1958 Enfield/Indian Trailblazer
Owner – Mark Dooley
Anaheim, California

1953 Brave
Owner – Vince Martinico
Auburn, California

Above: Some Braves were left over in Indian shops in 1954, and were sold at near cost. The second version of the 250cc single, with swingarm suspension, was not imported.

Left: The Super Meteor or Apache was a handsome British twin, but suffered with unreliable electrics and clutches. The model later became known as the Constellation in Britain, and subsequently became the 750cc Interceptor.

Above: The Royal Enfield, without the strong support of traditional Indian dealers, faced an uphill battle against Triumph, Norton and BSA. Ultimately a losing battle.

1957 Enfield/Indian Apache
Owner/restorer – Bob & Robin Markey
Etters, Pennsylvania

1959 CHIEF

SPECIFICATIONS
ENGINE/DRIVETRAIN
Engine: OHV vertical twin
Displacement: 42ci (693cc)
Bore & stroke: 2.75 x 3.54in
(70 x 90mm)
Horsepower: 43
Carburetor: Amal
Transmission: 4-speed
Primary drive: Chain
Final drive: Chain
Brakes: F & R. Drum
Battery: 6-volt
Ignition: Coil/points

CHASSIS/SUSPENSION
Frame: Steel, single downtube
Suspension: F. Telescopic forks.
R. Hydraulic shocks
Wheelbase: 60in (152.4cm)
Weight: 460lb (209kg)
Fuel capacity: 5gal (18.9lit)
Oil capacity: 2qts (1.9lit)
Tires: 5.00 x 16in
Top speed: 110mph (177km/h)
Colors: Red, black
Number built: Approx. 400
Price: $995

Above: Apparently the New York City Police Department was convinced that Royal Enfield Indians were suitable for law enforcement.

Right: In a last-ditch attempt to Americanize the Royal Enfield twin, the Brockhouse bunch introduced the new Chief in 1959. And with its skirted fenders and 5.00 x 16in tires, the British bike did indeed resemble a Yankee cruiser.

CHIEF (1959) AND POLICE CHIEF (1959)

While the V-twin had for 40 years been the Standard American Motorcycle (Uncle SAM), European machines developed differently. Throughout those decades there were always some dozen British and/or European builders working with singles and twins in other configurations; vertical, horizontal, inline and transverse opposed. And since racing in Europe meant road-racing, the considerations of weight, horsepower, suspension and handling were important concerns. American dirt-track, by comparison, was well suited to the tradition of the torque-strong V-twin with an unsprung rear wheel.

Most of the imports were equipped with overhead-valve engines, hand-operated clutches and foot-shift gearboxes. The motorcycles were generally lighter, easier to ride and handled better than their American counterparts. None of which guaranteed them great success in the USA, but their differences surely offered American riders more choices than they had ever known. And while many Indian enthusiasts would have liked to see their cherished V-twins remain on the menu, as many others were pleased to finally see a selection of something completely different.

In the absence of a home-built model, Indian had lost most of its police motorcycle business to Harley-Davidson. The attempt to regain a measure of the law enforcement market, and to win back some of the disaffected civilians, created the Royal Enfield Chief. The Americanized version of the Meteor featured 5.00 x 16in tires, larger and more skirted fenders and Stewart-Warner speedometers.

But the Royal Enfields, Americanized or not, faced an uphill battle against the established names of Triumph and BSA. Indian dealers experienced problems with the ignition systems and clutches on the British twins, and most were not unhappy when the Enfield line was discontinued a year later.

In the fall of 1959, the Indian Sales Company was sold to Britain's Associated Motor Cycles, Ltd., which owned AJS and Matchless. So, for 1960, the few remaining Indian dealers were supplied with Matchless motorcycles. The AMC machines were advertised as Matchless-Indians, and were named the Apache (650cc twin), Westerner (500cc single) and Arrow (250cc single), but carried no Indian identification on the tanks. Some showrooms also included leftover Royal Enfield Chiefs and an occasional Matchless G-50 roadracer.

This arrangement lasted three years, until AMC was acquired by Norton-Matchless, and Berliner Motor Corporation became the US Matchless distributor. The Indian name lapsed for a few years, until Floyd Clymer attempted to revive it.

Below: With its dual fishtail pipes and stylish bumpers, the police model was styling in 1959.

Right: The Enfield Chief was a stretched version of the Meteor 700 twin. A longer swingarm stretched the wheelbase to 60 inches (152.4cm). Larger wheels, tires, fenders and accessories added some 60 pounds (27kg) to the weight.

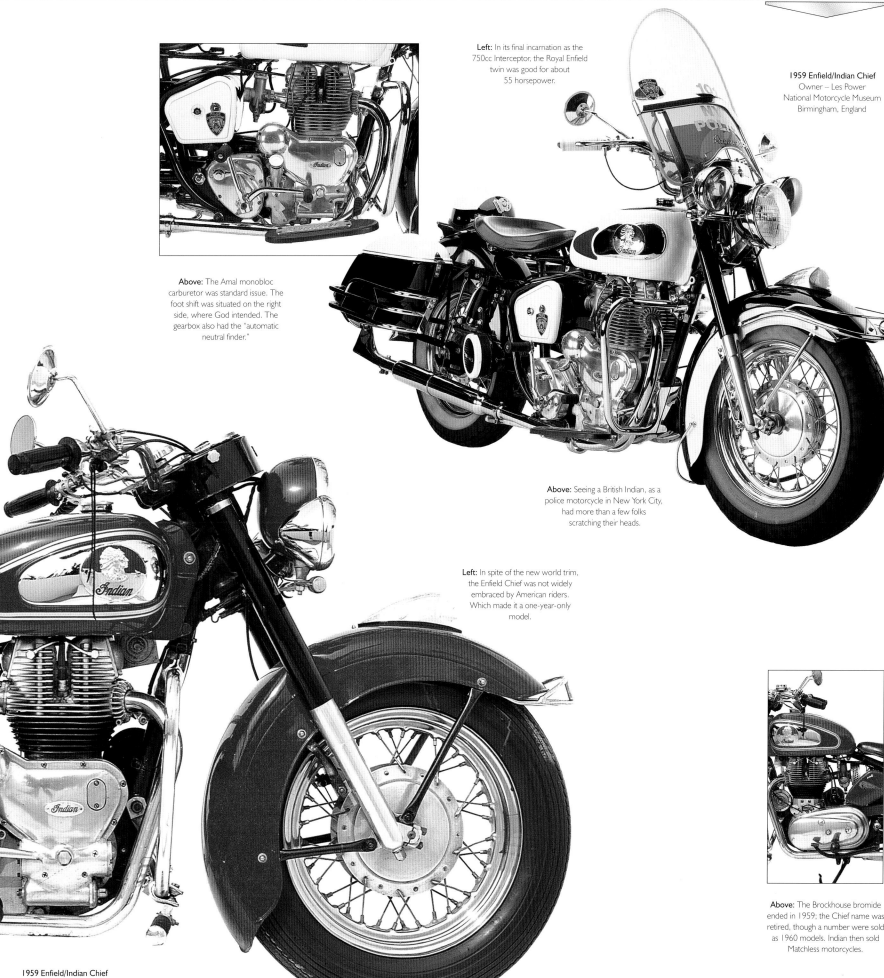

Left: In its final incarnation as the 750cc Interceptor, the Royal Enfield twin was good for about 55 horsepower.

1959 Enfield/Indian Chief
Owner – Les Power
National Motorcycle Museum
Birmingham, England

Above: The Amal monobloc carburetor was standard issue. The foot shift was situated on the right side, where God intended. The gearbox also had the "automatic neutral finder."

Above: Seeing a British Indian, as a police motorcycle in New York City, had more than a few folks scratching their heads.

Left: In spite of the new world trim, the Enfield Chief was not widely embraced by American riders. Which made it a one-year-only model.

Above: The Brockhouse bromide ended in 1959; the Chief name was retired, though a number were sold as 1960 models. Indian then sold Matchless motorcycles.

1959 Enfield/Indian Chief
Owner – George Gray
Los Angeles, California

MINI-MINI (1969), PAPOOSE (1967) AND JUNIOR CROSS (1971)

1969 MINI-MINI

SPECIFICATIONS
ENGINE/DRIVETRAIN
Engine: Two-stroke single
Displacement: 3ci (47.6cc)
Bore & stroke: 1.5 x 1.65in (38 x 42mm)
Horsepower: 1.3
Carburetor: Dell'orto
Transmission: Centrifugal clutch
Primary drive: Helical gear
Final drive: Chain
Brakes: F & R. Drum
Ignition: Magneto/points

CHASSIS/SUSPENSION
Frame: Steel backbone
Suspension: F. Telescopic forks. R. Hydraulic shocks
Wheelbase: 30.5in (77.5cm)
Weight: 70lb (32kg)
Fuel/oil capacity: 0.5gal (1.9lit)
Tires: 2.25 x 8in
Top speed: 12mph (19km/h)
Colors: Silver, red, blue
Number imported: 457
Price: $185

The first version of the Papoose was manufactured by Brockhouse Engineering in England, and called the Corgi. This was a gas-engined mini-scooter with folding handlebars, designed to be easily transported in the trunk of a car. The Papoose, priced at $260, failed to generate much interest in the United States.

The second generation Papooses (gas and electric versions) were imported from Italy by Floyd Clymer, former Indian racer,

dealer, entrepreneur, publisher and whatever took his fancy. Only one prototype of the battery-powered Papoose was ever built, the machine shown here that is now owned by Bob Stark of Perris, California.

The more conventional Papoose was powered by a 50cc Minarelli 2-stroke with a 4-speed transmission. It was fairly beefy for a mini-bike – 45-inch (114cm) wheelbase, 130 pounds (59kg)

1967 Indian Electracycle
Owner – Bob Stark
Perris, California

Left: One of Floyd Clymer's projects was the battery-powered version of the Papoose. Only one prototype was made and this is it.

Right: The Mini-Mini was the base model in Floyd Clymer's ambitious roster of imported motorcycles. In 1969 he sold his interest in the German Münch enterprise to concentrate on the mini-bike market.

Right: The Indian Mini-Mini was powered by a 50cc Minarelli two-stroke. The horsepower rating was 1.3 at 5000rpm. Clymer also sold a stronger 50cc engine (5hp at 7000 rpm) for those who wanted to build their own mini-bike.

1969 Mini-Mini
Owner – Bob Stark
Perris, California

Left: The Junior Cross represented an international collaboration between American, Italian and Czechoslovakian interests. The frame and running gear came from Italy, with a Jawa/CZ 50cc engine. Floyd Clymer was the American marketing maven.

Above: Quite a few youngsters were introduced to the thrills of motocross competition by the Indian Junior Cross. Second generation designs included 100, 125 and 175cc engines.

1971 Junior Cross
Owner – Bob Stark
Perris, California

Left: The Mini-Mini, also known as the Bambino, was just as cute as a bug. And about the same size. It became a popular pit bike among portly fellows, who appeared to be motoring about on a roller skate.

Left: The most popular seller during the Clymer declension, the Mini-Mini became the first motorized ride for hundreds of tiny tykes. Many of those children went on to ride real motorcycles, which, of course, was Floyd's plan.

– and sold for $345. The machines were constructed by the Italian company Italjet.

The Bambino "Mini-Mini" was a miniature 75-pound (34kg) machine for tiny tykes, with a 50cc engine and automatic clutch. The Bambino was also available with a sidecar. Clymer also offered an entry-level dirt bike for young motocross enthusiasts called the Boy Racer. The 100-pound (45kg) competition bike had a 50cc engine, 3-speed transmision and 20-inch wheels. The bike was powered by a CZ engine from Czechoslovakia. This model was later replaced by the Junior Cross with an Italian engine and 4-speed gearbox.

Floyd Clymer's grand plan was to revive the Indian Scout. The 750cc, 50-degree side-valve V-twin was to be built in Germany in collaboration with constructor Friedl Münch. The motorcycles were to be assembled in Italy using mostly Italian components. Ambitious plans were made for racing and dirt-track models, but only one prototype of the road version was produced in 1967.

In the October, 1969 issue of *Cycle Guide* magazine, Clymer bought a full-page ad soliciting dealers to "CASH IN on the magic word 'INDIAN,' the oldest name in U.S. motorcycling. Just display INDIAN models on your floor against any other make. Then and only then will you get public reaction." The ad boasted that numerous car dealers had joined the Indian tribe, and that Indianapolis 500 winner Mario Andretti and his two sons (ages 5 and 7) were owners of Indian mini bikes.

Indian fans were offended by Clymer's use of the traditional Indian logo, and cursed him as a blatant opportunist, poltroon, buffoon, snake oil salesman, toady and other pejoratives not fit for print in a library book.

1969 VELO

SPECIFICATIONS
ENGINE/DRIVETRAIN
Engine: OHV single
Displacement: 30ci (499cc)
Bore & stroke: 3.38 x 3.38in (86 x 86mm)
Horsepower: 37/41
Carburetor: Amal
Transmission: 4-speed
Primary drive: Chain
Final drive: Chain
Brakes: F & R. Drum
Battery: 12-volt
Ignition: Magneto

CHASSIS/SUSPENSION
Frame: Steel, double downtube
Suspension: F. Telescopic fork. R. Hydraulic shocks
Wheelbase: 56in (142.2cm)
Weight: 365lb (166kg)
Fuel capacity: 5.1gal (19.7lit)
Oil capacity: 2.4qts (2.27lit)
Tires: F. 3.00 x 18in. R. 4.00 x 18in
Top speed: 105mph (169km/h)
Colors: Bronze/white, black/blue, black/purple
Number imported: Approx. 200
Price: $1,450 (Venom), $1,550 (Thruxton)

VELO 500 (1969), SE 70 (1973) AND "FOUR" (1978)

Probably the best genuine motorcycle of Floyd Clymer's five-year chapter as the so-called Indian Motorcycle Company, was the Indian 500 Roadster. This was a British/Italian *bitsa*, but they were some of the best bits available at the time. The engine was from the British Veloce Company, which had built Velocette motorcycles for 65 years. The firm had pioneered overhead-cam engines and foot-shift, and in the Sixties their Venom and Thruxton models were widely regarded as the finest 500cc overhead-valve road machines ever built.

Clymer offered the Roadster with either Venom (37hp) or Thruxton (41hp) engine in an Italian Tartarini frame. The overhead-valve 500 was of squared displacement (equal bore and stroke) with a 4-speed transmission. Some models had a Marzocchi fork, some a Ceriani, with 18-inch Borrani aluminum rims and a twin leading shoe Grimeca front brake. Campagnola twin front discs were available as an option. Ready for the road, the motorcycle weighed 365 pounds (166kg).

sion, and the street-legal machine was rather more stout than the earlier Italian bikes.

Within three years Japanese machines dominated the market, and the mid-Sixties boom in motorcycle sales was over. Newman bowed out and the Indian trademark reverted to a bank, which assigned it to a California company called American Moped Associates. This firm imported a 50cc four-stroke moped from Taiwan, with the unfortunate name of Indian Four.

That project expired in 1981, and the Indian trademark was ostensibly abandoned. The famous mark has been reclaimed several times since, but without the appearance of new Indian motorcycles. The real Indians were gone years earlier, when, as Oscar Hedstrom would say, up to his 90th year, "Indian stopped winning races."

1969 Indian Velo
Owner – National Motorcycle Museum
Birmingham, England

A handful of these chassis were also fitted with both Royal Enfield and Norton 750cc twin engines, but few reached the U.S. Unfortunately this experiment in multi-national badge engineering came too late in the game for all concerned. The British motorcycle industry was approaching extinction and the Japanese manufacturers had rewritten the rules worldwide. Floyd Clymer died in 1970 and the Veloce Company expired the following year.

The marketing rights were next secured by Alan Newman, a Los Angeles lawyer, who liquidated Floyd Clymer's inventory and settled the debt with the British financial backers. With British engines no longer available, and the Italjet source growing more expensive, Newman designed the SE 70 and arranged for the assembly of Indian mini-bikes using Italian engines in a chassis built in Taiwan. The 70cc Minarelli powerplant had a 4-speed transmis-

Above: The Venom Thruxton engine first appeared in 1965, and was a genuine 100mph (161km/h) single. Velocette had a strong racing history.

1978 Four-Stroke
Owner – Bob Stark
Perris, California

Right: The so-called Indian "Four" of 1978 was a 50cc four-stroke single made in China. American Moped Associates imported these machines until 1981. The bikes fared poorly against the Japanese and Italian models, which both had well established dealer networks.

1973 SE 70
Owner – Bob Stark
Perris, California

Left: The SE 70 was one of the first machines produced by the reformed Indian Motorcycle Company after the death of Floyd Clymer. The Italian 70cc engine was rated at 8 horsepower and had a 4-speed transmission. Later models had an optional 6-speed.

Above: A motocross version of the 70, which was about 30 pounds (14kg) lighter, was also offered by the new company. Control of the Taiwan factory was assumed by Italjet in 1976.

Above: The overhead-valve Velocette engine was one of the smoothest running singles ever built. Riders on Venom Thruxtons finished 1-2 in the 1967 Isle of Man 500cc production race.

Above: Nearly 50 pounds (23kg) lighter than a Velocette Thruxton, the Indian Velo was a harmonious blend of British motorwork and Italian running gear.

Left: Veloce, Ltd. of Birmingham was in business from 1904 to 1971. In addition to overhead cams and positive-stop foot shift, the company pioneered hydraulic rear suspension. Among other records, a Velocette was the first to achieve a 100mph (161km/h) average for 24 hours.

1999 CHIEF

SPECIFICATIONS
Engine/Drivetrain
Engine: 45° OHV V-twin
Displacement: 88ci (1442cc)
Bore & stroke: 3.625 x
4.25in (92 x 108mm)
Compression ratio: 9.4:1
Horsepower: 65
Carburetor: S&S
Transmission: 5-speed
Clutch: Dry
Primary drive: Belt
Final drive: Belt
Brakes: F & R. Disc
Battery: 12-volt
Ignition: Electronic

CHASSIS/SUSPENSION
Frame: Steel cradle, single
downtube
Suspension: F. Showa fork. R.
Progress Suspension shock
Wheelbase: 69in (175cm)
Weight: 650lb (295kg) dry
Fuel capacity: 5gal (18.9lit)
Oil capacity: 3qts (2.84lit)
Tires: 130/90-16
Top speed: 115mph
(185km/h)
Colors: Black, black/gray,
black/cream, red, red/black,
red/cream, maroon/cream, yel-
low/cream, medium metallic
blue/gray, dark metallic
blue/gray, medium metallic
red/black, medium metallic
red/black, dark metallic red/gray
Number built: 1,100
Price: $23,995

CHIEF (1999/2000)

The Indian name receded from the public platform in the early 1980s, though a handful of enterprising salesfolk marketed clothing and accessories under the original logo. American and international trademarks and copyrights were disputed, and sometimes litigated, but never finally resolved.

This situation prevailed for ten years, until the number of players and the dollar amounts reached more serious proportions, and several independent entrepreneurs announced plans to build a new Indian motorcycle. One reached the running prototype phase, but these projects all succumbed to varied mixes of financial, legal and personal problems, and set the stage for a binding court decision on the Indian imprint.

By the late 1990s the contest had narrowed to a Canadian group with some marketing rights and the California Motorcycle Company (CMC). The Gilroy, California, company subsequently bought out the Canadians, and manufacture of the modern Indian motorcycle was underway. As a well-established builder of custom Harley-style V-twins, CMC was positioned with existing tooling, parts and suppliers. Using the 88-cubic inch (1442cc) S&S 45° twin, a number of proprietary components and new Indian body work, the 1999 Chief was on the road.

The S&S engine featured belt primary and final drive, a dry clutch and 5-speed constant-mesh gearbox. At 650 pounds (295kg), the Chief was solidly in Harley territory, but the long-stroke V-twin developed sufficient urge to get it down the road in reasonable haste. Four-piston caliper disc brakes were fitted front and rear on

16-inch chrome spoked wheels. The front fork was from Showa and a Progress Suspension gas shock damped the rear wheel action.

Only 1,100 of the first Limited Edition Chief were built for 1999, and CMC announced that plans for a new engine were in the works. The 2000 model year showed no changes in the engine or running gear on the Chief, but the accessory roster expanded with windshields, chromed shocks and optional cast alloy wheels.

Solid blue fell from the color menu for 2000, leaving red and black as the only solid color options. Black/cream, blue/blue, blue/gray, yellow/cream, metallic blue/cream, metallic red/black and dark metallic red/gray were the two-tone choices. Double mocha was discontinued for 2000.

The 1940s-style skirted fenders showed no signs of going out of style, since the art deco theme had recently entered its latest revival, and easily distinguished the Indian from the multitude of other cruisers on the road. And if the Indian head fender lamp or script logo on the tank didn't catch the eye, there was a new war bonnet design engraved on the teardrop aircleaner cover. The Mike Corbin saddle with rivets and fringe put the finishing touch on the first new Indian Chief in more than 45 years.

Below: Corbin seats adorned the first run of Indian Chiefs that appeared in 1999 and 2000. The new Chief was 100 pounds (45kg) heavier than the 1953 model, but also made half again as much horsepower.

Right: The fully skirted fenders would, as the originals had 60 years earlier, distinguish the Indian from every other motorcycle. The fish tail mufflers are another design cue from the old days, as are the pillion pad and scooped seat. The oversized taillight is not.

1999 Chief
Indian Motorcycle Company
Gilroy, California

2000 Chief
Indian Motorcycle Company
Gilroy, California

Below: Blue/gray was one of the most popular color combinations on the Chief.

Left: The war bonnet fender lamp was a natural carryover on the new Chief, though it has been postitioned farther forward. On the upcoming Scout model, the lamp would be fitted in the original spot.

2000 Chief
Indian Motorcycle Company
Gilroy, California

Left: Spoked chrome wheels and fat tires carry on an Indian tradition. The front disc brakes are a considerable improvement over the drum units fitted to the last of the original Indian Chiefs in 1953.

Below: One thing that distinguished the Indian Chiefs of the 1950s was the color selection from owner Paul Dupont's paint manufacturing business. The tradition of lively color schemes has been continued.

2000 Chief
Indian Motorcycle Company
Gilroy, California

2001 CHIEF

SPECIFICATIONS
Engine/Drivetrain
Engine: 45° OHV V-twin
Displacement: 88ci (1442cc)
Bore & stroke: 3.625 x
4.25in (92 x 108mm)
Compression ratio: 9.4:1
Horsepower: 65
Carburetor: 47.6mm S&S
Transmission: 5-speed
Clutch: Proprietary wet
Primary drive: Chain
Final drive: Belt
Brakes: F & R. 4-piston disc
Ignition: CDI

CHASSIS/SUSPENSION
Frame: Steel, single downtube
Suspension: F. Telescopic
41mm fork. R. Gas shock
Wheelbase: 69in (175cm)
Weight: 650lb (295kg) dry
Fuel capacity: 5.8gal (22lit)
Oil capacity: 3qts (2.84lit)
Tires: 130/90-16
Top speed: 115mph
(185km/h)
Colors: Black Hills black,
Yellowstone/Aspen white, Red
Rock/Aspen white, Nashville
green/Bonneville silver
Number built: n/a
Price: $23,995

Above: All the new Indians
are given real-world test rides
before being shipped to
dealers. Quality control gets
high priority in the new
company.

Right: Fish tails, fins and
riveted seats and bags
maintain the traditional look.
Contemporary tires, brakes,
suspension and chassis add up
to many more trouble-free
miles on the road.

CHIEF (2001)

For 2001 the Chief engine swapped its dry clutch/belt primary for a wet/chain configuration. Final drive was still handled by a belt. The model featured a new fork with cast covers and a neck lock. The rest of the running gear and chassis was unchanged, but a new instrument panel featured LED indicator lights and a VDO analog speedometer with digital odometer and trip meter. The staggered dual exhausts of the first Chief had been replaced by a two-into-one system for 2000.

Narrower stainless steel handlebars came standard, with the original bars available as an option. New color options were Black Hills black, Yellowstone/Aspen white, Red Rock/Aspen white and Nashville green/Bonneville silver.

A new fuel tank increased capacity from five to 5.8 gallons (22lit), adding about 40 miles (64km) to the cruising range. The suspension was unchanged and wheelbase remained 69 inches (175cm), but

seat height had gone from 24 to 26 inches (61 to 66cm). The Chief, priced at $23,995, was offered with a comprehensive two-year/24,000-mile warranty.

Indian asserted that all the components in the new machines were built to the most exacting standards. The frames were hand-welded and certified by a Coordinate Measuring Machine to make sure they were plumb and true. The fenders were hand-welded as well. The engines were assembled in Gilroy, each one balanced and blueprinted, tuned and run in for at least 20 miles (32km) before going to shipping.

While the Chief showed no major design or engineering changes for 2001, the several refinements enhanced both the classic look and functional appeal of the big twin. With the addition of the new Scout, and Centennial special editions of both the Scout and the Chief, the new Indian Motorcycle Company appeared ready to reaffirm its purpose – to make the grand old Indian name a player in the new century.

Right: The rivets and fringe were
retained on the saddle for 2001, and
a back support can be added to
make the passenger's ride a little
more comfortable.

2001 Chief
Indian Motorcycle Company
Gilroy, California

Below: For 2001 the Chief fuel tank
gained four-fifths of a gallon (3lit) in
capacity, which provided a
corresponding increase in the
cruising range.

Above right and Right: Indian motorcycles are still largely hand-built. Fenders are welded up and painted in the Gilroy factory, where the S&S engines are also assembled.

Below right: Spoked wheels are carefully trued before final assembly. Indian also offers cast alloy wheels as optional equipment.

2001 SCOUT 100

SPECIFICATIONS
Engine/Drivetrain
Engine: 45° OHV V-twin
Displacement: 88ci (1442cc)
Bore & stroke: 3.625 x
4.25in (92 x 108mm)
Compression ratio: 9.4:1
Horsepower: 65
Carburetor: 47.6mm S&S
Transmission: 5-speed
Clutch: Dry
Primary drive: Chain
Final drive: Belt
Brakes: F & R. 4-piston disc
Battery: 12-volt
Ignition: CDI

Chassis/Suspension
Frame: Steel, single downtube
Suspension: F. Telescopic
41mm fork. R. Gas shock
Wheelbase: 67in (170cm)
Weight: 585lb (265kg) dry
Fuel capacity: 3.5gal (13.2lit)
Oil capacity: 3qts (2.84lit)
Tires: F.100/90-19.
R.130/90-16
Top speed: 120mph
(193km/h)
Colors: Black Hills black,
Mojave, Red Rock,Bonneville
silver, Yellowstone
Number built: n/a
Price: $18,995

SCOUT 100 (2001)

The Scout 100 debuted as a new model in 2001, designating Indian's 100-year history. The original Scout of 1920 had revived Indian's flagging fortunes when competition with Harley-Davidson had put a serious dent in Springfield's sales. The seminal 600cc Scout was born of engineer Charles Franklin's certitude that Americans were ready for a sporting middleweight V-twin. Sport riders and racers proved him correct, while Harley's 600cc opposed twin found few takers in the domestic market.

The Scout later grew to 750cc and Milwaukee eventually responded with a 750 V-twin, which was developed over the decades and became the Sportster. The new Indian Scout is more light-heavyweight than middleweight, weighing in at 585 pounds (265kg), 85lb (38.5kg) fewer than the Chief. With mini-skirted fenders, 3.5-gallon (13.2lit) fuel tank, exposed fork tubes and 40-spoke wheels, the Scout looks considerably leaner and lighter than the Chief. The round headlight and narrower front rim contributed to the Scout's more athletic profile.

Given its lighter load, and the same engine as the Chief, the Scout accelerated and stopped more adroitly than its larger sibling. But although the Scout was somewhat shorter and narrower, and had four degrees steeper steering angle, ground clearance was slightly less than that of the Chief. Still, with its power-to-weight factor and quicker steering, the Scout proved more agile on the twisty back roads and gave up little stability on the open highway. Lower handlebars with less pullback also put the Scout rider in a more aggresive riding posture.

The Scout corresponded more closely with Harley's FX series than with the Sportster. Indian had planned a rigid-frame Sport Scout model for 2001, but the chopper/cruiser was postponed pending development of the new engine. The 2001 Scout was offered only in solid colors; Black Hills black, Mojave, Red Rock, Bonneville silver and Yellowstone. The suggested retail price was $18,995.

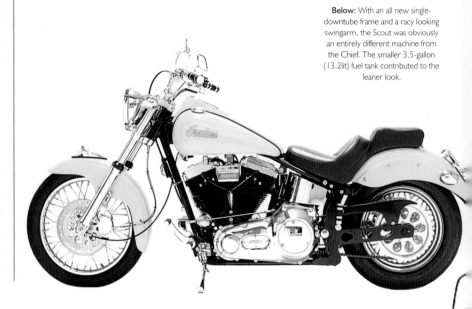

Below: With an all new single-downtube frame and a racy looking swingarm, the Scout was obviously an entirely different machine from the Chief. The smaller 3.5-gallon (13.2lit) fuel tank contributed to the leaner look.

2001 Scout 100
Indian Motorcycle Company
Gilroy, California

Right: Less fully skirted fenders recalled the bobbers of the 1940s and 1950s. The color is called Yellowstone.

Right: The new Scout, consistent with the original version, presented a lower and more sporting profile than the Chief. Carrying 85 fewer pounds (38.5kg) and different frame geometry, the Scout was significantly more agile than its larger sibling. Plans for a rigid frame version to be called the Sport Scout were shelved, at least temporarily.

Right: Early Scouts were fitted with the teardrop headlight of the Chief. Production models got a round lamp more consistent with the Scout's sporting profile. The front tire is a 19-incher compared to the 16-hoop on the Chief.

Left: The Scout's narrower look was obvious coming or going. The rear got the same 16-inch tire as the Chief, and a twin-shock, softail-style suspension. At $18,995, the Scout qualified as the economy model in the Indian lineup.

Right and Below right: Red Rock and Black Hills are two of the colors used with the Scout 100. The names of each summons up some of the famous locations in the history of America's western frontier.

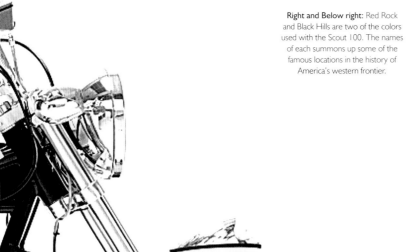

CENTENNIAL CHIEF AND SCOUT (2001) AND SPIRIT (2001)

Indian bannered the centennial of the marque with special editions of both the Chief and Scout, and a new model called the Spirit. The Chief, in black and gold, was equipped with narrower handlebars and four-inch (10cm) pullback risers. Front folding footpegs and 100th Anniversary commemorative clutch inspection covers completed the special edition of 2,001 motorcycles.

Set off by Avon whitewall tires and a 19-inch (48cm) custom windshield, the Centennial Chief sold for $25,995. The Scout centurion, by comparison, listed for $19,995.

The Scout was distinguished from its non-commemorative brethren by black powdercoating on the rims, triple trees, headlight and taillight. The cream paint was set off by red pinstriping, and the Scout also wore the commemorative clutch inspection cover. Both centennial models were delivered with a century seal and certificate of authenticity.

The Spirit provided Indian with another version of the Scout, with which it shared all the components except the fuel tank, handlebars and wheels. With 16-wheels at both ends, a 5.8-gallon (22lit) fuel tank and 60-spoke chrome rims, the Spirit fit nicely between the Scout and Chief. Thirty-five pounds (15.9kg) heavier than the former, and 50 pounds (22.7kg) lighter than the Chief, the hybrid Spirit weighed in as an all-purpose cruiser. Several fraternal brotherhoods showed interest in the Spirit as their next parade bike. The Spirit, offered in four solid metalflake colors, sold for $20,995.

Below: The Centennial Scout featured taller and narrower handlebars with more pullback, custom pinstriping and black powdercoated rims, headlight, taillight and triple trees. Only 2,001 of the specials were made.

2001 SPIRIT

SPECIFICATIONS
Engine/Drivetrain
Engine: 45° OHV V-twin
Displacement: 88ci (1442cc)
Bore & stroke: 3.625 x 4.25in (92 x 108mm)
Compression ratio: 9.4:1
Horsepower: 65
Carburetor: 47.6mm S&S
Transmission: 5-speed
Clutch: Proprietary wet
Primary drive: Chain
Final drive: Belt
Brakes: F & R. 4-piston disc
Battery: 12-volt
Ignition: CDI

CHASSIS/SUSPENSION
Frame: Steel, single downtube
Suspension: F. Telescopic 41mm fork. R. Gas shock
Wheelbase: 67in (170cm)
Weight: 620lb (281kg) dry
Fuel capacity: 5.8gal (22lit)
Oil capacity: 3qts (2.84lit)
Tires: F & R. 130/90-16
Top speed: 120mph (193km/h)
Colors: Monterey blue, Seattle silver, Springfield green, Sedona red
Number built: n/a
Price: $20,995

Below: The Spirit, with a frame common to the Scout, was set apart by its seat, larger fuel tank and 60-spoke wheels. Only 35 pounds (15.9kg) heavier than the Scout, the Spirit was about equal in terms of performance.

2001 Centennial Scout
Indian Motorcycle Company
Gilroy, California

Right: In a surprise move, Indian quickly produced a custom version of the Scout called the Spirit. With its two-into-one exhaust system, and fenders somewhere between the Scout and the Chief for coverage, the Spirit weighed in as the first sport-cruiser from Indian.

Below: The Centennial Chief was set off by the black and gold color scheme, Avon whitewalls and 19-inch (48cm) windscreen. The special edition added $2,000 to the price.

2001 Centennial Chief
Indian Motorcycle Company
Gilroy, California

Below: The Spirit was obviously designed for those who wanted Scout performance with some of the Chief's style and substance. More variations on the theme are expected.

Right: The clutch cover on both the Scout and Chief Centennial editions featured the badge proclaiming Indian's 100th anniversary. No bets were being made on the 2101 edition, but hopes were high that Indian would be first to reach the bicentennial mark.

2001 Spirit
Indian Motorcycle Company
Gilroy, California

INDEX

INDEX

INDEX

BIBLIOGRAPHY

Emde, Don, *The Daytona 200*, Infosport, 1991.
Hatfield, Jerry, *American Racing Motorcycles*, Motorbooks International, 1989.
Ibid, *Indian Motorcycle Buyer's Guide*, Ibid, 1995.
Ibid, *Indian Motorcycle Photographic History*, Ibid, 1993.
Ibid, *Indian Motorcycle Restoration Guide*, Ibid, 1995.
Hatfield, Jerry & Halberstadt, Hans, *Indian Motorcycles*, Ibid, 1996.
Hendry, Maurice D., *Harley-Davidson*, Ballantine Books, 1972.
Pagé, Victor, *Motorcycles, Sidecars & Cyclecars*, Norman W. Henley, 1917.
Prior, Rupert, *Motorcycling: The Golden Years*, CLB Publishing, 1994.
Rafferty, Tod, *The Complete Harley-Davidson*, Motorbooks International, 1997.
Sucher, Harry, *The Iron Redskin*, Haynes Publishing, 1997.
Wright, Stephen, *American Racer, 1900-1939*, Motorbooks International, 1989.
Ibid, *American Racer, 1940-1980*, Ibid, 1989.